BRIAN LONG & PHILIPPE CLAVEROL

PEUGEOT

CLASSIC BICYCLES

1945 to 1985

VELOCE PUBLISHING
THE PUBLISHER OF FINE AUTOMOTIVE BOOKS

Other titles by Brian Long:

Daimler SP250
Datsun Fairlady Roadster to 280ZX – The Z-car Story
Dino – The V6 Ferrari
Honda Acura NSX – Honda's Original Supercar
Kawasaki W, H & Z – The Big Air-cooled Machines
Mazda MX-5 Miata – The book of the world's favourite sportscar
Mazda Mx-5 Miata Roadster – Design & Development
Mercedes G-Wagen
Mercedes-Benz SL – R129 series 1989 to 2001
Mercedes-Benz SL – R230 series 2001 to 2011
Mercedes-Benz SL – W113-series 1963-1971
Mercedes-Benz SL & SLC – 107-series 1971 to 1989
Mercedes-Benz SLK – R170 series 1996-2004
Mercedes-Benz SLK – R171 series 2004-2011
Mercedes-Benz W123 series: all models 1976 to 1986
Mercedes-Benz W124 series – 1984-1997
Mitsubishi Lancer Evo – The road car & WRC story
Nissan 300zx/350z The Z Car Story
Porsche 911 – The Definitive History 1963 to 1971
Porsche 911 – The Definitive History 1971 to 1977
Porsche 911 – The Definitive History 1977 to 1987
Porsche 911 – The Definitive History 1987 to 1997
Porsche 911 – The Definitive History 1997 to 2005
Porsche 911 – The Definitive History 2004 to 2012
Porsche 914 & 914-6 – The Definitive History Of The Road & Competition Cars
Porsche 924
Porsche 928
Porsche 944
Porsche Boxster – The 986 Series 1996-2004
Porsche Boxster & Cayman – The 987 Series 2004 to 2013
Porsche Racing Cars – 1953 to 1975
Porsche Racing Cars – 1976 to 2005
RX-7 Mazda's Rotary Engine Sports Car
SM – Citroen's Maserati-engined Supercar
Subaru Impreza – The road car & WRC story
Suzuki Motorcycles – The Classic Two-stroke Era
The Book of the Ford Thunderbird from 1954
The Book of the Honda S2000
The Book of the Jaguar XJ-S
The Book of the Leica R-series Cameras
The Book of the Mazda MX-5 Miata – The 'Mk1' NA-series 1988 to 1997
The Book of the Mazda MX-5 Miata – The 'Mk2' NB-series 1997 to 2004
The Book of the Mazda MX-5 Miata – The 'Mk3' NC-series 2005 to 2015
The Ultimate Book Of The Air-Cooled Porsche 911
The Ultimate Book of the Porsche 356
Toyota Celica & Supra – The book of Toyota's sports coupés
Toyota MR2 Coupe & Spyders

See our website for more details about all of these books, and to view or purchase the latest titles from Veloce Publishing. Many of our books are also available in ebook format.

www.veloce.co.uk

First published in June 2022 by Veloce Publishing Limited, Veloce House, Parkway Farm Business Park, Middle Farm Way, Poundbury, Dorchester DT1 3AR, England.
Tel +44 (0)1305 260068 / Fax 01305 250479 / e-mail info@veloce.co.uk / web www.veloce.co.uk or www.velocebooks.com.
ISBN: 978-1-787112-15-5; UPC: 6-36847-01215-1.

Readers with ideas for automotive books, or books on other transport or related hobby subjects, are invited to write to the editorial director of Veloce Publishing at the above address. British Library Cataloguing in Publication Data – A catalogue record for this book is available from the British Library. Typesetting, design and page make-up all by Veloce Publishing Ltd on Apple Mac. Printed in India by Parksons Graphics.

RECORD
DU MONDE
PEUGEOT
Spidel

Contents

Introduction & acknowledgements

In my office, amongst other things, there are paintings and models of old racing cars, photographs of horses I've been involved with, and a couple of bicycles hanging on the wall. In pride of place is a 'Super Competition' Peugeot in colours familiar to any fan of cycle racing, with a 1971 PX10 frame next to it. There's also a PA10L on the same wall, with a replica World Champion jersey worn by a hero who died six weeks before I was born, and a model of a Peugeot service van in the same livery as the bike on the floor below it. These treasures have been a great source of inspiration.

During the golden age of road racing, an era I fell in love with in my 20s, Peugeot was almost unique in its stature, its bicycles competing at the top level with legendary riders, whilst also campaigning its cars in the upper echelons of motorsport, particularly in the budding rally arena. The links were bolstered by corporate colours and graphics, and sponsorship deals that bridged the gap between the two- and four-wheel teams.

Granted, Bianchi had made a number of cars before the Second World War and some beautiful motorbikes before and just after the conflict, but they were hardly world contenders, and while the Raleigh brand's efforts were similar, they're even less well-known. When all is said and done, for wide-eyed teenagers in the sixties, Peugeot seemed to have it all – superstars like Tom Simpson and Eddy Merckx riding bikes that you yourself could buy, and the 404 dominating the gruelling Safari Rally in Africa.

As such, as a motoring enthusiast, bitten by the classic car bug at an early age, and a huge fan of the Tour de France (inspired for life having seen the real thing while on holiday as a youngster), the Peugeot marque holds special appeal for me, hence my little shrine in the office, and another part of my collection in the hallway. The bikes are works of art with components that can't help but interest me as an engineer, while the cars have been there since the dawn of the horseless carriage, one constantly helping to promote the other. One visit to the museum in Sochaux, and it's easy to see in just a few minutes that Peugeot is much more than simply a manufacturer of products: it's a French institution.

For a change, even though my regular warblings centre on four-wheeled machines with engines, I am not going to write about cars, other than a passing comment here and there. Instead, I am going to write the book I wanted to buy but couldn't find – an in-depth celebration

of Peugeot bicycles and their place in history through the eyes of an enthusiast. I am hoping you will join me on a journey of unfettered nostalgia, briefly looking at the early history of the brand and the way its bicycles developed in the pre-WWII years, moving on to the core subject of the book, before a lighter review of what Peugeot has been marketing in more recent years to complete the story.

Acknowledgements

For this book, as with one of my earlier car titles, I've been blessed with the help of a dear friend, Philippe Claverol. Philippe and I met when he was the President of Citroën Japan, many years ago, and we hit it off immediately, being two foreigners of a similar age and with surprisingly similar interests. We stayed in touch when he moved up the corporate ladder and returned to Paris, and he has done a huge amount of work behind the scenes for this project, personally scanning old documents and sourcing photographs in France during his spare time. As such, this book simply would not have been possible without him, and while it has been written in a style that makes it look like mine alone, with references to 'my hometown' and so on, it should be stated from the off that this volume is a true joint-venture. In his efforts in making this book into something to treasure, Philippe was as big a hero as any rider tackling the Col du Tourmalet.

We are both grateful for the level of help given by Hervé Charpentier at the Peugeot Museum. Hervé opened up the archive for Philippe, with his staff giving us access to material that hasn't been seen in many years. With Philippe being a cycling enthusiast of the highest order (regularly riding both road and MTB bikes), I am sure this kind gesture brought many hours of fun – a trade-off for all the hard work!

We also received a great deal of help from Offside Sports Photography – the UK agent for Presse Sports, with its photography credited to *L'Equipe* on these pages. The many archive pictures from the *L'Equipe* files really have added a special aura – the very atmosphere that got Philippe and I hooked on bikes in our younger days. This particular link also brought fellow cycling enthusiast Dean Asbury into the frame, with him coming to the rescue as only old mates can. Hope we can talk about this little episode over a pint or two of Orion in the near future – there's no way COVID-19 will keep us apart forever.

Now all that remains to be said is that we hope you will enjoy this book as much as we have enjoyed putting it together ...

Brian Long & Philippe Claverol

(Courtesy *L'Equipe*)

1. PEUGEOT'S ROOTS

Ask any youngster today to say the first word that comes into their head at the mention of the Peugeot brand, and it will almost certainly be 'cars' or something relating to that trade, such as a specific model, or rallying perhaps. And why not? Cars are, after all, the company's staple product of late. Not so long ago, though, a lot of respondents would doubtless have quoted a number of bicycle connotations in amongst the motor vehicle ones …

Beautiful poster from a bygone era …

By the time the world returned to a semblance of normality following the 1939-1945 conflict, the European bicycle trade had become more of a specialist industry, dominated by a few big names and a gaggle of also-rans. It's amazing to watch the way the car and bike industries evolve, constantly whittling down the weakest to leave only the strongest, just like nature.

My hometown, Coventry – in the English Midlands, and the heart of UK engineering for decades – is a perfect example of this. Earlier research for a different project came up with a list of 260 different companies involved in making bicycles within the city. Even allowing for the renaming of firms and badge-engineering, we can safely say there were over 200 businesses in the game, starting with the Coventry Machinists Co Ltd building Swift-branded velocipedes (or boneshakers as they were aptly known, of the type invented by Pierre Michaux) way back in the latter half of the 1860s. Nowadays, you can count those involved in the trade on the fingers of one hand!

Interestingly, given the subject of this book, in amongst those early makers based in Coventry was Starley & Sutton, with one of its founders, John Kemp Starley, giving birth to the 'Safety Cycle' in 1885, named as such simply because it was a damned sight safer than a 'Penny Farthing' with its strikingly odd wheel diameters and high seating position! Anyway, this was not only the starting point of the Rover brand, as the first commercially successful Safety Cycle, it also provided a foundation stone for the modern cycle industry as we know it today, being an evolution of the Michaux machine, with the pedals moving from the front wheel hub to a central location. As an aside, Barr's Hill House, Starley's home, provided my form room for a little while, as the local council ultimately acquired it for use as a school.

The general increase in cycling's popularity had allowed manufacturers to refine production techniques as

The first Rover Safety Cycle had Michaux-type unmatched wheels, with the front one being slightly larger than the rear one. They were quickly brought closer in diameter, giving the world the first truly modern bicycle. This is JK Starley sitting on an early Rover bike.

demand picked up, and thus reduce costs – a necessity if the bicycle's reach was to expand beyond the middle and upper classes. The enhanced safety and comfort offered by the latest machines, combined with lower pricing, increased their appeal even more, and before the end of the century, in an era of peace for the majority, Europe was well and truly being gripped by bike fever. Many entrepreneurs set out to cash-in on the cycling boom, but surprisingly few made the most of it.

So why did so many fall by the wayside? Perhaps there were just too many makers trying to compete against each other, narrowing profit margins to critical levels on run-of-the-mill bicycles that failed to attract any kind of brand loyalty. In addition, albeit to a lesser extent, some of the failure rate can be attributed to the rise of the motorcycle and affordable automobiles, putting a lot out of business. Of course, there were others who switched their attention to these newer forms of transport, which had the potential of being more lucrative if one got in on the game from the start – one has to remember, investors were behind many ventures at this time, often with little interest in the product beyond its ability to generate cash.

In the midst of all this carnage, a few held steady, though, emerging in the postwar years as legendary names in the industry – the likes of Bianchi in Italy, Raleigh in England, and Peugeot in France being amongst them. Along with their contemporaries, they would fight for sales in the showrooms, and fight for glory in the classic races. It truly was a golden era. Before going on to this wonderful period, however, this chapter will look at how the Peugeot brand came about, and how the powerful Peugeot family originally became involved in the bike business …

Peugeot's origins

Unlike some French automotive companies, like De Dietrich and Hotchkiss, with their roots firmly in heavyweight industries, the business empire founded by the Peugeot family can be traced back to Jean-Pierre Peugeot, who was famous for making hand tools until his death in 1814. It was his sons, Jean-Pierre II and Jean-Frédéric, who established a metal foundry (Peugeot Frères) in the Doubs province on the Swiss border in 1810, and went on to invent the cold rolling mill. They were already in their 60s by the time Société Peugeot Frères Aînés was formed in 1832, but their three factories, with the main works at Valentigney, were producing a wide range of goods, from hand tools to saw blades, as well as things like coffee mills and other items for the kitchen.

With the familiar lion trademark already registered, the next generation (Emile and Jules) renamed the company Les Fils des Peugeot Frères in 1876, but it was Emile's son, Armand, that was to change the firm's direction. Armand (1849-1915) joined the firm at around the time it gained its new moniker, having spent some time in England to hone his engineering skills. He was the one that had bicycles added to the Peugeot catalogue (the first model appearing in 1882), and was also the key person behind a move into the automotive trade a few years later. Peugeot's prompt entry into this arena, initially via the use of Daimler gasoline engines

The main Peugeot works at Valentigney, seen here long before cars, bicycles and motorcycles came along.

built under licence by Panhard & Levassor after a short experiment with Serpollet steam vehicles, allows it to rightfully claim the honour of being the second oldest surviving car manufacturer in the world, with its support of motorsport being recorded as early as 1891. More serious racing exploits followed, with successful entries on the 1894 Paris-Rouen Trial and the 1895 Paris-Bordeaux-Paris event, refining the product, and also bringing the company closer to the Michelin brothers in the process.

However, a disagreement with the Germans regarding sales areas led to Peugeot dropping Daimler power for a new engine designed by Gratien Michaux – the man behind the Gladiator voiturette displayed at the 1895

Steadily evolving over the years, the lion logo was said to represent strength, with its sharp teeth also highlighting a practical link to items like saw blades. It was no coincidence that a 'lion rampant' was also the heraldic mark of the Doubs department in which the Peugeot family resided.

Salon du Cycle. This rift sparked a move to a new car factory at Audincourt, with a second opened further north in Lille in 1898, thus allowing La Société Anonyme des Automobiles Peugeot to become one of the largest car manufacturers in Europe. Meanwhile, Armand's cousin, Eugène, continued to run things in Valentigney with his three sons (Pierre, Robert and Jules), able to concentrate on more traditional fare, which naturally included bicycles by this time.

Peugeot's first bicycle – the Grand-Bi Penny Farthing (or Ordinary, to give the Penny Farthing breed, named after the old English coins, its proper title) – gave little clue as to the importance two-wheelers would have on the French company's fortunes. Yes, the car business would become the strongest element of the marque in time, but one wonders if its creation would have been possible had Armand Peugeot not brought bicycles into the fold first. Ultimately, motorcycles would follow as a natural progression, but not until close to the turn of the century, unlike Rover and Triumph in the UK, for instance, whose owners put an engine into a bicycle

Armand Peugeot in later life.

Pictured here at the Peugeot museum in Sochaux, the Grand-Bi was priced at a princely 325FF – the equivalent of three months' wages for the average working man. (Courtesy Wikimedia Commons: Alf van Beem)

The old mill at Beaulieu was actually an important part of Peugeot's transformation into a metalworking family, providing a successful stepping stone that would allow greater things in grander buildings in nearby Valentigney. The small plant established around the mill would ultimately become the home of Peugeot's bicycle business.

frame long before tackling automobiles. As such, the jump to motorised transport cannot be credited to motorbikes at Peugeot – the manufacturing foundation on which the empire was formed is therefore definitely the bicycle.

Within a couple of years of the Grand-Bi's debut, Peugeot was making Safety Cycles, with enough orders in hand to employ 300 people on the bicycle side of the business once series-production got under way in 1886. Although several components were shipped in,

A French bicycle advert from 1890.

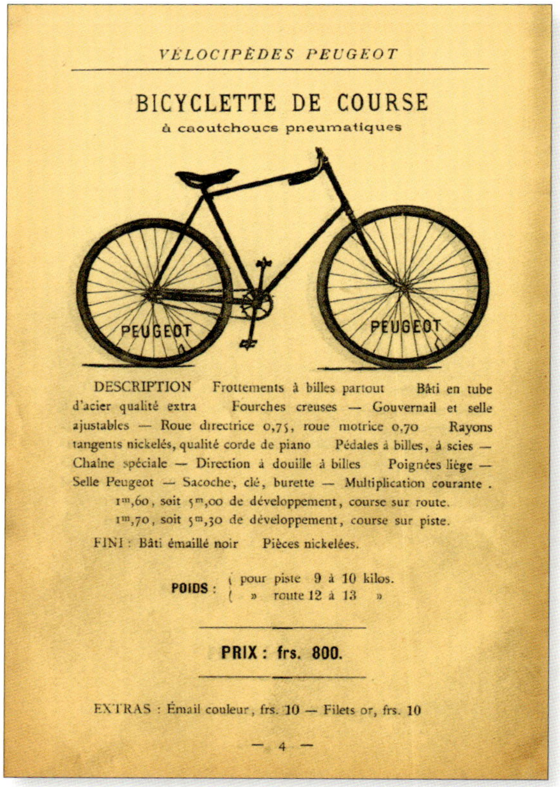

VÉLOCIPÈDES PEUGEOT

BICYCLETTE DE COURSE

à caoutchoucs pneumatiques

DESCRIPTION Frottements à billes partout Bâti en tube d'acier qualité extra Fourches creuses — Gouvernail et selle ajustables — Roue directrice 0,75, roue motrice 0,70 Rayons tangents nickelés, qualité corde de piano Pédales à billes, à scies — Chaîne spéciale — Direction à douille à billes Poignées liège — Selle Peugeot — Sacoche, clé, burette — Multiplication courante.

1m,60, soit 5m,00 de développement, course sur route.

1m,70, soit 5m,30 de développement, course sur piste.

FINI : Bâti émaillé noir Pièces nickelées.

POIDS : pour piste 9 à 10 kilos.
» route 12 à 13 »

PRIX : frs. 800.

EXTRAS : Émail couleur, frs. 10 — Filets or, frs. 10

— 4 —

Picture from the 1891 Peugeot catalogue, showing the contemporary 'Course' model.

construction was based in an old mill in Beaulieu (the southernmost of the three factories owned by Les Fils des Peugeot Frères, to the east of Besançon), and as demand increased, more models were added to the range, including tricycles.

The 1889 Exposition Universelle, which opened in Paris on 6 May and brought about the creation of the Tour Eiffel, witnessed the first use of the lion badge on a Peugeot cycle. Over 30,000,000 people went to the fair, and as people crowded into the first Exposition de Velocipédie (a specialist cycling event held in the summer of 1892 in the Champ de Mars next to the Eiffel Tower), the lasting success of the Peugeot bicycle was sealed once and for all.

Poster celebrating Peugeot's success on the 1892 Paris-Nantes event, won by Marius Allard, one of the top French riders at the time. There is more than a little artistic licence in the bike design, but it would be a shame to omit such a beautiful painting.

With sales already hovering around 10,000 units per year as the 1890s began, further boosted by an order from the military, annual production surged towards the 20,000 mark a decade later, by which time four-wheel quadricycles and other novelties, such as an elegant shaft-drive bicycle and a Gérard-type folding bike, had been marketed. There were also motorised versions of the two-, three- and four-wheelers (initially equipped with De Dion engines, rated at between 3bhp and 4.5bhp), although an average asking price of 2200FF as good as put the quadricycles well beyond the reach of anyone outside the landed gentry and their ilk.

The interaction between the two Peugeot firms was best illustrated by the production of chain, which was centred at the Valentigney works now being run by Robert Peugeot (Eugène Peugeot had given up the reins to his second son, and died in 1907), with various grades made available to suit the different cycle types and the cars being punted by Armand Peugeot's outfit. In addition, De Dion engines would ultimately give way to Peugeot power-units in the motorised machines built in Beaulieu and Valentigney.

Interestingly, although 'Cycles Peugeot' was still the dominant marque name for the bicycle business,

These catalogue images from 1896 show the rapid progress being made in cycle design.

Paul Bourillon pictured after winning the Grand Prix de Paris in 1898. (Courtesy Wikimedia Commons: Collection Jules Beau)

by now booming thanks to a varied range of quality machines, the 'Cycles Lion' trademark was often seen on paperwork from the turn of the century, and the 'Lion-Peugeot' moniker was adopted for the smaller-engined voiturettes built by Robert Peugeot until the outbreak of the First World War, thus distancing them

The interior of the Beaulieu works pictured in 1898.

from the vehicles made by his uncle, Armand. Naturally, though, there was a lot of common ground, and the two companies ultimately merged with the foundation of the Société Anonyme des Automobiles et Cycles Peugeot in 1910. Motor vehicles were now being built in Audincourt, Lille, Paris, Valentigney, and soon after, Sochaux, too.

Meanwhile, Peugeot exponent Paul Bourillon was crowned the world sprint champion in Copenhagen in 1896, bringing yet more welcome publicity to the brand at a time when it was establishing itself as a leading light in the cycling arena. Many more sprint records and championships fell to the French maker, although it wasn't until the end of the century that an official works racing team was created. As it happens, the Peugeot family had always been keen on sport, its early cars competing in the first town-to-town road races at the dawn of motoring (the company's first entry was actually in the Motor Vehicle Class in the inaugural 1891 Paris-

A magnificent poster from 1899.

Brest-Paris cycle race). Peugeot – and Lion-Peugeot for that matter – would remain heavily involved in motorsport in the ensuing years, so naturally, the bicycle races, which were now starting to become increasingly well-organised and well-publicised events, also held great appeal.

The first Tour de France had only six stages – Paris to Lyon, Lyon to Marseille, Marseille to Toulouse,

THE INFLUENTIAL TOUR DE FRANCE

Bicycle sales were booming at the turn of the century, with the popularity of these machines being easy to gauge – around 50,000 bikes were registered in France in 1890, but the figure had grown to almost a million by 1900, and easily topped 3,000,000 by the outbreak of the Great War.

Thanks to this popularity, a certain newspaper called *Le Vélo* was managing to sell 80,000 copies a day – enough for the publisher to justify the creation of the gruelling cobble-strewn Paris-Roubaix race in 1896 as a further means of promoting cycling and the title, which also covered sports, motoring and a fair bit of political comment. This latter element proved to be its undoing, however, for Pierre Giffard's editorials enraged a number of advertisers, including some very influential people, who duly walked away from *Le Vélo* and instead threw their support behind a new publication.

This split came about thanks to the Dreyfus affair, a scandal involving a soldier accused of selling secrets to the Germans, which ultimately had the effect of polarising French society – one camp thought he was innocent of the crime, and the other believed he was guilty. But cycling enthusiasts, whatever their views on the incident, had to be grateful for it, for the formation of the new paper – known as *L'Auto* – duly gave the world the Tour de France race, and, after a year or so, *Le Vélo* had fallen by the wayside, eventually being relaunched as *Le Journal de L'Automobile*.

Those behind *L'Auto* read like the proverbial who's who of the early French motor industry. Leading protagonists included the wealthy Count Albert de Dion (the sporting gentleman behind the pioneering De Dion-Bouton marque, who also joined the league of cycle manufacturers later on, in 1909 it seems), Édouard Michelin of Michelin tyre fame, and Adolphe Clément, another sporting industrialist behind cars, bicycles, motorbikes, and even aeronautical machines; the Clément tyre concern was another arm of his sprawling business empire, incidentally.

De Dion and Clément certainly loved their racing, with the Count using motorsport to amuse himself and promote his wares, and Clément partnering Albert Lemaître to a win in the 1894 Paris-Rouen race – the first proper car race ever held (based on the route of an old cycle race), and Peugeot also able to claim victory as their chosen mount. With the racing cyclist Henri Desgrange taken on as editor of *L'Auto*, the organization of the Tour de France cycle race was a natural progression – a poke in the eye of their rivals, being bigger and better than the Paris-Roubaix in every respect.

Thanks to Géo Lefèvre's sterling work behind the scenes (the ex-*Le Vélo* cycling correspondent did much of the organising, and would also act as clerk of the course) and some last minute changes by Desgrange to make the event more attractive for the riders, the first Tour de France started on the 1st July 1903. The grandest of all the Grand Tours had been born (with Maurice Garin winning this opening edition on a Diamant made by the Paris-based La Française concern), and the rest, as they say, is history. Interestingly, *L'Auto* was printed on yellow paper to distance itself from rival *Le Vélo*, and this is what gave rise to the famous yellow jersey on the Tour de France.

The end of the first stage of the 1903 Tour de France.

Toulouse to Bordeaux, Bordeaux to Nantes, and Nantes back to Paris. Whilst deliberately avoiding the north-east (the Paris-Roubaix was too well established), each stage had a hint of the one-day classics to it (such as the Bordeaux-Paris, the Marseille-Paris, and Nantes taking the place of Brest in the stage title) or featured a destination used for the Tour de France Automobile, inaugurated in 1899, and organised by *Le Matin* and the Automobile Club de France (or ACF), the latter co-founded by none other than Albert de Dion. This is where the phrase 'small world' jumps to mind, for it was indeed a close-knit society of enthusiasts who got the ball rolling in many spheres of sport, motorised or otherwise.

Of course, racing bikes back then would hardly be classed as racing bikes as we know them today (unless one thinks of the keirin racers that originate from Japan), although the basic frame shapes and drop handlebars look familiar enough to most of us. Being as heavy as lead was one thing, but having just a single gear and often no brakes, well that called for a special kind of toughness – and bravery! – and things would improve for riders at a fast pace. The 1901 'Course-Piste' was a regular Peugeot bike with drop handlebars, but within a couple of years, the model was given more dramatic frame geometry to allow the rider to crouch lower over the handlebars, and, according to contemporary official paperwork, was tipping the scales at just 10kg (22lb) – that would make it a full 15kg (33lb) lighter than the bike that won the first Paris-Rouen race in 1869!

In fact, it's quite amazing how quickly things had evolved by 1903, with only detail changes made to traditional steel frames over the next century or so – adapting to components, adding strength and reducing weight would be the main areas of development. The 1904 catalogue showed 'Course-Piste,' 'Course-Route' and 'Modèle Stayer' variants on the road-racer theme, with steel rims being an option to replace the traditional wooden items combined with metal spokes. Thankfully, various braking systems were starting to spread amongst the makers, too, looking at pictures of the TdF entries (although not shown on the racing bikes in the Peugeot brochure, photos of the works team members in 1905 clearly show a front brake), this perhaps being another example of racing improving the breed …

Anyway, after the stunning success of the first Tour

The fabled Danish sprinter Thorvald Ellegaard aboard a Peugeot racer.

de France, as it happens, the second running of the great event was marred by controversy, with the top four finishers all being disqualified for various forms of cheating, including hopping on a train at one point! Thankfully, while enraged by all the cheating, Desgrange stood by the Tour, and the 1905 edition had a much happier outcome, especially for fans of the Peugeot brand. Indeed, with shorter stages but more of them to give a longer Tour distance, along with a revised scoring system, the Peugeot team riders (managed by Léopold Alibert) dominated the French classic that year, with Louis Trousselier claiming a stunning victory, and Paris-Roubaix winner Hippolyte Aucouturier coming home in second. In typical swashbuckling style, Trousselier gambled away his winnings within 24 hours of receiving them!

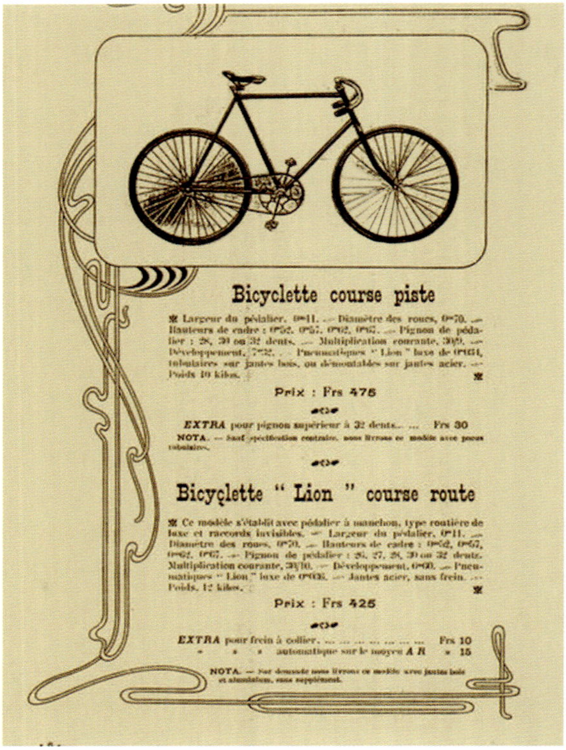

Bicyclette course piste

Prix : Frs 475

EXTRA pour pignon supérieur à 32 dents... ... Frs 30

Bicyclette " Lion " course route

Prix : Frs 425

EXTRA pour frein à collier. ... Frs 10

Page from the 1901 catalogue showing the 475FF 'Course-Piste' bike, and details of the strict road racer, priced 50FF cheaper.

By 1906, still basking in competition success on the TdF, Paris-Roubaix and Bordeaux-Paris races, the Peugeot line-up had settled into a range of two-wheelers based on the Safety Cycle, including the basic Type A at 225FF, a version with drop handlebars at 240FF, and one for the ladies at 245FF, which featured mudguards and a front brake, and was also available in Luxe form (with two-speeds) for 360FF. The 330FF Routière Luxe version of the men's bike provided mudguards and a brake (the Peugeots had a front brake that acted directly on the top of the tyre's contact surface via a lever on the handlebar, something that had been a feature on the maker's Penny Farthing models of yore and duly carried over to the Safety Cycles that followed), while the 'Touriste' added two gears and 10FF to the invoice. Oddities included the 'Ecclésiastique,' an unusual two-speed 'Rétro à Chaîne' model, chainless and folding bikes, one for kids, and single- and twin-cylinder motorcycles. One could also emulate the TdF heroes by securing a 380FF 'Course-Piste' model, with a single speed and no brakes, but a stronger frame, rims in wood and aluminium shod with

Louis Trousselier – winner of the 1905 Tour de France for Peugeot. Known as 'Trou-Trou' to his friends and fans, he was famous for his sense of humour, which perhaps explains the front fork positioning. (Courtesy Wikimedia Commons: Agence Rol)

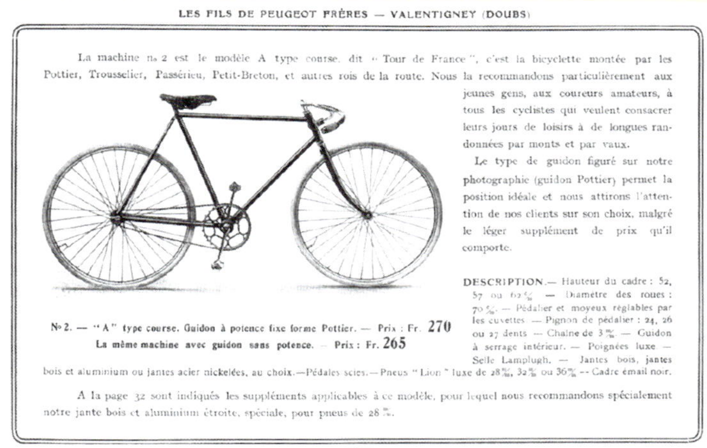

LES FILS DE PEUGEOT FRÈRES — VALENTIGNEY (DOUBS)

La machine n° 2 est le modèle A type course, dit « Tour de France », c'est la bicyclette montée par les Pottier, Trousselier, Passérieu, Petit-Breton, et autres rois de la route. Nous la recommandons particulièrement aux jeunes gens, aux coureurs amateurs, à tous les cyclistes qui veulent consacrer leurs jours de loisirs à de longues randonnées par monts et par vaux.

Le type de guidon figuré sur notre photographie (guidon Pottier) permet la position idéale et nous attirons l'attention de nos clients sur son choix, malgré le léger supplément de prix qu'il comporte.

N° 2. — "A" type course. Guidon à potence fixe forme Pottier. — Prix : Fr. 270
La même machine avec guidon sans potence. — Prix : Fr. 265

DESCRIPTION. — Hauteur du cadre : 52, 57 ou 62 m/m. — Diamètre des roues : 70 m/m. — Pédalier et moyeux réglables par les cuvettes. — Pignon de pédalier : 24, 26 ou 27 dents. — Chaîne de 3 m/m. — Guidon à serrage intérieur. — Poignées luxe. — Selle Lamplugh. — Jantes bois, jantes bois et aluminium ou jantes acier nickelées, au choix. — Pédales scies. — Pneus "Lion" luxe de 28 m/m, 32 m/m ou 36 m/m. — Cadre émail noir.

A la page 32 sont indiqués les suppléments applicables à ce modèle, pour lequel nous recommandons spécialement notre jante bois et aluminium étroite, spéciale, pour pneus de 28 m/m.

— 4 —

LES FILS DE PEUGEOT FRÈRES — VALENTIGNEY (DOUBS)

Dès l'origine des épreuves sur piste, les préférences des grands cracks sont allées aux Bicyclettes Peugeot qui résistent mieux que toutes autres aux à-coups des démarrages, et rendent le maximum de l'effort dans les virages, grâce à leur grande rigidité.

Les Morin et les Bourrillon s'adjugèrent nombre de fois le Grand Prix de la Ville de Paris sur bicyclette Extra-Piste Peugeot; les principaux grands championnats courus en France et à l'Etranger ont été gagnés sur Peugeot, et en 1906, notre supériorité était à ce point consacrée que les plus fines pédales de la saison, les Kramer, les Ellegaard, les Friol, les Schilling, les Rettich, etc. confièrent leur chance à la Peugeot, et ajoutèrent à notre Livre d'Or, parmi tant d'autres épreuves, le Grand Prix de Paris, le Championnat du Monde, le Championnat de France, etc., etc.

N° 5. — Bicyclette "Extra-Piste". — Prix : Fr. 400

Notre modèle « Extra-Piste » (cliché n° 5 ci-dessus) dont nous donnons ci-après la description succincte,

— 11 —

LES FILS DE PEUGEOT FRÈRES — VALENTIGNEY (DOUBS)

se classe en dehors de toute comparaison et s'impose à tous les cyclistes attirés par les réunions des Vélodromes.

DESCRIPTION. — Hauteur du cadre 52, 57 ou 62 m/m. — Diamètre des roues 70 m/m. — Pignon de pédalier 28 ou 30 dents. — Chaîne de 3 m/m. — Guidon à serrage intérieur. — Poignées liège. — Selle de course. — Serrage de selle à l'avant. — Jantes bois. — Pédales scies. — Pneus collés. — Cadre tube supérieur incliné à l'avant. — Email noir.

La bicyclette « Extra-Piste » se monte exclusivement avec jantes bois, pneus collés.

Aux cyclistes qui, sans s'adonner aux épreuves sur piste, participent parfois à des courses sur route, locales ou régionales, ou ne pratiquent la bicyclette que sur de belles routes, nous conseillons notre modèle de course à serrage de selle conique, monté soit avec jantes bois ou jantes acier, pneus démontables, soit avec pneus collés.

En passant commande, bien préciser le genre choisi.

Ce type constitue la bicyclette Course route et se facture au prix de la bicyclette « Extra-Piste ».

— 12 —

Cover and selected pages from the 1907 catalogue.

removable pneumatic tyres, and a racing saddle to justify the added expense; this duly became the 400FF 'Course Extra-Piste' model in the following year.

Meanwhile, the 1906 Tour de France became a significantly longer event, exceeding 2800 miles (4500km) for the first time, broken up into 13 stages. René Pottier gave Peugeot the double that year, with another Peugeot exponent, Lucien Petit-Breton (aka Lucien Mazan), winning this most famous of races in 1907 and 1908. While some would question the 1907 victory, following a huge penalty for Emile Georget whilst leading and Alcyon's withdrawal from the race as a sign of protest, no-one could doubt the 1908 win, or Peugeot's dominance, as François Faber and Georges Passerieu made sure that the brand secured all three places on the podium. The Peugeot-Wolber team also won the Paris-Tours race in 1906 and 1907, the Paris-Robaix and Milan-San Remo in 1907, the Tour of Lombardy in 1907 and 1908, and the Tour of Belgium in 1908; Peugeot riders were also crowned Road Race Champion of France in 1907 and 1908, and secured the first of four similar pre-WWI titles in Italy from 1908 onward.

Alcyon won the next four editions of the Tour de France, combining with the likes of La Française, Armor and Griffon to hold Peugeot at bay in most of the other big races, too, that now included the Giro d'Italia, or Tour of Italy. Ironically, the man behind the Alcyon

Lucien Petit-Breton (left), photographed with Henri Cornet on the 1908 Tour de France. Peugeot riders dominated the event, with Petit-Breton silencing those critical of his 1907 victory. (Courtesy Wikimedia Commons: Collection Jules Beau)

marque was an ex-Peugeot worker by the name of Edmond Gentil. Having made 3000 bicycles in 1902, by 1909 the figure had risen to 40,000 units (half of Peugeot's annual tally, but a huge number nonetheless), calling for expansion and a new factory at Courbevoie, on the outskirts of Paris, and on the other side of the Seine to the company's Neuilly birthplace. Gentil tried his hand at cars and motorcycles over the years, and even had a go at making radios, but it was bicycles that provided him with success, with his Alcyon-Dunlop racing team being the stuff of legend.

Calliper brakes were starting to filter through on a few bikes by this time, and were fitted to the Peugeot that took Philippe Thys to victory in the 1913 running of the Tour de France, when competitors once again rode against the clock. The Belgian made it a double in 1914, handing Peugeot its sixth Tour win, although the 'Extra-Piste' was still listed without brakes in the catalogues from the time, as was the 'Lion Course'. The new 275FF 'Trophée de France' model had the old style front brake to make it more suitable for regular use, but lost the feature again when the 265FF 'Tour de France' variant replaced it in 1914. All of these road racers had a single-speed drive, with wooden rims still being the norm on the more serious machines.

Poster making the most of Peugeot's success in 1908.

A promotional piece for Peugeot motorcycles, dating from around 1910.

Belgian rider Philippe Thys looking decidedly dirty and weary on the 1914 Tour de France. Like Petit-Breton, Thys twice won the classic French race for Peugeot – in 1913 and 1914. (Courtesy Wikimedia Commons: Agence Rol)

As well as one-two-three wins on the TdF in 1913 and 1914, the rejuvenated Peugeot team picked up another Paris-Roubaix trophy in 1913, and a third Paris-Tours victory the following year. Peugeot riders were also declared champion of Belgium and champion of Switzerland before Europe plunged into four long years of bloody conflict, which brought the joys of cycling and all forms of sport to a complete standstill.

The interwar years

Although the Peugeot family had emerged strongly from the Great War on the back of Allied orders for all manner of military vehicles, from motorcycles to half-tracks, the relentless march of foreign-made cars and bicycles was at last making inroads to the French market – until now, as with so many other countries, almost reliant on homegrown machinery. Ultimately, in the case of the latter, as the bicycle movement evolved from a hobby for the well-heeled into a cheap form of transport for the masses, price wars cut profits, and the whittling down we mentioned earlier in the chapter took its toll on the smaller firms, with mergers (the Aiglon brand had been absorbed by Peugeot in 1922, for instance, with Griffon following a few years later), bankruptcy, or a change of direction being the only choices available for many.

Peugeot was safe enough on the face of things. The racing team livery had changed from a blue jersey with a yellow stripe to yellow with blue bands, but Peugeot could claim a new French champion, and picked up another Tour de France victory in 1922, thanks to Firmin Lambot (Lambot actually won the first postwar TdF in 1919, when riding for the La Sportive equipe put together by a French manufacturer's consortium that included Peugeot, Alcyon, Automoto, La Française,

Firmin Lambot on the way to victory on the 1922 Tour de France. Belgium recently released a postage stamp to commemorate his achievements in the saddle. (Courtesy *L'Equipe*)

Left: Peugeot exponent Léon Despontin pictured in the summer of 1923. (Courtesy Wikimedia Commons: Agence Rol)

Armor, Griffon, Thomann, Labor, Gladiator, Clément, Liberator and Hurtu). It could be said that this was the first real Tour after the Great War, as this is when the familiar team rivalries kicked off again, with Peugeot managed by ex-Alcyon man, Alphonse Baugé, who had overseen Thys' two wins before the conflict.

Granted, Automoto won the next four editions of the Tour de France (with Alcyon dominating after that before an era of national teams fighting for glory), but the Peugeot brand was as popular as ever, with annual production of around 100,000 bicycles of various shapes and sizes (including racing bikes, by now modern in design, despite the single speed gearing, being fitted with cable-operated calliper brakes at both ends, and wood or steel rims with early 'quick-release' hubs), plus a range of motorcycles, and a huge showroom in Paris. As it happens, the car and commercial vehicle business was in a similar position, making everything from the lightweight Type 172 through to expensive sleeve-valve limousines, as well as a line of trucks. One should never judge a book by its cover, though, as the French giant was starting to feel the pinch, and ultimately split the car and bicycle operations once more.

There was nothing unusual in this. Most makers were hiving off sections with wildly different production and marketing requirements in the post-WWI era, allowing them to concentrate on products that seemed to have a better future (with Humber bicycle production separated from the automotive side of the business, and moving to Raleigh as a good example of the standard practice from the time). Interestingly, Peugeot closed the motorsport department and dropped the bigger trucks in favour of light commercials at the same time, but for the sake of this narrative, the most important thing to come out of this corporate streamlining was the formation of the Société Anonyme des Cycles Peugeot, or simply Cycles Peugeot in official publications and suchlike, in 1926.

The first Cycles Peugeot catalogue, noting the plush address on the Avenue de la Grande Armée in the capital (badging had used 'Peugeot Paris' wording for some years as a result of this property) but proudly showing Beaulieu as the base of the operation (there was even a picture of the now vast factory on the back cover), contained no less than 14 bicycles, including the Model 9 'Sport', duly refined through racing according to the blurb, although the 'Course' was no longer listed as a regular item. While the flimsy 'Cyclo-Moto' was dropped, there was a pair of new 175cc and 350cc motorcycles made available, along with a number of accessories for connoisseurs of cycling, including an early electric lighting set invented by Lucien Rosengart – Peugeot's PR man who would soon after go on to form his own car company.

Metal rims became the norm in the second half of the 1920s, with the Peugeot racing team changing its allegience from Wolber to Dunlop tyres at the same time – John Boyd Dunlop being the de facto inventor of the pneumatic tyre, of course. This move was reflected in the

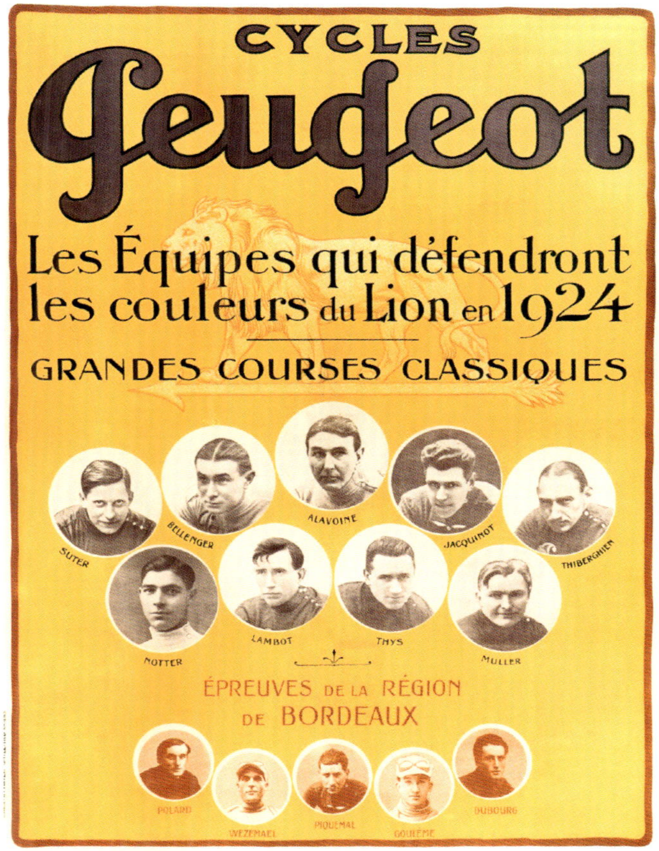

Poster showing the works team for 1924.

1927 catalogue, which saw a welcome return of the PS7 'Course' (priced at 610FF), listed alongside a basic PU7 variant, and the 'Tour de France' (code P8, or P10 with wood rims) and 'Sport' (P9) models. The same bikes were shown in the 1929 brochure, by which time, a big thing was being made of the use of stainless steel spokes.

In the early days of the Tour de France, cheating had been rife, and, following the incident involving Maurice de Waele of the Alcyon equipe in the 1929 edition of the race, an infuriated Henri Desgrange decided once and for all to take away the power of the bike factories by introducing a new team format for 1930 – one that would bring together riders via their nationality and/ or regional background, which ultimately lasted until 1962. Desgrange may have seen this as good for the TdF, but the likes of Peugeot, Alcyon, Armor and Automoto would struggle to reap any benefits that could translate into sales of regular bikes. Indeed, with hard times

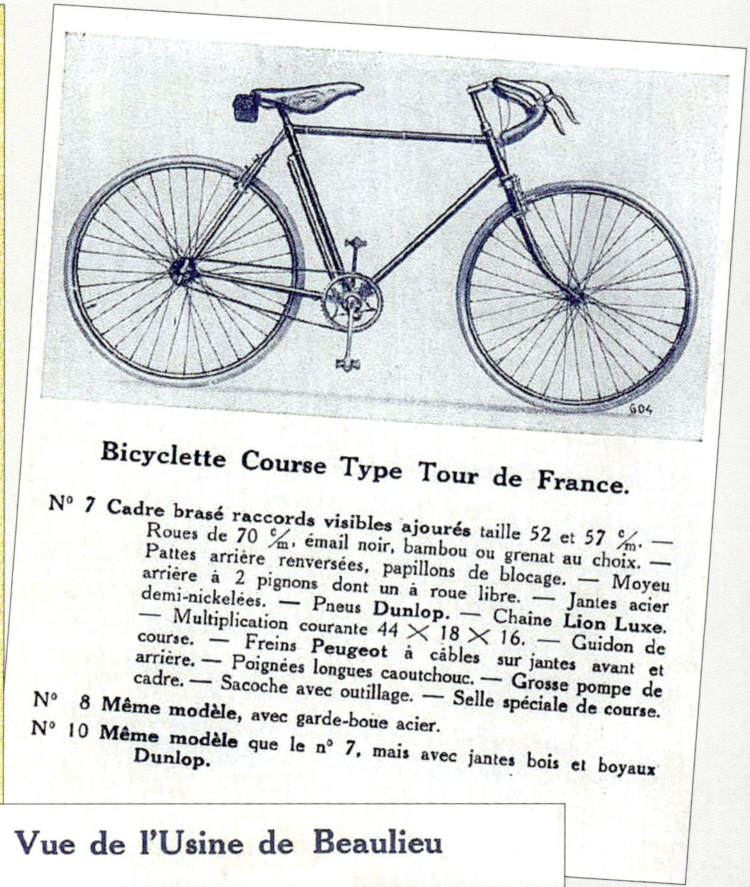

Bicyclette Course Type Tour de France.

N° 7 **Cadre brasé raccords visibles ajourés** taille 52 et 57 c/m. —
Roues de 70 c/m, émail noir, bambou ou grenat au choix. —
Pattes arrière renversées, papillons de blocage. — Moyeu
arrière à 2 pignons dont un à roue libre. — Jantes acier
demi-nickelées. — Pneus **Dunlop.** — Chaine **Lion Luxe.**
— Multiplication courante 44 × 18 × 16. — Guidon de
course. — Freins **Peugeot** à câbles sur jantes avant et
arrière. — Poignées longues caoutchouc. — Grosse pompe de
cadre. — Sacoche avec outillage. — Selle spéciale de course.

N° 8 **Même modèle,** avec garde-boue acier.

N° 10 **Même modèle** que le n° 7, mais avec jantes bois et boyaux **Dunlop.**

Cover of the 1926 Peugeot catalogue, along with the Course Type 'Tour de France' page, and the rear cover, which perfectly illustrates the immense growth at the Beaulieu site since the turn of the century.

promised in the wake of the Wall Street Crash and no real chance to get any decent publicity, Automoto had to resign itself to working alongside Peugeot from 1930 onwards in order to survive.

Meanwhile, the familiar Peugeot PS7 and P8 continued into the 1930s, with the more specialised P0 'Course Spécial' making its debut in 1932, and featuring a horizontal top tube that would duly become the norm. However, the Peugeot line-up was overhauled in 1933, with the 'PC' code taking the place of the 'P' one on the regular sporting machinery, but the P0 became the

Left: Art Deco-style advertising from the early part of 1928.

Below: The French team posing for a Tour de France publicity shot in 1932. The new format gave the TdF a completely different spirit that was appreciated by some, although not necessarily the manufacturers who could gain sales on the back of a good showing in the major races. (Courtesy Wikimedia Commons: Agence de presse Mondial Photo-Presse)

Action from the 1936 Tour de France. (Courtesy Wikimedia Commons: Agence Rol)

COURSE ET SPORT

P. C. 9. - Cadet grand sport, cadre de 50 %, émail rouge vif ou bleu roi. Machine spécialement montée pour jeunes gens de 13 à 16 ans . . **350f**

P. C. 7. - Demi-course jantes 1/2 nickelées , 2 freins course, moyeu arrière 2 pignons, longues poignées caoutchouc. Se fait en grenat, vert, bleu, bambou ou gris. **495f**

P. C. 8. - Course amateur, cadre gabarit spécial, pédalier attache trois branches, 2 freins spéciaux course, jantes et guidon chromés, rayons fins émaillés noir, poignées para, pédales course, selle course, porte-pompe et guide-câbles brasés au cadre, pneus para. Se fait en bleu turquoise, grenat ou havane. **575f**

P. C. 10. - Course à boyaux, même modèle que le précédent, mais avec jantes bois et boyaux sans garde-boue. Émail métallisé comme P. C. 10 Sp. **650f**

COURSE
SPÉCIAL PROFESSIONNEL

P. C. 10 sp. - Cadre brasé gabarit spécial, tubes Rubis, raccords ajourés, fourche spéciale, pédales de piste, moyeux super-piste extra-légers, roue libre à double denture et pignon fixe à l'AR avec papillons de blocage; selle de course graissée avec dispositif de démontage rapide du cuir; guidon émaillé noir avec poignée tressées et embouts de caoutchouc; attaches de freins soudées au guidon; guide-câbles brasés au cadre, freins sport, jantes bois spéciales course, boyaux demi-recouverts 700 × 32, rayons fins émaillés et ligaturés, graisseur de chaine brasé au cadre, émail transparent métallisé grenat, vert clair, vert foncé, bleu, or ou argent. **790f**

Pages from the 1933 catalogue.

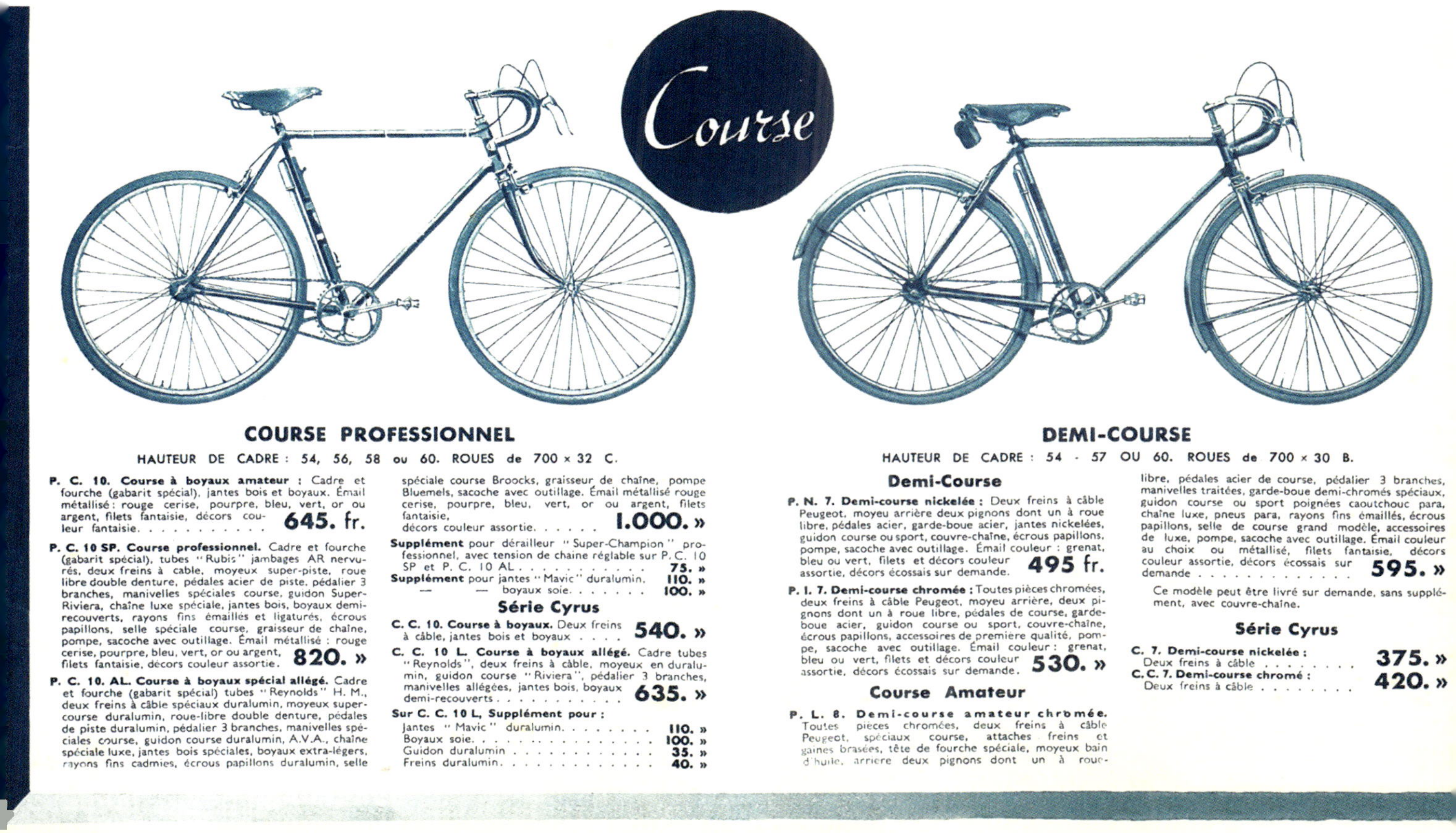

COURSE PROFESSIONNEL

HAUTEUR DE CADRE : 54, 56, 58 ou 60. ROUES de 700 × 32 C.

P. C. 10. Course à boyaux amateur : Cadre et fourche (gabarit spécial), jantes bois et boyaux. Émail métallisé : rouge cerise, pourpre, bleu, vert, or ou argent, filets fantaisie, décors couleur fantaisie. . . . . **645. fr.**

P. C. 10 SP. Course professionnel. Cadre et fourche (gabarit spécial), tubes "Rubis" jambages AR nervurés, deux freins à cable, moyeux super-piste, roue libre double denture, pédales acier de piste, pédalier 3 branches, manivelles spéciales course, guidon Super-Riviera, chaîne luxe spéciale, jantes bois, boyaux demi-recouverts, rayons fins émaillés et ligaturés, écrous papillons, selle spéciale course, graisseur de chaîne, pompe, sacoche avec outillage. Émail métallisé : rouge cerise, pourpre, bleu, vert, or ou argent, filets fantaisie, décors couleur assortie. **820. »**

P. C. 10. AL. Course à boyaux spécial allégé. Cadre et fourche (gabarit spécial) tubes "Reynolds" H. M., deux freins à câble spéciaux duralumin, moyeux super-course duralumin, roue-libre double denture, pédales de piste duralumin, pédalier 3 branches, manivelles spéciales course, guidon course duralumin, A.V.A., chaîne spéciale luxe, jantes bois spéciales, boyaux extra-légers, rayons fins cadmies, écrous papillons duralumin, selle spéciale course Broocks, graisseur de chaîne, pompe Bluemels, sacoche avec outillage. Émail métallisé rouge cerise, pourpre, bleu, vert, or ou argent, filets fantaisie, décors couleur assortie. . . . . . **1.000. »**

Supplément pour dérailleur "Super-Champion" professionnel, avec tension de chaine réglable sur P. C. 10 SP et P. C. 10 AL . . . . **75. »**
Supplément pour jantes "Mavic" duralumin. **110. »**
— — boyaux soie. . . . . . . **100. »**

Série Cyrus

C. C. 10. Course à boyaux. Deux freins à câble, jantes bois et boyaux . . . . **540. »**

C. C. 10 L. Course à boyaux allégé. Cadre tubes "Reynolds", deux freins à câble, moyeux en duralumin, guidon course "Riviera", pédalier 3 branches, manivelles allégées, jantes bois, boyaux demi-recouverts . . . . **635. »**

Sur C. C. 10 L, Supplément pour :
Jantes "Mavic" duralumin. . . . . **110. »**
Boyaux soie. . . . . **100. »**
Guidon duralumin . . . . **35. »**
Freins duralumin. . . . . **40. »**

DEMI-COURSE

HAUTEUR DE CADRE : 54 - 57 OU 60. ROUES de 700 × 30 B.

Demi-Course

P. N. 7. Demi-course nickelée : Deux freins à câble Peugeot, moyeu arrière deux pignons dont un à roue libre, pédales acier, garde-boue acier, jantes nickelées, guidon course ou sport, couvre-chaîne, écrous papillons, pompe, sacoche avec outillage. Émail couleur : grenat, bleu ou vert, filets et décors couleur assortie, décors écossais sur demande. **495 fr.**

P. I. 7. Demi-course chromée : Toutes pièces chromées, deux freins à câble Peugeot, moyeu arrière, deux pignons dont un à roue libre, pédales de course, garde-boue acier, guidon course ou sport, couvre-chaîne, écrous papillons, accessoires de première qualité, pompe, sacoche avec outillage. Émail couleur : grenat, bleu ou vert, filets et décors couleur assortie, décors écossais sur demande. **530. »**

Course Amateur

P. L. 8. Demi-course amateur chromée. Toutes pièces chromées, deux freins à câble Peugeot, spéciaux course, attaches freins et gaines brasées, tête de fourche spéciale, moyeux bain d'huile, arrière deux pignons dont un à roue-libre, pédales acier de course, pédalier 3 branches, manivelles traitées, garde-boue demi-chromés spéciaux, guidon course ou sport poignées caoutchouc para, chaîne luxe, pneus para, rayons fins émaillés, écrous papillons, selle de course grand modèle, accessoires de luxe, pompe, sacoche avec outillage. Émail couleur au choix ou métallisé, filets fantaisie, décors couleur assortie, décors écossais sur demande . . . . **595. »**

Ce modèle peut être livré sur demande, sans supplément, avec couvre-chaîne.

Série Cyrus

C. 7. Demi-course nickelée : Deux freins à câble . . . . **375. »**
C. C. 7. Demi-course chromé : Deux freins à câble . . . . **420. »**

A couple of pages from the 1936 catalogue.

PC10SP 'Course Spécial Professionnel' in the reshuffle, listed at 790FF – well over double the cost of a PC9 model, but with Rubis frame tubes, an uprated freewheel mechanism, and a number of chrome-plated parts to justify the premium. By 1934, the PS7 was replaced by the PC7, making the 'Course' range consist of the basic PC9, the PU7 and PC7 'Demi-Course' models, the PC8 and PC10 for amateur racers, and the elegant PC10SP. These continued into 1935, and were joined by the PC10AL. Priced at 980FF, the latter was a lightweight model using Reynolds tubing, duralumin hubs, wheel release wingnuts and pedals (duralumin, sometimes shortened to dural, being the moniker given to a high-quality aluminium alloy, some three times lighter than steel), wooden wheels with racing tyres, and a Brooks racing saddle.

At a time when wages were averaging 5FF an hour, and over double the cost of a regular runabout model like the PU22, the PC10AL really was a top-end machine, with the accessories list confirming this, for the model (and the PC10SP, for that matter) was available with duralumin wheels for 110FF, duralumin handlebars for 15FF, duralumin brakes for 30FF, lightweight chrome-plated and perforated cranks for 20FF, a three-speed 'Super Champion' derailleur from Oscar Egg's workshop for 75FF, and a duralumin derailleur for 90FF. The Mavic 700C alloy rims were certainly a novel item back then, but the derailleur was also rather special.

Before the birth of the derailleur, the ability to change gears on the move had been a rarity, with the Sturmey-Archer three-speed hub being by far the best option available, and offered by Peugeot from before WWI until well into the thirties. For a time, it was listed alongside several other hubs from France and Britain, but it was the hub named after Henry Sturmey and James Archer that prevailed. Ironically, the production

Domestic advertising from 1937.

version was based on a rival design by William Reilly rather than the aforementioned pair, but Sturmey's name was held in high esteem, and Frank Bowden of Raleigh fame made a deal to keep his vanity intact and also corner the market in conjunction with BSA. In reality, it was another example of how interlaced the cycling and automotive worlds were in the early days, for Sturmey was a keen cyclist that went on to be the editor of *Autocar*. He was also closely connected with Harry J. Lawson, who got Daimler off the ground in Coventry, and floated more bicycle and car firms than almost anyone else in the two industries worldwide. Anyway, while the elegantly-engineered Sturmey-Archer hub may have been ideal for raddoneurs and suchlike, it was not suited to racing applications, even though Comiot (France's Sturmey-Archer distributor) supplied one to Lucien Petit-Breton for the 1913 TdF to prove its worth. But no matter how good the epicyclic gear hubs were, competition work is where the derailleur came into its own.

An early type of derailleur had been used on the 1933 Giro d'Italia, the Italian organisers allowing their use long before those behind the Tour de France. Indeed, it was 1937 before one was seen on the TdF, but nonetheless, it signalled in another new era. Until then, innovative professional racers of the 1930s often had a second chain sprocket installed on opposite sides of the rear wheelhub, thus providing them with two gear ratios if they were willing to get off the bike, remove the chain, flip the wheel, and reattach the chain. This was a lengthy procedure, and no matter how primative the first derailleur designs were, they were still an improvement on traditional methods of getting a second speed. What's more, the derailleur often allowed a third gear (as offered by Peugeot), thus enabling the rider to more readily choose the right ratios for the job in hand – an important thing for those chasing the King of the Mountains titles recently introduced on both the Tour and the Giro.

In the background, 1935 witnessed the first running of the Vuelta a España – the Spanish race that with the Tour de France and Giro d'Italia makes up the three major classics, or Grand Tours. Unlike the high-profile French race, though, or the Italian one where domestic makers like Legnano and Bianchi were the dominant force and able to make the most of the marketing opportunities success brought, La Vuelta didn't really take off until after the Second World War, as the Spanish Civil War brought it to a grinding halt after being held for just two years.

The 1936 catalogue was fascinating for fans of Peugeot road bikes, as the range was expanded via the entry-level CC10 and CC10L (the latter having a lightweight Reynolds frame), both being available with the PC10 accessories for racers on a budget. This so-called 'Serié Cyrus' line was also available in the 'Demi-Course' range, with the C7 and chrome-adorned CC7 joining the PN7, the PI7 (with chrome parts) and PL8. For the record, the PC10, PC10SP, PC10AL and the two CC10s were supplied with wood rims, despite the otherwise modern specifications; opting for the Mavic rims would provide the buyer with a bicycle that wouldn't have looked out of place decades later.

Just as the bikes, and the components and accessories fitted to them for that matter, were evolving into decidedly modern articles (Peugeot was even working on an all-aluminium bicycle that was incredibly avantgarde), once again, the world was drawn into a war that put everything else on hold. From September 1939 to September 1945, cycling was basically the last thing on anyone's mind, even though certain Nazi-occupied countries were told to continue holding events to give an impression of normality. Things were far from normal, however, with factories turned over to the war effort, and virtually anything metal being melted down to keep the lines going.

One often wonders about the fate of the various French factories in the witch-hunt that followed the war, with the likes of Renault and Berliet being excellent examples of victims of an interim government (led by Charles de Gaulle) that was keen to show strength and reap revenge for even the slightest hint of collaboration long before VE Day materialised. Citroën escaped De Gaulle's wrath because Pierre Boulanger, who headed the company at the time, was found to be on a Nazi list of people to arrest on the grounds of a lack of co-operation, while Peugeot's loyalty was never questioned due to Rudolphe Peugeot aiding the French Resistance in sabotaging his own factory, not just once, but twice! Unlike Renault, which became a nationalised company in January 1945, the future of the Peugeot brand was safe, remaining in the hands of the founding family …

Cover of a 1942 issue of the famous Argentian sports magazine, *El Gráfico*, giving the Peugeot brand useful publicity.

2. POSTWAR REVIVAL

While the opening chapter covered the birth of the Peugeot brand and the development of the bicycle in general, this one takes the story from the end of WWII through to 1959, by which time, the bikes, the teams and the various suppliers had just about fallen into line, once and for all giving us the names we came to recognise in the golden era of cycling ...

The bicycle industry, like so many others, was never quite the same after the war, with many of the smaller firms consigned to the history books. The bigger concerns, bolstered by military orders to take the place of civilian goods, remained as strong as ever, though, with most reviving prewar lines to get things moving again as Europe's conglomerates adjusted to peacetime manufacturing.

The Peugeot cycle catalogue was a case in point, with the PC8 and PC10AL being rolled out for service once more, although there were now four-speed gearsets on the back, and alloy 700C rims and hubs were standard fare. The chain guard on the PC8 looked a little out of place, but the PC10AL was a work of art, with a Stronglight headset and pedal straps included in the package. Of special interest was the Type PRH 'Grand Randonneur', which although not a racer by any stretch of the imagination, is worth a mention due to its two gears at the front, that combined with four at the back

Cover and the PC10AL section of the 1947 catalogue, below which was a list of the Peugeot team's successes during the 1946 season.

Camille Danguillaume was one of many riders to provide Peugeot with a deep pool of talent after WWII. The brother of fellow Peugeot racers André and Roland, and the uncle of Jean-Pierre Danguillaume (who would also don a Peugeot shirt in his day), unfortunately his life was cut tragically short by an accident in 1950.

gave an eight-speed model. The final parts of the jigsaw were falling into place, and the modern road bike was therefore just around the corner.

Peugeot actually retained a racing team throughout the war years, so found itself in a relatively good position when events started up again. Under the direction of Robert Pahin (a champion motorcyclist and Peugeot exponent), Camille Danguillaume, Maurice de Muer, Gaby Gaudin, Gilbert Martin, Robert Dorgebray, René Lafosse, Albert Dolhats, Jean de Gribaldi and Victor Joly picked up some decent results in 1946, ably assisted by 15 other riders. The Peugeot-Dunlop team was back in yellow with blue jerseys after the conflict, but reverted to blue with yellow as the forties came to an end (by which time, Camille Narcy, a professional rider in the interwar years, had established himself as Directeur Sportif), and stuck with these colours until the definitive white with a chequered flag design came through in the early sixties.

The Tour de France came back to life in the middle of 1947, although a lot of water had passed under the bridge since it was last run. Not least, the organiser had changed, albeit on face value, as the publishing house Henri Desgrange was so readily associated with had been closed down due to some trumped-up charges of collusion during the war. As it happens, Desgrange had given up his post as editor and director of the Tour de France long before as a result of failing health, and had died in August 1940. However, his successor (Jacques Goddet, the son of Victor Goddet, *L'Auto*'s first finance chief) carried on the same policies as Desgrange without question, both on paper and in the sporting arena. As such, the first Tour de France under his guidance (the 1936 edition) was exactly as Desgrange would have done it.

Ultimately, as a way forward, *L'Equipe* was born out of the *L'Auto* title in February 1946, printed on white paper at the request of the French authorities, who wanted any sign of *L'Auto* gone for good. The journal was actually much the same in reality, with the same staff by and large, and it was printed at an office that once belonged to the now-defunct title. But Goddet was told to keep a distance, allowing the paper's survival and Goddet to continue as organiser of the TdF via the *L'Equipe* offices. A point had been made, with the largely sympathetic arrangements leaving all parties happy enough at the end of the day ...

When the great race was revived for 1947, Goddet, teaming up with resistance fighter and publishing magnate Émilien Amaury, decided the 21-stage event was to be run in the same format as the prewar era (or at least from 1930 to 1939), meaning teams were selected according to countries and French regions, so the Peugeot-Dunlop banner couldn't really be raised. There wasn't much to celebrate anyway. Albert Bourlon, Peugeot rider and winner of the one-day Paris-Bourges race that year, won the 14th stage from Carcassonne to Luchon after a stunning solo break, but it was his team-mate and compatriot, Paul Giguet, that finished highest of the Peugeot men in the general classification (GC) in 1947, coming 19th overall after 4642 gruelling kilometres (a fraction over 2900 miles); Bourlon was 21st.

Paul Giguet, who rode for Peugeot almost exclusively throughout his lengthy career. He is seen here showing his approval of a certain aperitif that would become synonymous with cycling in the near future.

A return to normality

The basic 1948 domestic catalogue saw the PC8 dropped in favour of the PH18, which was called a 'Sport' bike, but the mixte-type frame design was too unusual for it to be classed as a proper road-race bicycle. While a men's version (the PH8) was available, the PC8 duly made a rapid comeback in the brochures. The PC10AL was also gone, but at least its replacement – the four-speed PH10 – was a pukka machine, and indeed, the picture used to illustrate it looks exactly the same as that used for the earlier bike. As before, it was available in 54, 56, 58 and 60cm frame sizes, and painted in red enamel.

Jacques Pras won the fourth stage of the 1948 Tour de France, but, like the year before, contemporary Peugeot-Dunlop team members had to be satisfied with a single stage win, and its top rider a long way down the general classification. At least the country/region format that remained in place until 1961 hid the disappointment to some extent, although with riders now clearly sporting the name of their mount on both their bibs and shorts, there was still a good chance to make the most of the marketing potential competition success brings.

Of course, across the border, the folks behind the Giro d'Italia had no qualms about the professional teams fighting it out in time-honoured fashion. Indeed, every running of this classic Grand Tour since the very first one back in 1909 has been a works team event: for sure, an individual is held up as the victor, but his team shares the limelight to keep sponsors happy. As it happens, this

Continued on page 36

Below: The PH10 featured in the 1948 catalogue.

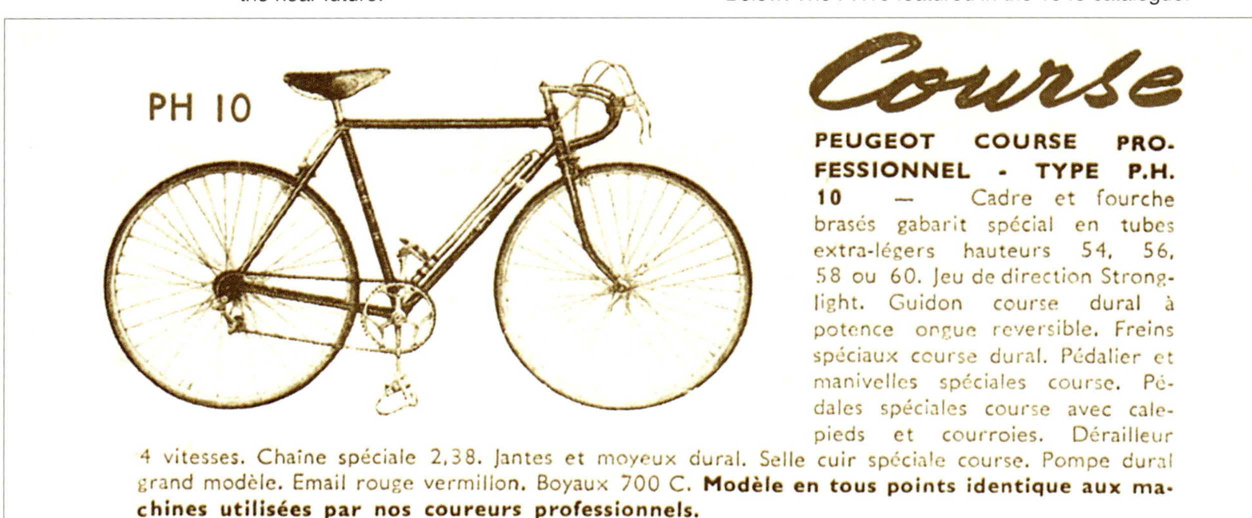

PH 10

Course

PEUGEOT COURSE PROFESSIONNEL - TYPE P.H. 10 — Cadre et fourche brasés gabarit spécial en tubes extra-légers hauteurs 54, 56, 58 ou 60. Jeu de direction Stronglight. Guidon course dural à potence ongue reversible. Freins spéciaux course dural. Pédalier et manivelles spéciales course. Pédales spéciales course avec cale-pieds et courroies. Dérailleur 4 vitesses. Chaine spéciale 2,38. Jantes et moyeux dural. Selle cuir spéciale course. Pompe dural grand modèle. Email rouge vermillon. Boyaux 700 C. **Modèle en tous points identique aux machines utilisées par nos coureurs professionnels.**

One of the Peugeot riders having some adjustments made to his bike on the 1949 Paris-Roubaix. (Courtesy *L'Equipe*)

Below: Émile Idée fighting away on the 1949 Tour de France. Idée had won the Critérium National for Peugeot a couple of months earlier, having come second to Camille Danguillaume in the previous year. (Courtesy *L'Equipe*)

Cover and selected pages from the 1950 catalogue.

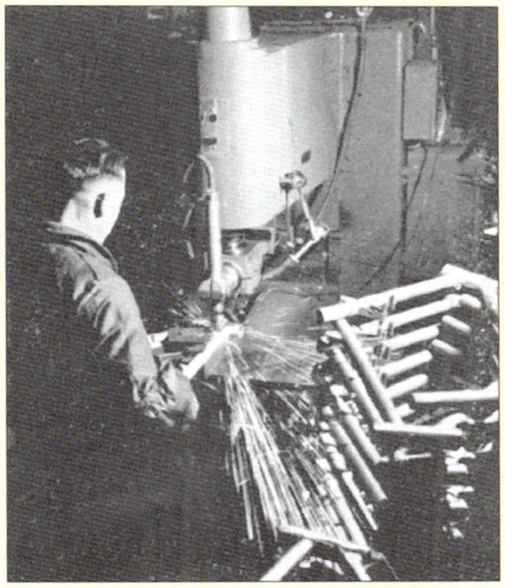

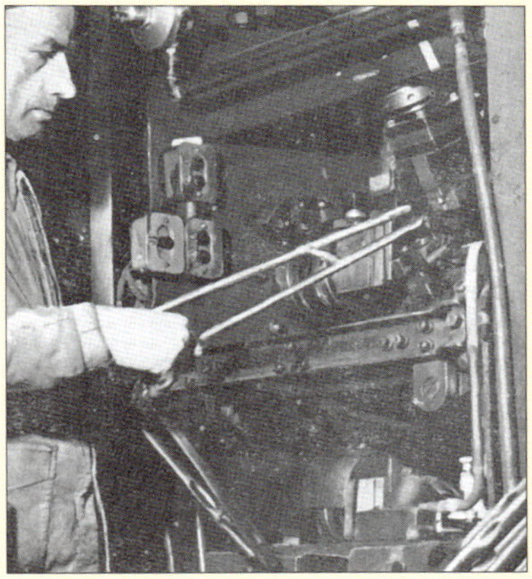

This page and spread overleaf: Details from a domestic brochure from 1952. As well as the attractive cover and the road racer sections in full (overleaf), we can see contemporary production methods, too. First we see the tube-making machine; tubes were then heat treated, machined, welded and painted. Various components were made in another part of the factory, including wheels for the lesser models, and then added with any bought-in parts to the frames. The final picture shows bikes being packed ready for shipping.

G^{DS} RANDONNEURS SPÉCIAUX

PH. 60. MODÈLE HOMME.

Tubes Vitus. Direction Stronglight. Pédalier Stronglight. Manivelles duralumin sans clavettes. Jantes « Ménal 51 indéformable ». Pneus 1/2 recouverts extra-légers. Moyeux spéciaux extra-légers à grandes ailettes (ou flasques allégés). Blocage Simplex compétition. Rayons acier inoxydables. Dérailleur AR. Simplex 4 vitesses. Dérailleur AV. type randonneur Simplex. Double plateau 46×32. Chaîne Yellorex de 2,38. Guidon course dural à potence reversible. Protège-frein AV. et porte-sacoche. Poignées tressées blanches. Pédales sport duralumin. Cale-pieds et courroies. Garde-boue Peugeot nervurés à bandeaux. Freins sécurité Mafac. Selle sport croupon clair 1er choix, chariot duralumin. Porte-bagages Peugeot sport cyclotouriste. Eclairage grand luxe. Phare duralumin modèle réduit sur garde-boue AV. Pompe extra-légère. Trousse d'outillage Mafac. Email : BLANC DE NEIGE.

PH. 65. MODÈLE DAME.

Même description que PH. 60, cadre triangulé, guidon duralumin type sport randonneur. Poignées caoutchouc blanches. Pare-chaîne sport métal léger.

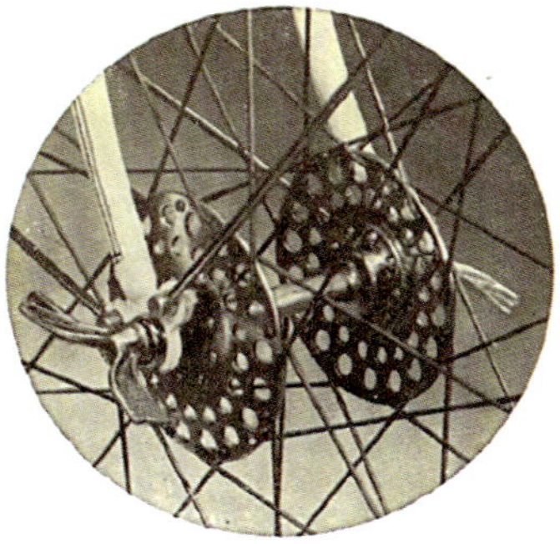

Moyeux à flasques allégées.

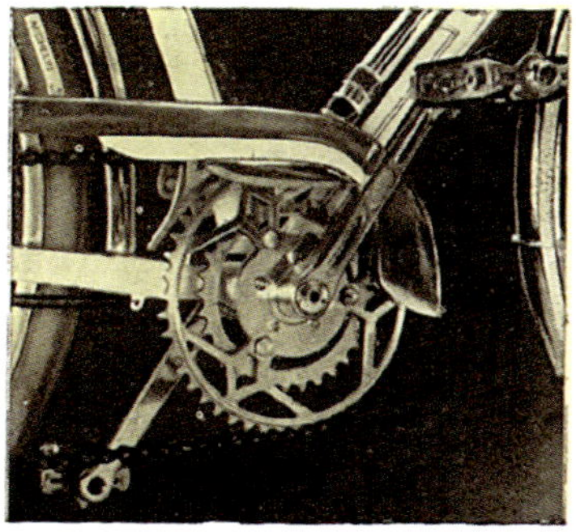

Double plateau et pare-chaîne sport.

is when Italian heroes, such as Gino Bartali and Fausto Coppi, were coming of age, with Bartali of Legnano (and later his own bike brand, made by Santamaria of Novi Ligure, to the south of Milan), and Coppi putting Bianchi firmly in the spotlight.

While the TdF was not being kind to Peugeot, Camille Danguillaume won the Critérium National again in 1948 (he was joint-first in 1946), with Émile Idée, now with Peugeot-Dunlop, claiming his fifth win on the event in the following year. This would be the last

SPORT ET COURSE

PC. 8. MODÈLE SPORT LUXE.
Pédalier 3 branches, manivelles allégées. Jantes acier. Pneus course de 700 C. Moyeux acier. Rayons acier inoxydables. Roue libre Moyne 3 dentures. Dérailleur Simplex type Tour de France, 3 vitesses. Chaîne Yellorex de 3,17. Garde-boue métal léger à bandeaux. Guidon course 1/2 dural. Poignées tressées couleur assortie au cadre. 2 freins sport acier. Pédales acier sport. Selle sport croupon 1er choix. Pompe duralumin. Trousse d'outillage Mafac.
Émaux : BLEU TRANSPARENT, VERT TRANSPARENT, ROUGE TRANSPARENT.

PH. 8. MODÈLE SPORT GRAND LUXE.
Comme le modèle précédent mais avec jantes « Ménal 51 ». Moyeux dural. Roue libre 4 dentures. Dérailleur AR. 4 vitesses. Dérailleur AV. double plateau 46×50. Chaîne Yellorex de 2,38. Eclairage luxe. Émaux : BLEU TRANSPARENT, VERT TRANSPARENT, IVOIRE.

PH. 10. MODÈLE COURSE
Modèle identique aux machines utilisées par nos coureurs professionnels.
Tubes Vitus. Direction Stronglight. Pédalier à manivelles Stronglight compétition. Jantes dural spéciales course 700 C. Boyaux course 700 C. Moyeux extra-légers. Blocage Simplex compétition. Roue-libre Moyne 4 dentures (14×16×18×20 ou 15×16×17×18). Dérailleur AR. Simplex type Tour de France 4 vitesses. Dérailleur AV. Simplex type compétition. Double plateau 46×50. Rayons acier inoxydable. Pédales course duralumin. Cale-pieds et courroies. Guidon course duralumin potence reversible, à poignées tressées. Freins course Lam duralumin type Tour de France. Selle spéciale course cuir traité, à chariot duralumin. Tige de selle duralumin. Pompe duralumin spéciale course. Trousse d'outillage Mafac.
Émail : ROUGE VERMILLON.

Peugeot victory in this race for a while, but there were plenty of other races providing the team with success. Peugeot riders claimed the Vuelta a España in 1948 (Bernardo Ruiz was declared winner in the GC and also crowned King of the Mountains), the second ever Tour de Romandie, the Grand Prix des Nations and the classic Liège-Bastogne-Liège (aka La Doyenne) in 1949, and were also declared champion of Spain in 1948 and champion of Switzerland in 1948 and 1949.

By 1950, further expansion at the Beaulieu factory

Ferdi Kübler pipping Peugeot's Stan Ockers to the post in the 1952 La Flèche Wallonne race. Kübler had ridden for Peugeot a few years earlier, but was now with the Frejus team. (Courtesy *L'Equipe*)

saw the facility covering over a million square feet (110,000m²) – it was totally unrecognisable from the old mill in which the Peugeot bicycle legend started, despite being on the same site. Production was up to 160,000 units a year by this time (aided by the recent acquisition of a small factory at Saint-Louis, to the east of Valentigney), and catalogues were at last being illustrated by photographs rather than drawings. The PC8 and PH10 were still there, augmented by the usual selection of regular machines for men, women and children, including elegant touring models like the PC40 and PH50 (the latter spawning a drop handlebar version known as the PHR50, with the PHR55 listed as a ladies version), and the sporty PH60 'Grand Randonneur' made with Vitus tubing, as used on the PH10.

The 1950 Tour de France will best be remembered for the clash between Gino Bartali and Jean Robic – it certainly wasn't for the success of Peugeot regulars, although Custodio Dos Reis did manage to take a stage win (after the two Italian teams quit, it should be said), and Belgian rider Marcel Verschueren finished the event in 15th overall. On the racing front at least, it was a disappointing year all-round for Peugeot fans. Despite wins on the Paris-Tours and Tour de Lombardie, plus two finishers in the top 20 of the TdF (Édouard Van Ende in 14th and Marcel Verschueren in 18th), as it happens, 1951 was another poor season for a top-flight

Wonderful shot from the 1952 Tour de France. From left to right we can see Gino Bartali, Bernado Ruiz, Stan Ockers, and Fausto Coppi. Coppi won the event on a Bianchi, with Ockers second on a Peugeot, and Ruiz third on a Le Perle. (Courtesy *L'Equipe*)

outfit, and would prove to be Camille Narcy's last as team manager.

Meanwhile, there were few surprises in the 1951 Peugeot bicycle catalogue, with much the same line-up, joined by a four-speed PH8 (the similar-looking PC8 had three gears), and the four-speed PC10 road bike with a frame made using 'extra-légers' tubing – a grade down from the PH10's Vitus tubes, but superior and lighter than the steel employed on the two models sporting an '8' suffix. The PH10 had four speeds at the back from day one, but, by 1950, had inherited a lever-activated Simplex Compétition front derailleur as well, thus making it into an eight-speed machine – another example of how racing continued to improve cycling in general; the PH8 also had a front derailleur as standard, further distancing it from the cheaper PC8. Oddly, even though Stronglight had been making steel and alloy cotterless cranksets since the 1930s, the PH10 had a steel crankset with a cotter pin, as this was still the setup favoured by the majority of top riders. It would be some time before cotterless cranks and alloy gearwheels caught on, but they were at least starting to make inroads into the scene.

For 1952, the three-speed PC8 continued with detail changes, plus new shades of the three existing paint schemes. While the short-lived PC10 was dropped from the line-up, the eight-speed PH8 was carried over, available with fresh blue, green or ivory colouring, as was the PH10, still listed in red only (a different shade of red to that used on the PC8, incidentally). The more civilised PH60 and PHR50 were still there, too, for sporty types that weren't really interested in racing. In fact, with the PC8 and PH8 having mudguards (albeit truncated, with lighting added on the PH8), and now rear carriers as well, it could be said that the eight-speed PH10 was the only bike truly worthy of the road-racer moniker for that year.

On the racing side of the business, Jean Lecocq took over as the Peugeot-Dunlop team boss, adding Belgian star Stan Ockers to the roster at the same time. It was to be another largely dry year, though, with the Tour de France providing the highlight of the 1952 season after

THE CLASSIC COMPONENT SUPPLIERS: FRAMES & SEATING

Peugeot's loyalty to French companies remained unflinching for decades, although the use of tried-and-tested Reynolds 531 steel tubing on certain premium models was forgiven, despite Reynolds being readily associated with British machinery, especially Raleigh due to its links with the TI (or Tube Investments) Group – owner of both the Reynolds and Raleigh brands by the middle of 1960. However, Columbus – the Italian equivalent to the English brand, and used on the frames of most of Italy's top class bicycles – was ignored almost completely. One had to wait until 1984 before a frame using Columbus tubing was offered, and even then, for one year only in France. It would make a comeback in the domestic market in 1989, but the 'Golden Age' was already well and truly over by this time.

Vitus, nowadays better known as a bike brand, began life as Ateliers de la Rive, turning to steel frame tube making in 1931. The company's Durifort and Rubis tubing was known for its quality, but it was the lightweight Vitus tube (used on the sporting PH10 and PHX10) that is of special interest to enthusiasts. In time, various Vitus grades would be introduced, such as the Vitus 171 and Super Vitus 971, and under Bador ownership from 1970, the St Etienne firm would become amongst the first to develop successful aluminium and carbonfibre frames, too. Incidentally, Vitus supplied unbranded machines for the Kas equipe, helping Sean Kelly and others on their way to stardom, and later provided branded bikes for the Lotto team.

Early advertising from Ateliers de la Rive – the company behind the Vitus brand. The text mentions an array of famous names to conjure with.

Reynolds and Vitus tubing may have been the obvious choice for the pure racers, but, blessed with its own foundry and manufacturing and machining experience built up over many decades, Peugeot employed homemade steel tubing on the vast majority of its bicycles from 1958 onwards (culminating in the manganese-rich HLE alloy of 1986), with in-house techniques being developed to give strong, invisible joints. On the subject of joints, lugs are something of a specialist subject, with stylish Nervex lugs being considered the ultimate when combining art and efficiency for many years, although their cost often meant lesser grades had to do with lugs sourced from other suppliers.

A 1977 advert from TI Reynolds.

As we reached the 1980s, technology started to replace tradition. The 1982 PX10DU was the first sign of this, employing a duralumin frame made of Vitus Duralinox 979 tubing, complete with bonded lugs. In time, this brought about the 'A'-series line, which took construction techniques to another level.

Next up was carbonfibre, brought out in 1983 on the

PY10FC model. This really was the beginning of the end for traditionalists – a new era for a new generation. In recent years, however, there has been something of a revival for steel-framed bikes, mostly made of Cr-Mo tubing, which is significantly more common than the aircraft-standard Reynolds 531 Mn-Mo alloy of yore.

Saddles were usually sourced domestically in the early years, with the Idéale range (from the Tron & Berthet concern, founded in Pont Saint Pierre in 1890, and basically following the design of the classic Brooks saddles) serving the company well until Peugeot started moving across to Gallet and the Spanish Arius brand in the late 1970s, followed soon after by Selle San Marco. Even then, the Idéale saddles retained their favour on the top stuff until 1982, when Tron & Berthet had closed its doors and Selle Italia products reigned supreme at the premium end of the market.

Advertising for the new Bima.

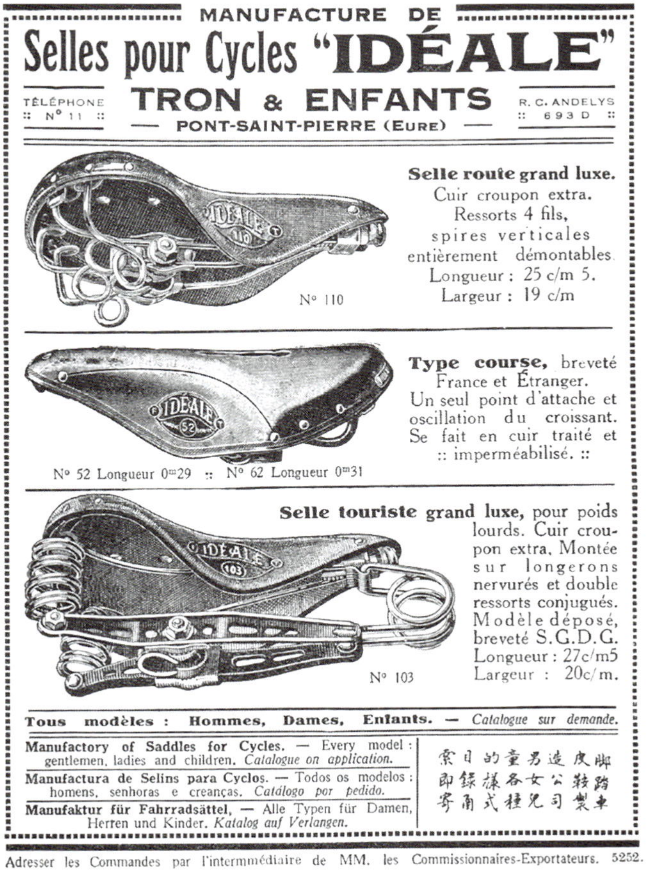

An advert for Idéale saddles dating from 1927.

Robert Vanderstockt rode well in the early stages, and Ockers finished the event in second, trailing an unstoppable Fausto Coppi.

For 1953, the vast majority of the bicycle range was given a fresh batch of code numbers, and duly joined in the catalogues by the 48cc Bima cyclemotor (an early type of moped) that had been originally introduced at the 1951 Paris Salon. For the record, the Peugeot Bima was also produced with Terrot, Automoto, Aiglon, Griffon and Ruche badging, but only the Terrot and Automoto variants made it past 1955, when the cyclemotor market fell into a sudden decline. The latter brands were dropped in 1961 and 1962, respectively, leaving only the Peugeot-branded models in the line-up.

Anyway, back to 1953, when the PC8 became the PX8 (with Hélium frame tubes), the PH8 was renamed the PHX8, and the PH10 transformed into the PHX10, although the newer models looked very similar to their predecessors at the end of the day. Basically, the 'X' suffix implies the use of rustproof materials, although the frame was not stainless

Cover and road racer pages from the 1953 French catalogue.

steel, simply regular tubing that was treated to help it withstand the rigours of time. Whilst not shown in the French catalogue (older illustrations were still being used – a common problem that acts as a cunning trap for historians), one big difference for 1953 lay in the use of chrome front fork ends on the PHX8 and PHX10, matched with chrome sections leading to and from the chrome dropout at the rear; the front lugs were painted yellow. All three sporting bikes were available in light blue, with the PX8 and PHX8 also coming in red or gold.

Incidentally, the PHX10's freewheel mechanism was changed from a Moyne unit to a Prior one at this stage in the proceedings. The frame tubing was still sourced from Vitus, while the duralumin wheel rims came from Mavic, the headset and crankset from Stronglight, the front and rear derailleurs from Simplex, the duralumin 'Béborex' braking system from Follis, the handlebars from AVA, and the toolkit from MAFAC.

In competition, despite a star-studded Peugeot-Dunlop team, a win for Robert Vanderstockt on the Tour of Luxembourg was the highlight of the 1953 season.

Start of the 1954 Tour de France, with Amsterdam chosen as the first TdF starting point outside French borders. Note the special Peugeot 203 course cars (the brand would be used in this capacity for many years), painted white, and sporting *L'Equipe* and *Le Parisien* signs down the sides. (Courtesy Wikimedia Commons: Joop van Bilsen/Anefo)

Alex Close deserves a special mention for coming fourth in the Tour de France (with Gerrit Voorting winning a stage in the same event), but overall, it was another year best forgotten by fans of the French marque.

For 1954, the PX8 morphed into the PLX8 'Luxe,' gaining a front derailleur to give eight speeds, plus chrome sections on the front and rear forks, and two-tone tyres now the norm. With the same chrome embellishments, the PHX8 'Grand Luxe' was now very similar to the lesser model at first glance, although lighter components separated the pairing with Hélium tube frames. Meanwhile, the Vitus-framed PHX10 'Course' continued pretty much unchanged, even down to the colouring. At least the catalogues confirmed the specifications this year, as the extra chrome provided a useful identifying feature when comparing the 1953 and 1954 models with their immediate predecessors.

Yves, the son of TdF hero Lucien Petit-Breton, took charge of the Peugeot-Dunlop racing team at this time, but still the results would not come. Indeed, Stan Ockers' second place in the points (green jersey) competition and sixth overall on the Tour de France was hardly a reflection of a top team. This was not a good situation, as the bicycle industry was starting to struggle, hit by a younger generation turning its back on pedal power in favour of cheap cars, scooters and mopeds. Fortunately, bicycle racing was still a firm favourite in Europe, but without competition success being reflected in sales, a few enterprising folks started turning to sponsorship in order to survive. It was ultimately a sensible idea for all concerned – an end to budget worries for the teams, and mobile advertising boards with plenty of press coverage to boot for the sponsors. Of course, with sponsorship deals on the increase, the face of the sport would change forever over the coming decades.

Indeed, there were new shirts for the 1955 season, similar in colour and style to the 1954 version, but with the Elvé name placed above the Peugeot one. Léon Van der Hulst had been making Elvé bicycles in Belgium since before the war, and had been involved in racing for some time. But it was as Belgium's Peugeot distributor that Van der Hulst made an impact,

Stan Ockers in his 'rainbow' jersey, showing him to be World Champion.

sponsoring the works racing team. Alex Close duly won the 1955 Tour of Belgium under Van der Hulst's management, and Émile Van Cauter was declared the champion of Belgium. Stan Ockers won the Liège-Bastogne-Liège and a couple of other big races in Belgium, as well as the UCI World Championship crown at Frascati in Italy.

Oddly, despite the lack of a win, the Tour de France overshadowed these results, with Jean Brankart taking second overall (as well as two stage wins and third in the climber's category), and Ockers claiming the green jersey – things were starting to head in the right direction at last. Things were looking up in Spain, too. The Vuelta a España had been held in fits and starts until now, but became a regular fixture on the international calendar from 1955 onwards. It wouldn't make much difference to the Peugeot riders that year, but at least another big part of the jigsaw puzzle had fallen into place ...

Meanwhile, with annual production standing at around 220,000 units, the 1955 range continued largely unchanged as far as the Peugeot road-racer specifications were concerned. On saying that, seemingly just to confuse folks, the PHX10 was renamed the PLX10 'Spécial Course' (still available in blue only), while the PHX8 model was dropped to leave only the PLX8, which now took on the 'Sport Grand Luxe' moniker. It was a sign of the times that a certain amount of rationalisation was called for, with the same two bikes rolled out again for 1956 and 1957.

The Elvé-Peugeot team got another shot in the arm in 1956, with another win on the Tour of Belgium (courtesy of André Vlayen), and, thanks to Alex Close, one on the Critérium du Dauphiné, too. At the same time, Vlayen was declared champion of Belgium (repeating the feat, again aboard a Peugeot, in the following year), and Rik Van Steenbergen was crowned the UCI World Champion in Copenhagen, Denmark, that August. As with Vlayen, Van Steenbergen (who'd joined the team in 1955) duly claimed a double in 1957 when the world championship was held in Waregem, Belgium.

In the three Grand Tours, Stan Ockers kept hold of his TdF green jersey for another year (finishing the 1956 event – the last before his untimely death – in eighth overall), and while there was nothing to write home about on the Giro d'Italia in 1956, at least Peugeot

Continued on page 50

Jean Brankart winning the Pau stage on the 1955 Tour de France. (Courtesy *L'Equipe*)

The 1955 TdF winner Louison 'Zonzon' Bobet flanked by his younger brother, Jean Bobet (left), and Elvé-Peugeot man Richard Van Genechten. (Courtesy *L'Equipe*)

THE SPORTING RIVALS

ALCYON (FRA)

This Paris-based maker was founded by Edmond Gentil in the 1890s, and was probably Peugeot's greatest rival in the pre-WWII era, and in the years immediately following the conflict. Gentil had also made cars and motorcycles, but it was the bicycles that he will be remembered for; Alcyon also took over the La Française, Thomann and Labor brands in due course, making the famous manufacturer even stronger. Alcyon riders are credited with 14 Tour de France victories (seven officially, and seven more in the national team years), and a similar number of wins on the Paris-Roubaix and Bordeaux-Paris races, in addition to countless other trophies and championship titles. Alcyon became part of the Peugeot empire in 1954, although the racing team continued for several years after that.

AUTOMOTO (FRA)

The Automoto marque, founded in Saint Étienne back in 1889, had built motorbikes and bicycles over a similar period as Peugeot, but found itself having to team up with the Doubs-based maker, and was taken over completely in 1931. The once-proud Automoto racing team, which could point to four consecutive wins on the Tour de France, finally disappeared by 1952, with the brand as a whole following ten years later.

WILIER (ITA)

The Wilier brand was founded by Pietro Dal Molin in 1906. He quickly established a reputation for building quality machines, and soon had to abandon his tiny workshop for bigger premises. After WWI, Pietro's son, Mario, took over the business, which become a vast enterprise – one that would emerge well from the Second World War via the Wilier Triestina racing team, which would win the 1948 Giro d'Italia thanks to Fiorenzo Magni. However, the Dal Molin family had to sell up in 1952, and motorcycles took priority. Guided by the romance attached to the name, Lino and Antonio Gasteldello duly stepped in to revive the brand in 1969, and became involved in racing again a decade later.

LA PERLE (FRA)

Based in Saint-Maur, close to Le Havre in northern France, the La Perle Cycle Co was a newcomer in relative terms, being founded in the 1930s, and thus too late to establish itself properly before the Second World War. Notwithstanding, after the conflict, and led by Francis Pélissier, the La Perle racing team was blessed with greats like Hugo Koblet and Jacques Anquetil (Koblet had won the 1951 Tour de France on a La Perle), going a long way towards explaining why Peugeot was largely left in the shadows during this period. By 1955, though, feeling the pinch that eliminated a lot of the smaller brands, the firm had filed for bankruptcy, and was duly consigned to the history books soon after.

An Alcyon poster from the late 1930s.

Fiorenzo Magni pictured aboard a Wilier in 1948.

Jacques Anquetil and the La Perle team car featured on the cover of a 1953 publication.

STELLA (FRA)

The Stella brand's origins can be traced back to 1909, when Pierre Fonteneau added bicycles to the family business, which until then had been building prams and sewing machines. His son, another Pierre, stuck to his father's policy of small volumes and high quality until the Second World War broke out. After WWII, in a bid to revive the brand, Paul le Drogo built a racing team around Louison Bobet, who won the 1953 and 1954 editions of the Tour de France on a Stella bike equipped with Huret components. Stella was offering over 20 different models by this time, but after Bobet left the team with another key member, Pierre Barbotin, it lost a lot of its shine. It did manage to limp into the 1970s with bikes that looked a lot like the contemporary Peugeots, but a devastating fire at the factory in 1975 proved to be the final nail in the coffin for the Nantes company.

BH (ESP)

The BH brand shares the honour of being Spain's leading bike manufacturer with Orbea, although its importance in later years cannot be underestimated. Founded in 1909 by three brothers, Domingo, Juan and Cosme Beistegui (with BH standing for Beistegui Hermanos), the company duly started building bikes in 1923. The first Vuelta was won by a BH rider, and rapid expansion followed on the back of this success into the 1950s. Cashing in on the BMX/ATB boom, as well as maintaining a presence in classic road-racing, BH would ultimately go on to be an important part of the Cycleurope project.

Richard Van Genechten keeping Mercier's Fred De Bruyne company on the 1956 Liège-Bastogne-Liège race. De Bruyne ultimately won, but was followed home by three Peugeot riders. (Courtesy *L'Equipe*)

Rik Van Steenbergen in his World Champion shirt. He can be seen in his more familiar Peugeot team colours in the introduction.

The Belgian team at the start of the 1957 TdF, which included many Peugeot riders. Pino Cerami is second from the left, with Alex Close on his left. Marcel Janssens is to the left of centre, while second and third from the right are Frans Schoubben and Joseph Planckaert respectively. (Courtesy *L'Equipe*)

Below: Marcel Janssens (right) keeping pace with 1957 Tour de France winner Jacques Anquetil. By the time they arrived in Paris, the Frenchman had nearly 15 minutes on the Belgian Peugeot rider, but second overall was still a fine achievement. (Courtesy *L'Equipe*)

The LX10 section from the 1958 catalogue.

exponent Raymond Impanis was third in the Vuelta a España that year.

In 1957, with Peugeot represented by the Peugeot-BP-Dunlop and Elvé-Peugeot-Marvan teams (although Léon Van der Hulst was DS for both, and almost half of the riders were shared), Marcel Rohrbach won the Critérium du Dauphiné, Pino Cerami was victorious on the Tour of Belgium, and Frans Schoubben was declared joint-winner of the Liège-Bastogne-Liège with a Faema squad member. In addition, Peugeot rider Marcel Janssens was second overall in the Tour de France.

Interestingly, Bertrand Peugeot (grandson of Robert Peugeot, and later architect of the Peugeot-Citroën merger) held a press conference in early October 1957 stating that a new level of effort would be made on the competition front under Gaston Plaud. While Van der Hulst had allowed Peugeot to turn a corner, this move signalled the true renaissance of the team, although it would take some time for the planted seed to grow into something worthwhile. For now, two equipes would continue to represent the marque in 1958 and 1959, but only the Peugeot-BP-Dunlop team would be wearing the famous blue and yellow jersey from 1960 onward ...

Peugeot had fielded the same pair of PLX8 and PLX10 eight-speed sports bikes for three straight seasons, backed up by the three-speed PL8 'Junior' and PLX50 randonneur. For 1958, however, the top model gained Reynolds frame tubing and MAFAC-sourced forged duralumin centre-pull brakes, the 'P' prefix was dropped from the model codes, and the colours were revised (albeit in the same red, blue and yellowish-gvold basic shades, just subtly different hues). In reality, other than the change in braking systems, it was still difficult to tell the 1958 models from those sold in the previous season, with the LX10 continuing in blue with yellow detailing only, and the decals above the front derailleur lever much the same, too.

In the background, sales were still falling off. Peugeot was in a better position than most, but still hurting nonetheless, so parts of the Cycles Peugeot operation turned to the manufacture of car components, while the Beaulieu factory started making its own

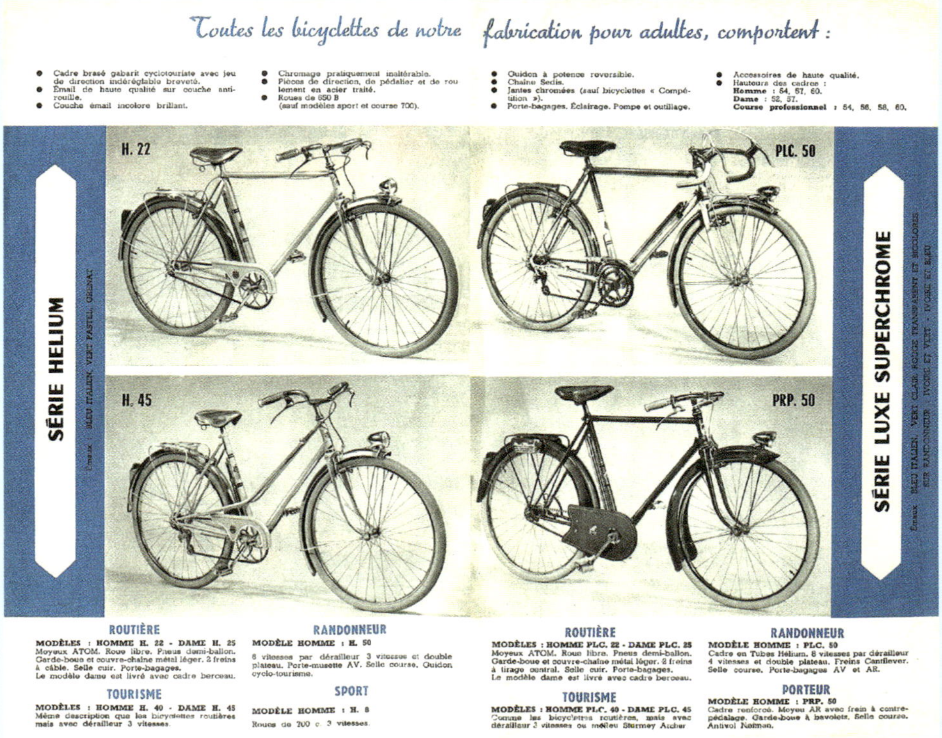

Toutes les bicyclettes de notre fabrication pour adultes, comportent :

- Cadre brasé gabarit cyclotouriste avec jeu de direction indéréglable breveté.
- Émail de haute qualité sur couche antirouille.
- Couche émail incolore brillant.
- Chromage pratiquement inaltérable.
- Pièces de direction, de pédalier et de roulement en acier traité.
- Roues de 650 B (sauf modèles sport et course 700).
- Guidon à potence reversible.
- Chaîne Sedis.
- Jantes chromées (sauf bicyclettes « Compétition »).
- Porte-bagages. Éclairage. Pompe et outillage.
- Accessoires de haute qualité.
- Hauteurs des cadres :
Homme : 54, 57, 60.
Dame : 52, 57.
Course professionnel : 54, 56, 58, 60.

SÉRIE HELIUM

Émaux : BLEU ITALIEN, VERT PASTEL, GRENAT

H. 22

H. 45

ROUTIÈRE

MODÈLES : HOMME H. 22 - DAME H. 25
Moyeux ATOM. Roue libre. Pneus demi-ballon. Garde-boue et couvre-chaîne métal léger. 2 freins à câble. Selle cuir. Porte-bagages.
Le modèle dame est livré avec cadre berceau.

TOURISME

MODÈLES : HOMME H. 40 - DAME H. 45
Même description que les bicyclettes routières mais avec dérailleur 3 vitesses.

RANDONNEUR

MODÈLE HOMME : H. 50
6 vitesses par dérailleur 3 vitesses et double plateau. Porte-musette AV. Selle course. Guidon cyclo-tourisme.

SPORT

MODÈLE HOMME : H. 8
Roues de 700 c. 3 vitesses.

SÉRIE LUXE SUPERCHROME

Émaux : BLEU ITALIEN, VERT CLAIR, ROUGE TRANSPARENT ET BICOLORES SUR RANDONNEUR : IVOIRE ET VERT - IVOIRE ET BLEU

PLC. 50

PRP. 50

ROUTIÈRE

MODÈLES : HOMME PLC. 22 - DAME PLC. 25
Moyeux ATOM. Roue libre. Pneus demi-ballon. Garde-boue et couvre-chaîne métal léger. 2 freins à tirage central. Selle cuir. Porte-bagages.
Le modèle dame est livré avec cadre berceau.

TOURISME

MODÈLES : HOMME PLC. 40 - DAME PLC. 45
Comme les bicyclettes routières, mais avec dérailleur 3 vitesses ou moyeu Sturmey Archer

RANDONNEUR

MODÈLE HOMME : PLC. 50
Cadre en Tubes Hélium. 8 vitesses par dérailleur 4 vitesses et double plateau. Freins Cantilever. Selle course. Porte-bagages AV et AR.

PORTEUR

MODÈLE HOMME : PRP. 50
Cadre renforcé. Moyeu AR avec frein à contre-pédalage. Garde-boue à bavolets. Selle course. Antivol Neiman.

The main pages from the 1959 domestic brochure.

SÉRIE HAUT LUXE INOXYDABLE

Émaux : BLEU ITALIEN, VERT CLAIR,
ROUGE TRANSPARENT ET BICOLORES SUR RANDONNEUR :
IVOIRE ET VERT, IVOIRE ET BLEU

GRAND TOURISME

MODÈLE HOMME : PHX. 40 — MODÈLE DAME : PHX. 45
Jantes chrolux. Pneus bicolores. 3 vitesses par dérailleur ou moyeu Sturmey Archer. Garde-boue en acier Peuginox. Freins à tirage central. Porte-bagages avec 2 sacoches et serre-paquets. Antivol Neiman.

PHX. 50

PHX. 40

PHX. 10

PHX. 45

GRAND TOURISME RANDONNEUR

MODÈLE HOMME : PHX. 50
Tubes Hélium. Bases, haubans et fourche AV chromés. Moyeux dural. 8 vitesses, par dérailleur 4 vitesses et double plateau. Porte-bagages AV et AR. Selle course. Antivol Neiman.

COMPÉTITION

MODÈLE COURSE PROFESSIONNEL : PHX. 10
Tubes Reynolds. Bases, haubans et fourche AV chromés. Jantes et boyaux course 700 c. Moyeux légers à blocage instantané. 10 vitesses. Double plateau AV 46 × 50. Cale-pieds. Guidon et freins course dural.
Émail : BLEU TRANSPARENT.
Cette machine est livrée avec un maillot.

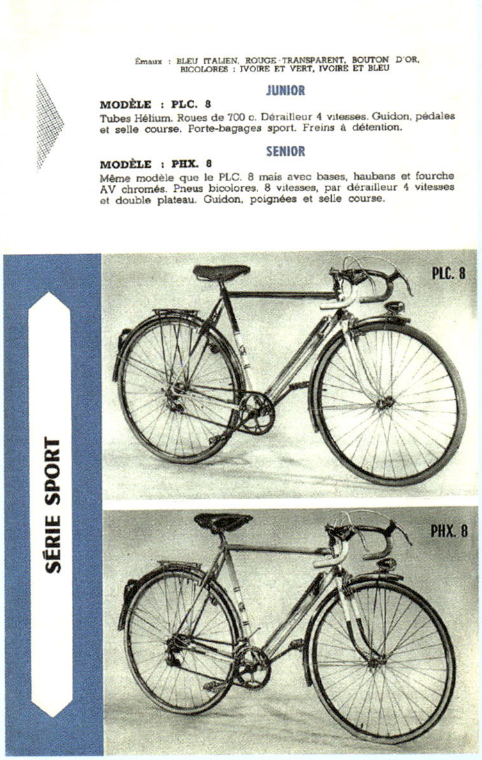

Émaux : BLEU ITALIEN, ROUGE TRANSPARENT, BOUTON D'OR,
BICOLORES : IVOIRE ET VERT, IVOIRE ET BLEU

JUNIOR

MODÈLE : PLC. 8
Tubes Hélium. Roues de 700 c. Dérailleur 4 vitesses. Guidon, pédales et selle course. Porte-bagages sport. Freins à détention.

SENIOR

MODÈLE : PHX. 8
Même modèle que le PLC. 8 mais avec bases, haubans et fourche AV chromés. Pneus bicolores. 8 vitesses, par dérailleur 4 vitesses et double plateau. Guidon, poignées et selle course.

SÉRIE SPORT

PLC. 8

PHX. 8

tubes, initially to suit the mainstream bikes, although the tubing would become more specialised as the years ticked by. Workers would later turn their hands to the fabrication of industrial items, like crates, and so on. It wasn't an ideal situation, but it was ultimately better than having to call for a spate of redundancies. The news from the racing front wasn't much brighter, with Richard Van Genechten's win on the Tour of Catalunya being the highlight of the 1958 season for Peugeot fans.

However, there was more subtle evolution in store for 1959, with the 'Junior' gaining an extra cog to become the PLC8, the LX8 becoming the PHX8, and the PHX10 replacing the LX10. While the latter remained in blue only and had to do without the new colour scheme options (variations of blue, red, yellowish gold, and two-tone ivory/green or ivory/blue, matched up with new decals), the PHX10 now had ten speeds, with the front derailleur becoming cable-operated at the same time. Interestingly, the blue paintwork offered on the top bike went back to being a unique lighter shade (the shared one offered in 1958 had been a touch deeper), and the graphics below the seatpost remained more subdued; the front lugs were still painted yellow at this stage.

Alfred 'Fred' De Bruyne signed up for Peugeot in 1959, and duly won that year's Liège-Bastogne-Liège race.

Hoping to attract a stronger field and some of the big names in racing from other parts of Europe, La Vuelta a España turned its back on the national team format in 1959, its organisers rightfully pointing out that sponsors expected a return on their investment, with the Grand Tours providing the greatest form of exposure for their teams – the spectacle provided by the Giro d'Italia being held up as the perfect example of why the Spaniards needed to change. Even the riders were in agreement, albeit from a different perspective, with one top Spanish race exponent stating that it was crazy to expect cyclists to be friends one day and rivals the next. Of course, there were some well-known personality clashes within the professional teams, with the one between Tom Simpson and Roger Pingeon in the mid-sixties being a perfect example, but one can certainly see the rider's point.

None of this made much difference to the Peugeot team, though, as its members failed to get on the podium (Manuel Busto was the top Peugeot finisher, in fifth). There was no silverware in the Tour de France or Giro d'Italia either. Alfred De Bruyne, having just joined the Peugeot-BP-Dunlop team with another good signing, Jan Adriaenssens, won the 1959 edition of the Liège-Bastogne-Liège in his native Belgium, but other than that and a few stage wins here and there, it was a quiet year. Indeed, the Elvé-Peugeot equipe, already much diminished in size, was disbanded at the end of the season, coinciding with the retirement of Alex Close, while André Vlayen went to the Molteni team. Fortunately, Peugeot didn't lose too many other big names amid the upheaval.

As the decade came to an end, Peugeot took over the Terrot business, closing the company's Dijon factory a couple of years later, in 1961. Terrot (named after founder, Charles Terrot) had been making bicycles since 1890, adding motorcycles to its range in 1902, which duly evolved into the mainstream Terrot product, spawning a successful racing team along the way. By the 1950s, Terrot was concentrating on mopeds and other lightweight motorbikes, although the bicycles, thanks to strong performances from the likes of Jean Malléjac and Jean Robic of the Terrot racing team, still had a following – a fact not lost on Peugeot's management, who furnished the Leroux and Solo equipes with Terrot bikes in the sixties, for instance, and duly kept the brand going until 1970 via some astute badge-engineering.

A beautiful poster from Terrot's earlier days.

3. THE SWINGING SIXTIES

If the fifties had been a golden age for cycling in general, with the likes of Fausto Coppi, Louison Bobet, Fiorenzo Magni, Charly Gaul and a young Jacques Anquetil thrilling the crowds, it was the sixties when Peugeot riders came to the fore, filling trophy cabinets for the French maker on bikes that enthusiasts could buy at their local dealer ...

1960 was a quiet year for the showroom models, with nothing much happening following the changes made to the line-up at the very end of 1958 in time for the 1959 season. It's interesting to note that the 1959 domestic catalogue was the first one in decades not to have a date on the cover, allowing it to be reissued over the following months and years, saving money on several fronts – an absolute necessity as the cycle industry as a whole tried to come to terms with falling demand. As such, the sporting range still consisted of the four-speed PLC8 'Junior,' the eight-speed PHX8 'Senior,' and the flagship ten-speed PHX10. It would continue this way into the autumn of 1961, as it happens, with the same colouring and specifications described at the end of the previous chapter.

Pino Cerami was the hero of the 1960 season as far as Peugeot fans were concerned, with his win on the Paris-Roubaix being celebrated for months.

Following on from the 'Cyrus' idea of prewar days, to protect Peugeot's good image, cheaper bicycles were fielded under the Hélium tradename during this period (from the 1959 season onwards, to be precise) and throughout the seventies. This move was quite common at the time, although a number of unscrupulous makers nowadays, across all manner of fields of endeavour, from cars to cameras and pretty much everything in-between, have turned this noble idea on its head, exploiting a hard-earned reputation to move lesser products that are far from worthy of the brand. For the record, the Hélium name appears both with and without an accent over the 'e' in official documents, so we are going to stick to the one style – the earliest – to avoid confusion.

Meanwhile, the appointment of Gaston Plaud as Directeur Sportif (DS) had failed to bring immediate results in the 1958 and 1959 seasons. Other than wins for Peugeot stalwart Pino Cerami on the gruelling Paris-Roubaix and La Flèche Wallonne, 1960 was also frustratingly short of silverware. The equipe was dealt another blow with Rik Van Steenbergen leaving at the end of the 1960 season to form his own racing team. Sponsored by Solo, a Belgian margarine company, the Van Steenbergen bikes were actually built by Peugeot, and a change in name to Solo-Terrot duly confirmed the Belgian's loyalty to his former masters.

As one team was born, another disappeared. Alcyon no longer posed a threat, the Neuilly-sur-Seine company founded by Edmond Gentil giving up car production in

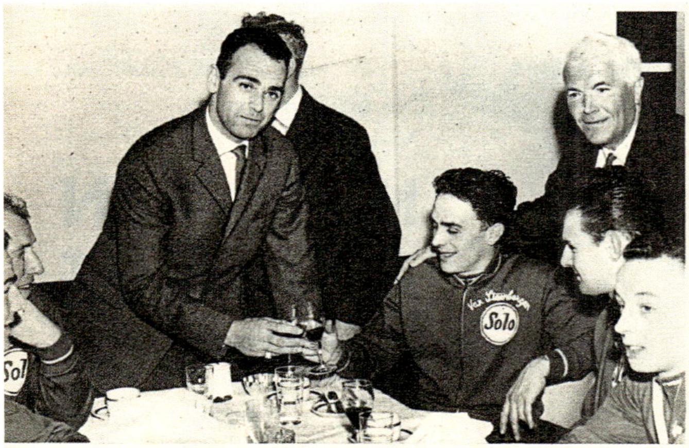

Rik Van Steenbergen klinkt op de komende successen van Stanny Goossens, streekgenoot en kampioen in de dop — Rechts van beiden Dhr Mouws, van de publiciteitsdienst van U.M.B.

RIK VAN STEENBERGEN

aan het hoofd van een nieuwe sportgroep

Rik Van Steenbergen, zal op 9 september aanstaande 37 jaar worden.

Hij, die in 1943 een seizoen begon waarin hij 16 overwinningen boekte, waaronder deze in het kampioenschap van België, heeft dus nog drie jaartjes te kloppen om te kunnen zeggen « Ik heb twee wielerdecades achter de rug en ik heb ze niet in ledigheid doorgebracht ».

Meteen zal Rik inderdaad fier het hoofd mogen opsteken. En wi' zullen er graag van getuigen, dat hij in de wielersport de grootste vakman aller tijden is geweest in zijn genre.

DE VOLLE OVERGAVE

Wat wij overigens op dit ogenblik reeds graag willen getuigen: de man, die in Arendonk werd geboren, maar sinds lange jaren als Borgerhoutenaar of Sinjoor « tout court » is aanvaard, doet sinds 1943 niets anders dan met volle overgave voor zijn stiel leven.

Rik Van Steenbergen is een renner apart. Hij alleen kon dag in, dag uit rijden, winter in, zomer uit, morgen in Aarhus, overmorgen in Milaan. Hij alleen moest niet, zoals sommigen, baron spelen in een zwitsers sneeuwlandschap om zogezegd te rusten. Hij alleen reed zesdagen aan de lopende band en wegkoersen zoveel ge maar wenste.

Dat hij hiermee een fraai fortuin heeft vergaard is niet meer dan juist. Hij deed het met werken hard en alle dagen. Anderen hebben er slechts een gelukkige beursspeculatie of een erfenis voor nodig. Zo hij dit fortuin vergaarde, dan was het tenslotte voor zijn vrouw en vijf kinderen. Het typeert hem allemaal niet alleen als renner, maar ook als mens.

Rik Van Steenbergen, met zijn naam en faam, zou op dit ogenblik kunnen stoppen een bedrijf opzetten of een wielerzaak dirigeren, ook wel op zijn renten gaan leven.

Maar ge ziet dat van hier

NON STOP

Het zit nog allemaal te diep in het bloed en er kan nog veel uitkomen. En instee van te stoppen heeft Rik zich bereid verklaard van nog wat hooi bij op zijn vork te nemen. Men is dynamisch of men is het niet. Men is Van Steenbergen of men is het niet.

Rik zal dus in de komende maanden de orkestmeester zijn van een jonge Belgische ploeg van 18 renners, die de fietsen zullen berijden waarop Rik's naam staat en de truien zullen dragen, waarop men behalve Rik's naam ook Solo zal vinden.

DE DOOP

Dat genoemde firma ineens maar een supernaam als leider van het team nam, strekt haar tot ere. Het moeten niet allemaal vreemden zijn die met onze beste spierkrachten uitpakken. En als Solo het doet, doet ze het ineens zo.

Wij hebben voor « Ons Land » de doop van de nieuwe sportgroep Van Steenbergen-Solo meegemaakt en we moeten eerlijk bekennen, dat het een prettig, inslaand doopfeest was.

In gloednieuwe rode sportpakken met de geelblauwe halsboorden (kleur die past bij de Solofabrieken) werden ons Rik's partners voor het komende seizoen voorgesteld. Het was alsof ze bewust waren dat het voor hen een eer is van door een « champion » als Rik te worden aanvaard. Langs de andere kant mogen ze er zich ook van bewust zijn dat ze iets in zich hebben, anders zouden noch Rik noch Solo hen in een team opnemen.

R. Van Steenbergen, Severeyns, Van Huyck, Cornelis, Vander Veken, Goossens, Wouters, Seneca, Van Gompel, Coppens, Colette, Maes G en R, Joosen, Van Buggenhout, Lelangue, Simon, Janssens, we wensen u veel succes voor het komend seizoen !

Rik Van Steenbergen, in het midden van de tweede rij, poseerde graag in een groep van Solo-hostessen — Solo-renners en Solo-dirigenten —

A newspaper cutting outlining the formation of Rik Van Steenbergen's new racing team.

the 1920s, and motorcycle production as good as died in the 1950s, ironically after a takeover from Peugeot. Alcyon's involvement in cycling gradually dropped off, too, with 1961 seeing the last year of participation by the archrival Alcyon-Leroux team, which had gone under the Alcyon-Dunlop banner before that, basically all the way back to the early 1920s.

Of course, the Tour de France was still being run with loosely put-together teams in a country/region format at this time. As a result, very little was made of the fact that Marcel Rohrbach was ninth overall in the 1960 edition, as well as second in the green jersey competition. Coming anywhere in the top ten is an achievement, even though we tend to hold up the victors as heroes and quickly forget the also-rans.

After a rethink in the *L'Equipe* offices, 1961 was thankfully the last year that the Tour de France was held for national teams, as opposed to professional trade-sponsored racing teams. For a little while, at least, manufacturers had a better chance of promoting their wares as having been proven in the heat of what was undoubtedly the world's toughest competition as the sixties progressed.

None of this made much difference to the Peugeot-BP-Dunlop riders in 1961 anyway, as the win by Henri Duez on the Tour of Catalunya was the only major result picked up by team members that year. Nonetheless, strong foundations were laid during this period, and ultimately, Plaud would retain his post with the Peugeot team well into the seventies. It's therefore fair to say that Plaud, who was born in Saint-Savin in March 1920, was the man behind Peugeot's revival in cycle racing, bringing together an all-star cast to propel the marque to greatness. In addition, in the PX10, Peugeot had a bike that would be able to take on the best the rest of the world had to offer ...

Atmospheric shot from the 1960 Tour de France, with Jacques Goddet sitting in the Peugeot 403 course car. (Courtesy Wikimedia Commons: Harry Pot/Anefo)

A legend is born

Looking through old pictures, it appears that bikes loosely conforming to recognised PX10 specifications had been supplied to works riders as early as the 1960 season. For example, the bike that Pino Cerami rode to victory on the Paris-Roubaix that year had its rear brake cable routed along the upper surface of the top tube, held in place by three clips – an easy to spot feature that distinguishes the PX10 from its immediate predecessor in the catalogues, the PHX10.

However, the earliest definitive record of the PX10 in paperwork appertaining to showroom models appears to be the domestic price list of October 1961. This had entry-level Hélium models ranging from 191 to 224FF, with the Peugeot-badged bikes starting at 226FF and going all the way up to 295FF in the regular lines; the

20

PX 10

PX 10 - CARACTÉRISTIQUES : Tubes Reynolds, jambages AR et fourreaux de fourche chromés, boyaux course 700 C, moyeux super compétition à blocages, dérailleurs AV et AR 10 vitesses, pédalier super compétition, freins MAFAC RACER.

21

N° des pièces	Nbre	DÉSIGNATION
		CADRE
V 4561	1	Cadre avec cône et cuvette de direction
V 3344	1	Cadre demi-façon (c'est-à-dire avec fourche, pédalier et direction)
		FOURCHE
V 6476	1	Fourche chromée à mi-hauteur
		DIRECTION
V 18123	1	Jeu de direction STRONGLIGHT
		PÉDALIER
420 A	1	Jeu de pédalier STRONGLIGHT, emmanchement carré, comprenant : axe, cuvettes et contre-écrou
57 ST	1	Manivelle droite dural
V 1018 B	1	Manivelle gauche dural
57-52	1	Grand plateau 52 dents
57-45	1	Grand plateau 45 dents
V 57-ST	5	Vis d'assemblage avec entretoise et écrou
		PÉDALES
455 A	1	Paire de pédales acier, course
		GUIDON
V 18129	1	Guidon course cintre acier Antonin Magne, potence SUPER DURA
V 18176	1	Potence SUPER DURA, L = 80 mm
V 18177	1	Potence SUPER DURA, L = 100 mm
V 18178	1	Potence SUPER DURA, L = 110 mm
524 A		Rubar pour guidon

N° des pièces	Nbre	DÉSIGNATION
		SELLE
658 A	1	Selle course
V 1223	1	Tige de selle dural, ⌀ 26,4 mm
		ou
V 18121	1	Selle sans chariot
V 18122	1	Tige de selle SIMPLEX
		FREINS
V 17886	1	Frein AV MAFAC RACER course
V 17887	1	Frein AR MAFAC RACER course
		ROUES
V 8048	1	Roue AV 700 C, moyeu SIMPLEX
V 8049	1	Roue AR 700 C, moyeu SIMPLEX
V 18125	2	Jante 700 C MAVIC Monthléry
V 18002	1	Moyeu AV SIMPLEX pour blocage
V 18003	1	Moyeu AR SIMPLEX pour blocage
BR 540 A	1	Blocage AV SIMPLEX
BR 540 B	1	Blocage AR SIMPLEX
		ROUE LIBRE
596 A	1	Roue libre 5 dentures 14 × 15 × 17 × 19 × 21
		DÉRAILLEUR
V 18278	1	Dérailleur AR JUY EXPORT 61
AV 207	1	Dérailleur AV à collier LJ 23
V 18059	1	Manette double à collier avec commande
		CHAINE
382 A	1	Chaine, largeur 2,38, 108 maillons
		POMPE
V 18134	1	Pompe 480 × 20, avec raccord BATAM
V 18133	2	Collier porte-pompe

The PX10 pages from the 1961 parts catalogue.

sporting PL8 and PX8 sat somewhere in the middle of the latter group. In another league altogether, we had the 470FF PL10, and the 720FF PX10. Perhaps its price explains why there was no hurry to get this legendary machine into public hands, as the average metalworker in Paris was earning just over 3FF an hour at this time!

Before looking at the PX10, though, it's worth seeing how the other road-racers evolved first, as we've already mentioned them in the prices, and the 'Saison 1961-62' range signified the first changes to the line-up in quite some time.

The PLC8 became the PL8. It was built with Peugeot's own lightweight tubing, and had four speeds (eight as an option), centre-pull MAFAC 'Racer' brakes, stronger graphics on the seat tube, resembling those of its contempories in the regular lines, and flashes framing the Peugeot badge on the down tube. The PHX8 morphed into the PX8, with the same frame tubing as the PL8, but with PX10-style decals on the seat tube according to brochure pictures, and augmented by extra decals on the front forks. This model had eight speeds as standard (lever or cable operation was listed on the front derailleur), more chrome (on the fork ends, for instance), better components, and a choice of 11 colours, against seven for the PL8.

The eight-speed PL10 was a newcomer, with Reynolds tubing, Nervex lugs, chromed ends at the front and rear, Mavic wheels, a Stronglight headset, AVA handlebars, a cable-operated front derailleur, a three-spoke chromed steel crankset, steel pedals with clips, and MAFAC 'Racer' brakes. Like the PX10 – and PHX10 before it – the PL10 was available in blue only according to official French documentation, and came with PX10-style graphics.

And so to the PX10 itself. Reynolds 531 tubing, chrome ends, and gorgeous Nervex 'Professional' lugs continued to be a feature, adding strength to the frame, as well as artistic appeal, with those on the head tube still painted yellow. There was a new head badge with a red shield behind the familiar Peugeot lion and fresh script (duly matched up with that on the down tube), and the rear brake cable was now placed on the top of the top tube, secured by three clips, as per the new PL10 model. In keeping with its works spec, the components were of the highest quality, with a Stronglight headset and five-spoke alloy crankset, the latest Simplex LJ 23 and Juy Export 61 front and rear derailleurs, Mavic 'Monthléry' 700C rims, Simplex hubs, a five-tooth freewheel, MAFAC 'Racer' brakes, an Idéale 59 saddle, Lyotard duralumin pedals complete with Christophe toe clips, and a lightweight pump, now held in place by clips, thus allowing the owner to readily choose its location (or leave it off); the pump had previously always been mounted on the upper surface of the down tube since the PH10 days of the early fifties.

Unfortunately, serial numbers are hit and miss to say the least. In reality, so many theories and myths exist on numbering, it's frankly better to say nothing, as one thing is for sure – there is no particular batch or code to identify a real PX10 (it appears there are an awful lot of spurious bikes out there), or any other Peugeot from the fifties and sixties for that matter.

In competition, the Tour de France organisers at last dropped the country/region team format in favour of one pitching professional racing teams against one another for 1962. In reality, then, even though there was some memorable racing (some of it naturally involving Peugeot bikes), that is the year when things start to get exciting for diehard fans of the French brand. Sadly, there were no Peugeot riders in the top 20 at the end of the 22 stages, and the other classics also failed to attract any trophies. Indeed, Ferdinand Bracke's Grand Prix des Nations win was the highlight of the 1962 season, with the Belgian rider sharing the podium with another Peugeot man, Claude Valdois, who finished the famous individual time trial event in third.

This was to be the final year of a decades-long relationship with Dunlop as a partner, and also the last for blue and yellow team jerseys. In fact, it's worth noting that the 1962 jersey featured altogether more modern graphics than the 1961 version, duly bridging the gap between the old and the new, with white becoming the corporate colour for 1963. As the history books go on to show, the switch would ultimately bring about a most welcome change in Peugeot's fortunes.

The French four-page catalogue produced to show the 1963 sporting line-up included the PX50 randonneur, and the PL8, PX8 and PX10 carried over more or less untouched. This makes sense, for while the team shirts may have been white, contemporary pictures show that many of the factory bikes were still blue for the early part of the 1963 season. Interestingly, the PL10 was not shown. Instead, a brand new ten-speed PA10 grade was listed, with Peugeot tubing combined with Nervex lugs, chrome on the front forks only, and components selected to deliver good performance whilst keeping the price in check. A slightly later brochure covering the entire 1963 domestic range featured the PL8, PX8, PA10, PL10 and PX10, all in familiar liveries.

A note should be made here that the US distributors (Franklin Imports of New York on the POE East Coast,

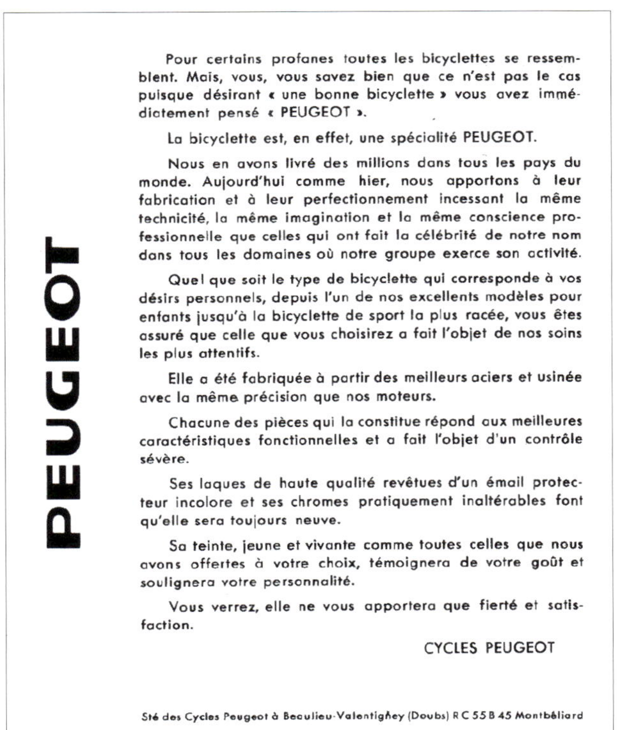
PEUGEOT

Pour certains profanes toutes les bicyclettes se ressemblent. Mais, vous, vous savez bien que ce n'est pas le cas puisque désirant « une bonne bicyclette » vous avez immédiatement pensé « PEUGEOT ».

La bicyclette est, en effet, une spécialité PEUGEOT.

Nous en avons livré des millions dans tous les pays du monde. Aujourd'hui comme hier, nous apportons à leur fabrication et à leur perfectionnement incessant la même technicité, la même imagination et la même conscience professionnelle que celles qui ont fait la célébrité de notre nom dans tous les domaines où notre groupe exerce son activité.

Quel que soit le type de bicyclette qui correspond à vos désirs personnels, depuis l'un de nos excellents modèles pour enfants jusqu'à la bicyclette de sport la plus racée, vous êtes assuré que celle que vous choisirez a fait l'objet de nos soins les plus attentifs.

Elle a été fabriquée à partir des meilleurs aciers et usinée avec la même précision que nos moteurs.

Chacune des pièces qui la constitue répond aux meilleures caractéristiques fonctionnelles et a fait l'objet d'un contrôle sévère.

Ses laques de haute qualité revêtues d'un émail protecteur incolore et ses chromes pratiquement inaltérables font qu'elle sera toujours neuve.

Sa teinte, jeune et vivante comme toutes celles que nous avons offertes à votre choix, témoignera de votre goût et soulignera votre personnalité.

Vous verrez, elle ne vous apportera que fierté et satisfaction.

CYCLES PEUGEOT

Sté des Cycles Peugeot à Beaulieu-Valentigney (Doubs) R C 55 B 45 Montbéliard

The 1961 brochure, featuring illustrations of the PX8, PX10 and PX50 shown here, along with other lesser models and bikes for children.

Ferdinand Bracke taking a lap of honour after winning the 1962 Grand Prix des Nations. (Courtesy *L'Equipe)*

and United Import Sales of Los Angeles on the West Coast) sold the PX10 in blue or lime green, priced at $150. Americans could also buy the UO8 'Trophée de France' model, which was similar to the PX8, but available in ten- or 15-speed guise for less than $100. Exchange rates helped keep the prices low (they didn't really jump until 1970), but they still sound ridiculously cheap, until you realise you could secure a well-trimmed Dodge Dart convertible for $2385 in the States at the time; a Volkswagen Beetle was listed at just $1595!

Anyway, as it happens, the later of the two catalogues mentioned some of the stars in the Peugeot-BP-Englebert team for 1963. These included Ferdinand Bracke and Rolf Wolfshohl, and important new signings in the shape of Charly Gaul, Tom Simpson, Raymond Mastrotto, Willy Vannitsen, Jean Forestier and Emile Daems.

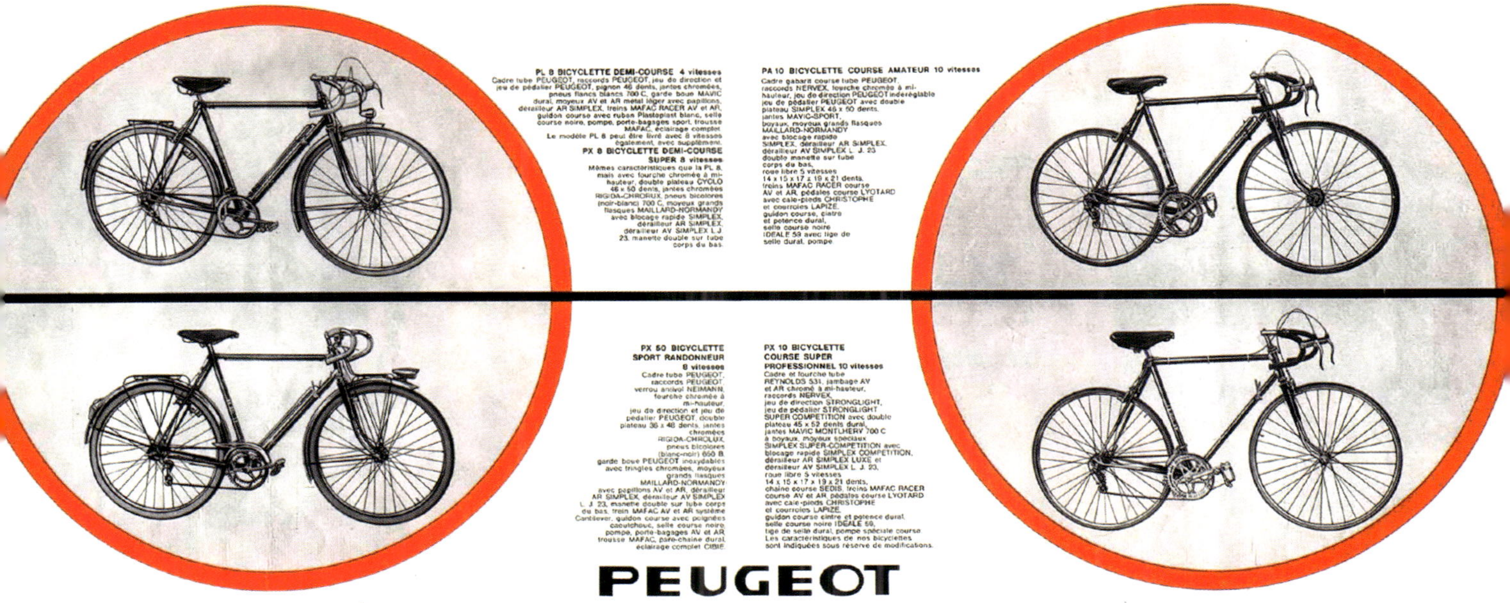

A lightweight but nonetheless interesting little brochure published at the end of 1962 in time for the 1963 season. A similar one was produced soon after, with riders sporting white shirts with chequers to fit in with the new team colours.

Of course, the likes of Pino Cerami, Claude Valdois and Henri Duez were still on the roster, too, so there was now a great deal of in-depth strength in the equipe.

It appears that most of the works bikes were in their iconic white with chequers paint scheme by the spring of 1963, with film footage showing Tom Simpson's win on the Bordeaux-Paris clearly showing the latest livery. Simpson also claimed victory on the GP du Parisien, while Emile Daems won the classic Paris-Roubaix event. With Pino Cerami picking up a stage win on the Tour de France, and a gaggle of decent finishes over the year for other Peugeot riders in top class events, it looked as if the patience shown towards Gaston Plaud was finally starting to pay off. In reality, this was just the beginning ...

Continued on page 64

Gaston Plaud signing up the legendary British rider, Tom Simpson. (Courtesy *L'Equipe)*

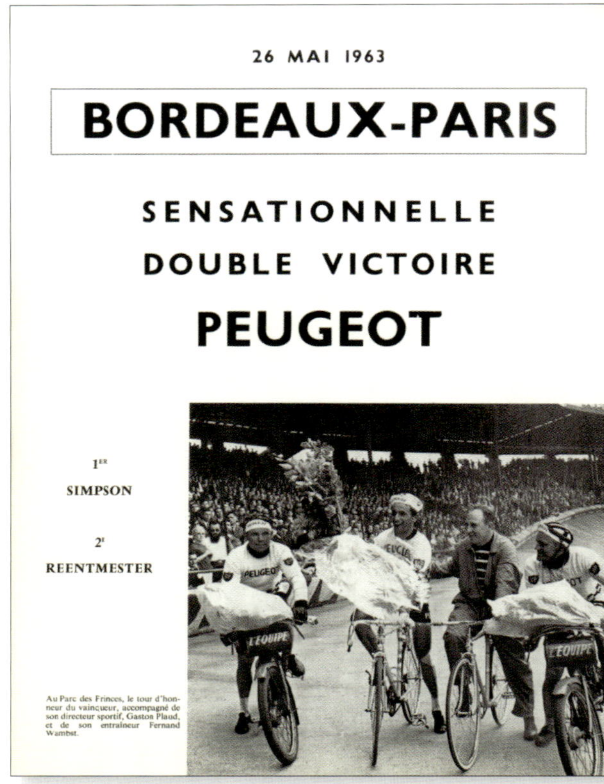

26 MAI 1963

BORDEAUX-PARIS

SENSATIONNELLE
DOUBLE VICTOIRE
PEUGEOT

1ER
SIMPSON

2E
REENTMESTER

Au Parc des Frinces, le tour d'honneur du vainqueur, accompagné de son directeur sportif, Gaston Plaud, et de son entraîneur Fernand Wambst.

Right: Peugeot's in-house newsletter, *Peugeot Commercial,* celebrating Tom Simpson's 1963 Bordeaux-Paris race win.

Emile Daems punching the air after winning the 1963 Paris-Roubaix. (Courtesy *L'Equipe)*

THE CLASSIC COMPONENT SUPPLIERS: STEERING & BRAKING PARTS

Tasteful advertising for MAFAC 'Racer' brakes.

For quite some time, AVA handlebars and stems (made by Henri Gormand's EMR company) were considered the norm on Peugeot's top road-racers, despite some branding the AVA stem as "the death stem!" Actually, even today, many keirin bikes have steel stems for safety, so one should not judge AVA too harshly, especially given metallurgy at the time. With the right leverage, a powerful man can break almost anything ...

Nonetheless, Peugeot gradually moved across to Philippe bars and Atax stems, with the latter sometimes carrying Peugeot markings, and actually made by the same firm following one of many mergers in the French cycle industry. Cinelli handlebars would find their way onto the spec sheets in the 1980s, but, not surprisingly, it was French makers that dominated during the classic years.

The attractive logo used by Guidons Philippe in the late 1970s, with the tricolour-based Atax badge is just visible in the background. Like many items from this time, the stem carried a 'Peugeot' badge as well as that of its maker; sometimes the Peugeot name was used exclusively.

One thing that remained pretty much constant throughout the postwar era, though, was the use of Stronglight headsets on the more expensive bikes. Based in Saint Étienne, Stronglight, with its roots in a business founded in Boën-sur-Lignon by Ets Vérot et Perrin in the 1920s, would also become France's number one supplier of lightweight chainrings and cranks. Despite a series of financial woes, the coveted brand name still exists to this day.

The evolution of Peugeot's post-WWII road-racer brakes is interesting to follow. LAM 'Tour de France' side-pull brakes were fitted on early PH10 models, which were duly replaced by Follis 'Béborex' type units from 1953 to 1957. After this, the iconic MAFAC centre-pull brakes became the norm on the top stuff, with subtle changes helping to keep the design current for decades.

MAFAC (short for Manufacture Auvergnoise de Freins et Accessories pour Cycles) was founded in Clermont-Ferrand just after the Second World War, specializing in cycle brakes and toolkits. It eventually joined Stronglight, Simplex and Maillard to become part of the Spidel enterprise that aimed to supply top quality groupsets to fend off the challenge of a growing number of strong rivals, but it was too little, too late. By the mid-1980s, the MAFAC name had been consigned to the history books.

In later years, brakes were sourced from Weinmann (the models ranging from cheap and cheerful to race spec), CLB (likewise), Modolo, and also Campagnolo and Shimano as part of their groupsets. Throughout the 'Golden Age' though, there was little to compare with the Gallic charm of the MAFAC 'Racer' family.

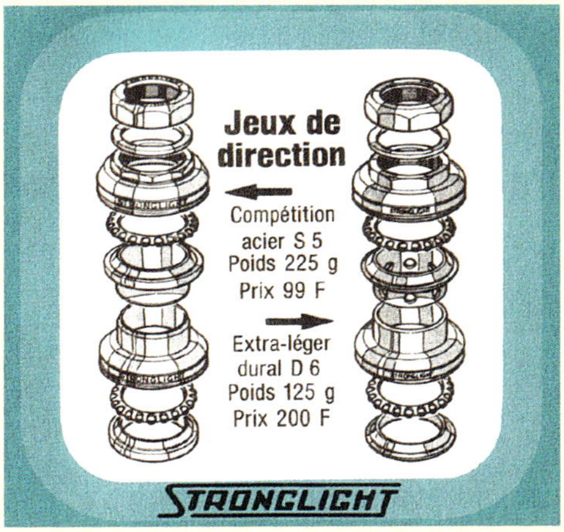

Left: Stronglight headsets illustrated in a 1977 Spidel catalogue.

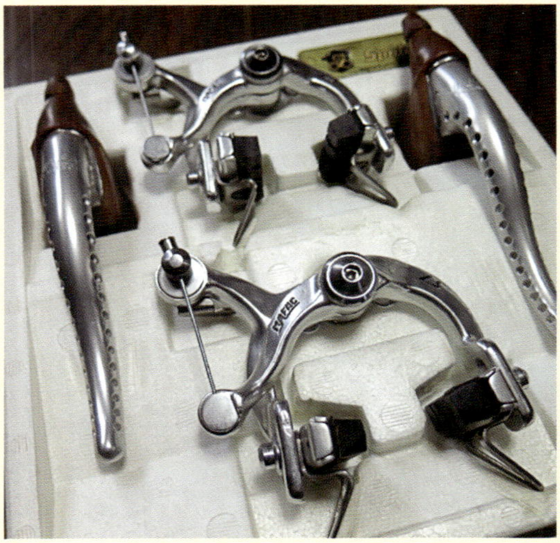

Right: An unused MAFAC brake set from the 1978 season, sold via the Spidel consortium. Made of forged alloy, the LS brakes were 300FF a pair (against 138FF for the traditional centre-pull items), while the levers were priced at 35FF a pair.

October 1963 marked the changeover from blue to white paintwork for the catalogue PX10 (now priced at 780FF, with slightly modified gearing, plus a change to lightweight but sadly flawed Simplex 'Prestige' derailleurs, new hubs, Englebert tyres, and a different saddle), and also the end of the PL10 run, dropped in favour of the more modest 405FF PA10 variant, just as earlier brochures hinted might happen. For the record, the head badge was subtly different by this time, with block lettering resembling that used on the contemporary team jerseys; the down tube decals also lost the joined up 'P' and 'g' in a bid to modernise the overall impression. One has to bear in mind, though, that bikes like the PX10 were never sold in high numbers, and graphics may not always tie-up with the more general sweeping changes made on other, faster moving models.

According to brochures and the master catalogue, the PL8 and PX8 gained a white chequer pattern section on the seat tube for the 'Saison 1963-64' line-up, along with block lettering on the down tube (framed by flashes on either side), fresh arrow-shaped fork decals (now on both grades), and the latest head badge. While the PX10 and PA10 were available in white only (with a chequer pattern on the down tube and black front lugs) in Europe, the lesser PL8 and PX8 could be bought in ten or 12 shades, respectively. For the record, other sporting models from this time included the three-speed Hélium H8, and the randonneur-type H50, PL50 and PX50 variants.

One of three brochures produced for the 1964 season, with the others covering touring bikes and those built for kids.

On the other side of the Atlantic, where Peugeot bikes were probably better known than the brand's motor vehicles, except amongst old car buffs, the Americans were offered a blue PX10 with black lugs for the 1964 season, in addition to the white version punted elsewhere. This is also about the time that the ubiquitous 'Trophée de France' badge appeared on a white background on the UO8's seat tube, framed by rainbow bands. There was a Terrot variant of the UO8, by the way, known as the AO8, and sold in three colours rather than the five listed against the Peugeot model.

The so-called PX10 'Super De Luxe' bikes are something of an oddity, as the Olympic rings emblem that seems to define the model would be there to coincide with the 1964 event, if one takes in the average vintages of bicycles put forward for appraisal and the various theories on the odd mix of logos and markings (including bands that some claim to represent a World Championship rainbow, although Olympic rings are altogether more likely, as they're of the same colours).

On saying that, the French maker had no tangible interest whatsoever in the Tokyo edition of the Games, so it's hard to determine a plausible link. Likewise, 1960 was lacking in meaningful Peugeot content, although at least Henri Duez was a member of the French team trial squad, which ultimately came seventh, and Robert Lelangue rode for Belgium, but finished a long way down the field – hardly justification for a special decal. Indeed, we have to go back to 1956 to find an Olympic year in which there was something to celebrate, however tenuous – a French team victory in the road racing. None of the riders were Peugeot men, but the industry would have welcomed anything to boost morale at that time, so it is possible.

However, it could well be that it was a US-only model, with the detailing carried out in the States, and it's starting to look as if it is. In that case, there's even less of a legitimate link with the Olympics, but since when has that stopped marketing types jumping on the bandwagon? With there being no reference to such bikes in available catalogues or price lists, and the same decal being used over so many years (regardless of the Olympics being held or not, it seems, only adding to the mound of question marks), pukka or not, the only thing one can say with any level of certainty is that the so-called 'Super De Luxe' PX10s are a complete mystery!

A flyer from America, with the PX10 now offered in blue or white.

They definitely don't appear to be an official sub-grade, unlike the 1964-onward PX8L, which gained a coat of clear lacquer on the forks in order to justify the 'L' suffix.

On the subject of designations, one should be aware of the PX10/E moniker, which also seems to have come into use at this time in European export markets. Indeed, with the specification being virtually identical to domestic models, one can assume the 'E' (initially separated by a forward slash, not used on the PX8L's 'L' suffix) is only there to distinguish an export bike. Models like the PA10/E (or PA10E further into the future) also appear in catalogues, although again, only in those produced for export markets, including mainland Europe, Britain, North America and Japan.

On the racing front, Tom Simpson won the 1964 Milan-San Remo, Michel Nédélec (one of the 1963 signings) claimed the silverware in the Bordeaux-Paris race, and Georges Vanconingsloo (also new to the equipe from 1963) won the Paris-Bruxelles one day event. While there was little to write home about on the Grand

Joining the team at the end of 1964, Roger Pingeon, would prove to be an important signing for Peugeot.

Tours, at least the white shirts had been in the thick of the action all year, and this is what keeps sponsors happy. Also, Roger Pingeon joined the Peugeot-BP-Englebert squad at the end of 1964, with the young Frenchman proving his worth as a team member over the ensuing years.

Meanwhile, Peugeot introduced the Trophée Peugeot in 1964, replacing an existing pro-am contest with an amateur-only series. It was a good way of selling extra bikes, as the amateurs now had a chance to shine. The first winner, Désiré Letort, was duly given a contract to ride for the works team, so it was a worthwhile exercise for all concerned. It later merged with the Tour l'Avenir, before pro riders from all teams were allowed to swell the ranks

Tom Simpson pushing hard on the 1964 Milan-San Remo. Ultimately, no-one else was able to match his pace on the event. (Courtesy *L'Equipe*)

Simpson being punished by the notorious Paris-Roubaix surface, and stocking up on food before signing all those photos in front of his boss. (Courtesy *L'Equipe*)

The Peugeot-BP team for the 1964 TdF, with (l-r) Ferdinand Bracke, Henri Duez, François Hamon, Pierre Le Mellec, Camille Le Menn, Raymond Mastrotto, Emile Daems, Michel Nédélec, Guy Seyve, Tom Simpson, Georges Vanconingsloo, and the DS, Gaston Plaud. (Courtesy *L'Equipe*)

Action from the 1964 Tour de France, with Peugeot's riders fighting hard in the middle of the pack. (Courtesy Wikimedia Commons: Dutch National Archives/Anefo)

in 1981. Fittingly, the winner that year was a Peugeot man, Pascal Simon.

Incidentally, Jean-Pierre Peugeot had stepped down after a long stint as the head of Peugeot at the end of July 1964, handing over the reins of the car business to Maurice Jordan, although it has to be said that the Peugeot family retained a tight grip on things in the boardroom, and would continue to do so long after the formation of PSA (Peugeot Société Anonyme) in 1966.

The same domestic catalogues were rolled out again for 1965, albeit with different background colouring on the product pages to give a fresh impression. This

Advert created to celebrate Ferdinand Bracke's pleasing GP de Lugano victory in October 1964.

PEUGEOT

au palmarès de

L'EAST AFRICAN SAFARI

pour la 5e année consécutive

1965 1er au Classement par Équipes (cinq 404 classées à l'arrivée) 2e au Classement Général

1964 1er, 2e, 3e, 4e et 5e de la catégorie 1600 à 2000 cm^3 2e au Classement par Équipes

1963 1er au Classement Général 1er et 2e de la catégorie 1600 à 2000 cm^3

1962 1er, 2e et 3e de la catégorie 1600 à 2000 cm^3 1er au Classement par Équipes

1961 1er, 3e et 4e de la catégorie 1600 à 2000 cm^3 2e au Classement par Équipes

Peugeot's motorsport exploits hardly need introduction, but it's worth noting that the main focus in the 1960s was on rallying, with rough road events being a Peugeot speciality. The works cars were often seen painted in the same colours used by the bicycle team.

naturally implies that the line-up was carried over from the previous year, which is hardly surprising given its recent makeover. It does appear, though, that block lettering had begun being used on the PX10's down tube, giving the bike an altogether more modern appearance. It should be noted, however, that the works bikes took a while to catch up with this revision, as the author has pictures of Tom Simpson in a rainbow jersey riding a bike with the older markings. Like so many things in industrial scenarios, changes are often made as and when rather than during specific calendar months or Model Year introductions.

In competition, 1965 saw Peugeot adopting new team jerseys to fit in with a change from Englebert to Michelin tyres. In reality, they looked very similar, but the addition of the tyre maker's name does at least help when it comes to dating photographs, even though the team colours stayed basically the same for the next decade.

It was an odd year, with Simpson easily winning the Giro di Lombardia, and taking the World Championship crown in Spain in September. At the same time, Winfried Bölke won the German title, Ferdinand Bracke the Belgian one, and Jean Raynal the French one. However, the big classics were still eluding the men in white. Three Peugeot riders finished in the top 20 of the Tour de France, but this fine performance, with Roger Pingeon leading the way in the Peugeot-BP-Michelin camp, failed to make headlines, and it was particularly ironic that Rolf Wolfshohl, who'd been with Peugeot in 1963 and 1964, won the 1965 Vuelta for the Mercier outfit. Onward and upward, as the saying goes ...

The main 1966 domestic brochures used some of the artwork from the two previous seasons, but the Peugeot version featured Tom Simpson and Jacques Botherel on the cover. And why not? After all, Simpson was reigning UCI World Champion in the professional ranks, and Botherel top amateur in 1965, giving both Peugeot riders the right to wear the coveted rainbow jersey. The Terrot version was much the same, even down to the product pictures and model codes, but with different covers to appease fans of the marque.

As it happens, it was the rainbow bands that helped distinguish the latest bikes from those of the previous season, added on the seat tube to the inside of the chequer decals to frame the Peugeot logo. The new graphics were adopted on the PL8, PX8/PX8L, PA10, PX10, and

Peugeot BB LT mopeds being built at Beaulieu.

the UO8/AO8 in the States; the PL50 and PX50 had chequers with no rainbow bands, and the Hélium-badged H8 and H50 had to make do with a fresh heraldic lion badge only. The home market PX10 was given slightly different gearing (with a 52/45t chain-ring setup at the front, rather than 51/45t) at this time, but was otherwise continued unchanged from a mechanical viewpoint.

The racing team scored something of a coup in 1966, bringing Eddy Merckx onboard. Securing 'The Cannibal' meant that the Peugeot-BP-Michelin equipe now had a stunning line-up, with the all-out attacking style of Merckx balanced by the more calculated approach of Simpson, Pingeon, Duez, Bracke, Mertens, et al. The outfit

Poster released after Tom Simpson was named World Champion. Behind him is Jacques Botherel, who was awarded the amateur crown.

Roger Pingeon (left) and Raymond Delisle tackling the mountains on the Tour de France in 1965. (Courtesy *L'Equipe*)

may have come up short on Grand Tour podiums again (there are only nine spots available over the year, after all), but Merckx duly won the classic Milan-San Remo, and the number of stage and overall wins gained by Peugeot riders in other races must have given Gaston Plaud and his assistant, Robert Naeye, a great deal of hope. There were also three national champions crowned in the squad, so all in all, it was a good, solid season.

Apart from new covers (with attractive artwork shared by Peugeot and Terrot), the French catalogues released in the spring of 1967 were virtually identical to the 1966 editions, with no changes made to the sporting line-up. Interestingly, the US market continued to list the PX10 in blue or white (white only elsewhere), fitted with different gearsets to the domestic models, and still augmented by the UO8 and AO8 variants not found in

Continued on page 74

The artwork on the front cover of the 1966 Terrot catalogue was actually the same as that used on the back cover of the Peugeot version. Later editions used identical pictures, with only the marque name changed to suit.

THE SPORTING RIVALS

BIANCHI (ITA)

Bianchi has always been an ever-present threat, be it in the showrooms or in racing. Founded by Edoardo Bianchi in Milan in 1885, the company began life building bicycles and was involved with racing from the start. Motor vehicles soon followed (including some magnificent motorcycles), with business booming until the Second World War. A strong revival could not stop the downward trend, however, and after 1964, only the bike manufacturing arm remained, boosted by racing success from the likes of Fausto Coppi. Felice Gimondi became the next Bianchi hero after the powerful Salvarani team moved across to Bianchi bikes in 1967, having previously used Magni frames, which one couldn't buy. The arrangement didn't last long, however, as the team quickly adopted De Rosa frames labelled as a Chiorda, but Gimondi would become the 'face' of Bianchi from 1973 to 1979, being crowned World Champion on one. More heroes followed, prompting Grimaldi Industri AB to secure the brand in the spring of 1997 and keep it going through the Cycleurope project.

Bianchi catalogue from the 1970s.

MERCIER (FRA)

Although Emile Mercier had been building bike frames (and then full bicycles) since 1924, and the Mercier-Hutchinson team had been around since the mid-1930s, because Mercier always seemed to be an outsider, at odds with Desgrange and his followers in the early days of the brand, it was probably not until the fifties that the Saint Étienne maker joined the fight as a worthy contender for French honour in racing. However, it was Raymond Poulidor's battles with Jacques Anguetil on the Tour de France in the early sixties that truly put the brand in the spotlight.

Emile Mercier had struggled to keep his business independent until his death in 1973, but with Mercier continuing to be a regular supporter of top class cycle sport (later via the GAN and Miko racing teams), it managed to limp along in his absense. Despite a fine performance from Sean Kelly on the TdF, though, the company was declared bankrupt in 1985. The Mercier marque name still exists, by the way, as does that of Hutchinson, who had been making bicycle tyres in France since 1890.

Team photo of the GAN-Mercier equipe of 1972.

MASI (ITA)

Faliero Masi was the man behind Cicli Masi of Milan, an ex-rider and an ex-Gloria worker before becoming a bespoke frame builder who was often approached by the best in the business, including Tom Simpson and Eddy Merckx. Faliero tried his hand in the States in the early 1970s, leaving his son Alberto in charge of things in Italy, but it was a short-lived venture from his point of view that ultimately led to frames being made in America with Faliero retiring back in Italy. The California enterprise still exists (via Haro nowadays), meaning Masi was not able to export to the US, although a handful of Italian frames, always made in low numbers, made their way across the Atlantic, some branded as a 'Milano'. The old workshop under the Velodromo Vigorelli is now a bicycle shop called Biciclette Masi.

LEGNANO (ITA)

Gino Bartali brought the Legnano name to world attention following his 1948 Tour de France win, but the Milan-based maker had already won the Giro d'Italia 13 times by then! It was Emilio Bozzi that was responsible for the creation of the Legnano legend, building on Vittorio Rossi's earlier work at the turn of the century after buying the company. Bozzi also owned the Pearl and Giro-winning Frejus brands, and joined forces with Franco Tosi to bring Wolsit into the fold – another famous name. Legnano, however, with its badge penned by a certain Alfredo Binda, would come to symbolise quality for decades. Sadly, with more money being made on parts distribution than bike production, after 60 years of history, the Legnano-Pirelli racing team folded in 1966, and things slowly started going downhill in the 1970s. Bianchi bought what was left of the business in 1987, which eventually became part of the Cycleurope Group.

The dandy fashions of the 1963 Legnano squad.

HELYETT (FRA)

Inspired by their father Alphonse's cycling exploits, the Helyett brand was established by Raymond and Gabriel Picard in Sully-sur-Loire in 1919, making parts, then bicycles and motorcycles under that name. At the time of the Second World War, Helyett was producing around 12,000 bikes a year. The firm also had a works racing team from 1932 to 1961, giving Jacques Anquetil a launchpad to stardom in its later years before the St Raphaël team (sponsored by the aperitif company of that name) took things over, first continuing with Helyett machinery, but switching to Gitane models for 1963. As it happens, after selling the factory to Griffon in 1962, Helyett was ultimately merged with Gitane in 1966, and sold as a badge-engineered bike for a while after. The brand has recently been revived, making steel bikes in a traditional manner.

GEMINIANI (FRA)

Named after Raphaël Géminiani, the famous French racer and later DS, Geminiani bikes were famously linked through sponsorship to the St Raphaël and Ford France equipes he ran in the sixties. Manufactured with Geminiani badging by a selection of French makers, because they were all made in the 'Golden Era', with some being of very nice quality, the bikes themselves have a strong following amongst collectors today.

PX10

PX 10 - CARACTERISTIQUES : Tubes Reynolds, jambages AR et fourreaux de fourche chromés, boyaux course 700 C, moyeux compétition à blocages, dérailleurs AV et AR PRESTIGE, pédalier super compétition, freins MAFAC RACER.

N° des Pièces	Nbre	DESIGNATION
		CADRE
V 4561	1	Cadre avec cône et cuvette de direction
V 3344	1	Cadre demi-façon (c'est à dire avec fourche, pédalier et direction)
		FOURCHE
V 6485	1	Fourche chromée à mi-hauteur
		DIRECTION
V 18123	1	Jeu de direction STRONGLIGHT
		PEDALIER
420 A	1	Jeu de pédalier STRONGLIGHT, emmanchement carré comprenant : axe, cuvettes et contre-écrou
57 ST 63	1	Manivelle droite dural avec vis d'assemblage plateaux
V 1018 B	1	Manivelle gauche dural
57-52-63	1	Grand plateau 52 dents
57-45-63	1	Grand plateau 45 dents
V 57-ST-63	5	Vis d'assemblage avec entretoise et écrou
		PEDALES
V 18120	1	Paire de pédales acier, course
91 A	2	Cale-pied sans courroie
92 A	2	Courroie de cale-pied
		GUIDON
V 9656	1	Guidon course dural potence SUPER DURA
V 18176	1	Potence SUPER DURA L = 80 mm
V 18177	1	Potence SUPER DURA L = 100 mm
V 18178	1	Potence SUPER DURA L = 110 mm
524 A		Ruban pour guidon

N° des Pièces	Nbre	DESIGNATION
		SELLE
658 A	1	Selle course
V 1223	1	Tige de selle alu Ø 26, 4 mm
		ou
V 18121	1	Selle sans chariot
V 18122	1	Tige de selle SIMPLEX
		FREINS
V 17886	1	Frein AV MAFAC RACER course poignée avec repose-main
V 17887	1	Frein AR MAFAC RACER course poignée avec repose-main
		ROUES
V 8124	1	Roue AV 700 C moyeu EXCELTOO compétiton
V 8125	1	Roue AR 700 C moyeu EXCELTOO compétiton
V 18125	2	Jante 700 C MAVIC Monthléry
V 18679	1	Moyeu AV EXCELTOO pour blocage
V 18680	1	Moyeu AR EXCELTOO pour blocage
BR 540 A	1	Blocage AV SIMPLEX
BR 540 B	1	Blocage AR SIMPLEX
		ROUE LIBRE
596 A	1	Roue libre 5 dentures 14 X 15 X 17 X 19 X 21
		DERAILLEUR
V 18983	1	Dérailleur AR PRESTIGE LUXE
V 18480	1	Dérailleur AV PRESTIGE LUXE
V 18475	1	Manette double à collier avec commandes AV et AR
S 2113	1	Collier tunnel à droite et butée de gaine à gauche
		CHAINE
382 A	1	Chaîne largeur 2,38 108 maillons
		OUTILLAGE
538 A	1	Trousse MAFAC avec clés
		POMPE
V 18134	1	Pompe 480 X 20 avec raccord BATAM
V 18133	2	Collier porte-pompe Ø 28 (54-56)
V 18508	2	Collier porte-pompe Ø 26 (58-60)

The PX10 pages from the 1966 parts catalogue.

Europe. Interestingly, the Terrot brand was not mentioned any more – the AO8 was batched in with the Peugeots to avoid confusion. In reality, as before, the choice of colours was the main difference between the UO8 and AO8, both now coming with flashes on the down tube and front fork decals, although the latter didn't have the 15-speed option; as it happens, the Peugeot UO8 sold in Canada was also offered with ten speeds only.

Eddy Merckx – probably the most famous rider of a generation.

SPÉCIAL CYCLISME

Sensationnelle Victoire de MERCKX dans MILAN-SAN-REMO

LE SURSAUT VICTORIEUX DE MERCKX FUT CELUI D'UN CHAMPION !

Encore une victoire PEUGEOT BP

1er MILAN-SAN REMO EDDY MERCKX

En cyclomoteur comme en bicyclette, QUALITÉ = PEUGEOT

PEUGEOT

La magnifique arrivée de MERCKX à San Remo

Photo Associated Press Photo

Peugeot's in-house newsletter celebrating Merckx's fine performance on the 1966 Milan-San Remo.

The Peugeot team for the 1966 Tour de France. (Courtesy *L'Equipe*)

The full domestic catalogue released in March 1967.

Meanwhile, in a bid to expand the US range, Americans were also treated to a UO18 for ladies, and the recently-announced D22 'Week-End' bike at this time – a rather cute two-piece runabout with a central joining clamp.

1967 and 1968 were strange years on the Tour de France, with the brief reintroduction of a national team format, although riders competed wearing an odd mixture of their country's colours overlaid with their regular team graphics, using bikes with full livery still in place! Despite the odd format, though, and a definite tinge of sadness, the champagne was flowing in rivers back in Doubs on 23rd July 1967, for, after 22 stages and 2987 miles (4779km) of road, Roger Pingeon had won the Tour de France. Pingeon had finished the 1966 edition in eighth, some eight minutes or so down on the winner – Ford France man Lucien Aimar. He'd also been 12th overall in 1965, again as the top Peugeot rider for the year, so this string of solid performances proves it was certainly no fluke. Eight minutes down, another Peugeot rider, Désiré Letort, was fourth.

Poster celebrating Roger Pingeon's win on the 1967 TdF.

As for the sad part, the world of cycling as a whole came together to mourn the loss of Tom Simpson, who collapsed on Stage 13 of the Tour de France whilst climbing Mount Ventoux, and died later that day. Simpson had won the Paris-Nice race, and claimed two stage wins on the Vuelta a España earlier in the year, and the fact that Pingeon had been named as his domestique showed the level of respect he'd garnered in the Peugeot camp. With our last memories of him being a haunted face, with drugs allowing him to keep pushing beyond the pain barrier in order to try and win the big race he'd set his heart on, it was a black day for the sport, albeit somewhat inevitable given the widespread use of amphetamines and other go-faster aids in the peloton at the time. At least the riders saw him off in their own way, allowing Barry Hoban of the British team to take the next stage in honour of the County Durham man ...

Merckx (left) and Simpson on the 1967 Paris-Nice, with a fantastic service car in the background. The Brit ultimately won the race. (Courtesy *L'Equipe*)

One of the last pictures of Tom Simpson. He will always be remembered as a hero. (Courtesy *L'Equipe*)

Right: Cover of *Peugeot Commercial* from September 1967.

Below: A vintage year for the men in white ...

PEUGEOT Commercial

SUPPLEMENT N° 77

SPORTS ACTUALITES

Cyclisme

deux belles victoires **PEUGEOT...**

PINGEON enlève le TOUR DE FRANCE 67

MERCKX CHAMPION du MONDE de cyclisme sur route

eddy MERCKX du groupe SPORTIF

PEUGEOT

CHAMPION du MONDE 'PROFESSIONNELS' de cyclisme sur route

Eddy MERCKX, champion du monde « professionnels ». En 1964, MERCKX avait remporté le championnat du monde « amateurs ».

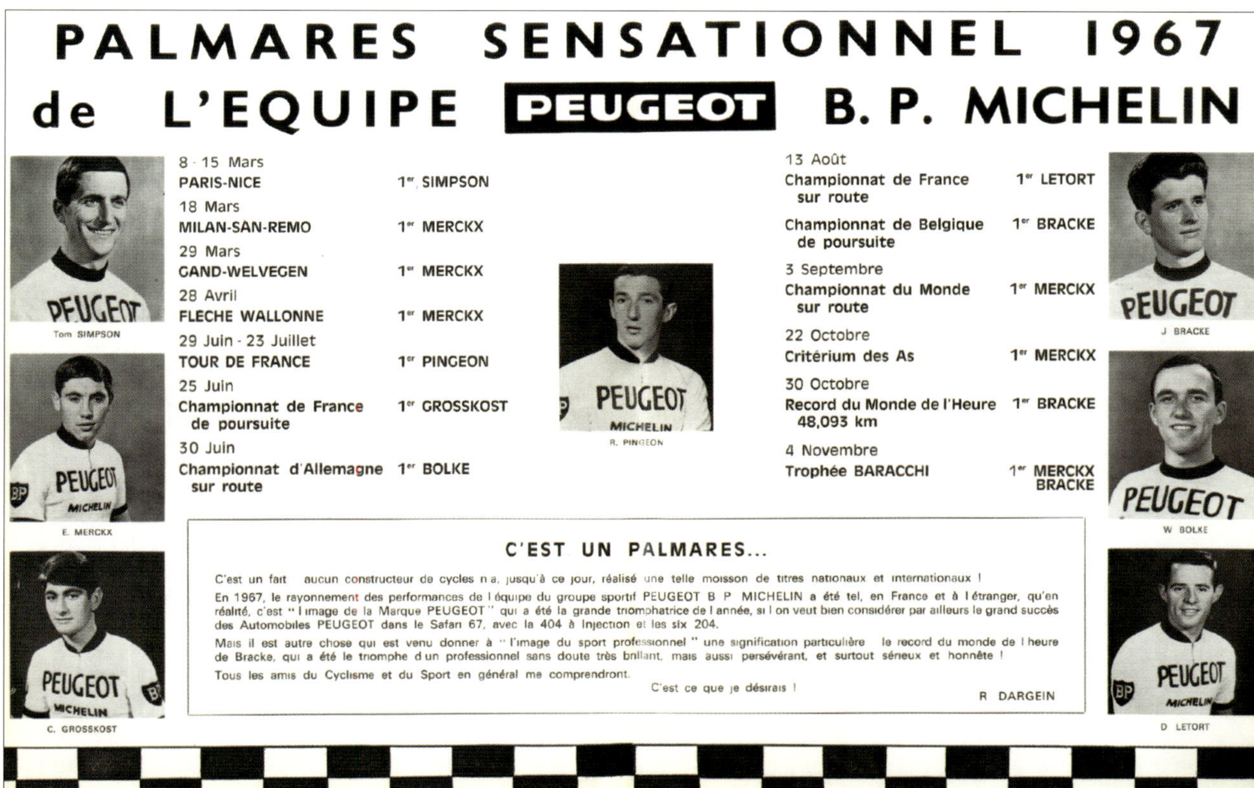

PALMARES SENSATIONNEL 1967 de L'EQUIPE PEUGEOT B. P. MICHELIN

8 - 15 Mars	PARIS-NICE	1er SIMPSON
18 Mars	MILAN-SAN-REMO	1er MERCKX
29 Mars	GAND-WELVEGEN	1er MERCKX
28 Avril	FLECHE WALLONNE	1er MERCKX
29 Juin - 23 Juillet	TOUR DE FRANCE	1er PINGEON
25 Juin	Championnat de France de poursuite	1er GROSSKOST
30 Juin	Championnat d'Allemagne sur route	1er BOLKE
13 Août	Championnat de France sur route	1er LETORT
	Championnat de Belgique de poursuite	1er BRACKE
3 Septembre	Championnat du Monde sur route	1er MERCKX
22 Octobre	Critérium des As	1er MERCKX
30 Octobre	Record du Monde de l'Heure 48,093 km	1er BRACKE
4 Novembre	Trophée BARACCHI	1er MERCKX BRACKE

Tom SIMPSON — E. MERCKX — C. GROSSKOST — R. PINGEON — J. BRACKE — W. BOLKE — D. LETORT

C'EST UN PALMARES...

C'est un fait aucun constructeur de cycles n'a, jusqu'à ce jour, réalisé une telle moisson de titres nationaux et internationaux !

En 1967, le rayonnement des performances de l'équipe du groupe sportif PEUGEOT B P MICHELIN a été tel, en France et à l'étranger, qu'en réalité, c'est " l'image de la Marque PEUGEOT " qui a été la grande triomphatrice de l'année, si l'on veut bien considérer par ailleurs le grand succès des Automobiles PEUGEOT dans le Safari 67, avec la 404 à Injection et les six 204.

Mais il est autre chose qui est venu donner à " l'image du sport professionnel " une signification particulière le record du monde de l'heure de Bracke, qui a été le triomphe d'un professionnel sans doute très brillant, mais aussi persévérant, et surtout sérieux et honnête !

Tous les amis du Cyclisme et du Sport en général me comprendront.

C'est ce que je désirais !

R DARGEIN

Poster produced to mark Ferdinand Bracke's world speed record.

Cover of the 1968 catalogue, with artwork that epitomises the swinging sixties.

In other races, Merckx (now using a Peugeot clone built by master frame builder Faliero Masi rather than a stock machine) won the Milan-San Remo again, as well as the Flèche Wallonne, Critérium des As and a gaggle of smaller events, and would also be crowned UCI World Champion in Holland in September 1967. In addition, Ferdinand Bracke took the world speed record for the hour, Winfried Bölke was named champion of Germany, and Désiré Letort the Road Race Champion of France.

The domestic 1968 Peugeot and Terrot catalogues featured all-new artwork, although the bikes themselves were more or less carried over, at least in the sporting category. However, the P10 grade was added in the spring (with painted front forks and other cost-cutting measures to keep the price down), and certain export markets (such as Canada, for instance) were offered a new PR10 model, which was like a ten-speed version of the now-defunct PL10, as it featured Reynolds tubing and a Stronglight crankset. American distributors also started selling the UE-8 at about this time, which was basically a touring version of the UO8, as well as a UE18 variant for the ladies.

1968 was surprisingly quiet on the racing front, given the team line-up. Granted, there was no Tom Simpson, of course, and Eddy Merckx, Henri Duez and Michel Nédélec had all gone, either for greener pastures or into retirement, but there was still a lot of talent in the squad nonetheless. This was confirmed by the 22 victories claimed in smaller races by team members, taking in events from France, Belgium, Holland and Switzerland. There were also stage wins on the Tour de France, with Ferdinand Bracke finishing third and Roger Pingeon fifth overall, so the lack of trophies from the classics was hardly a fair reflection of the season as a whole.

On the subject of the Tour, this was to be the final year of the national team format, albeit a looser variation than earlier editions from a manufacturer's point of view. Ultimately, though, the Olympic Games were there for team events. Makers, sponsors and riders wanted individual glory, and their wishes were duly taken on-board. A lot of this can probably be put down to Émilien Amaury, who was pulling strings in the background. Amaury, who'd backed Jacques Goddet in his bid to relaunch the Tour de France after WWII, became the event's main sponsor in 1962 in return for Goddet allowing Félix Lévitan (the sports editor of *Le*

Ferdinand Bracke on the 1968 Tour de France, riding for the Belgian team on this occasion, although, thankfully, the Peugeot logo is still much in evidence. (Courtesy *L'Equipe*)

Parisien Libéré, one of Amaury's flagship publications) in as co-organiser. He eventually bought a controlling interest in *L'Equipe* in 1968, and therefore owned the rights to the Tour de France as a result. Regardless of Amaury's input, thankfully, the silliness came to an end, and starting with the 1969 edition, the event was once and for all contested by riders in commercially-sponsored professional teams thereafter.

Meanwhile, the French catalogue released in the spring of 1969 featured a new cover and fresh product photography, although the sporting line-up remained unchanged from the previous year, with the H50, PL50, PX50, H8, PL8, PX8, PX8L, P10, PA10 and PX10 models listed. Interestingly, there doesn't appear to be a Terrot version of this brochure, signalling the imminent end of the brand, which by this time was simply an unnecessary extravagance in the marketing budget. European export markets gained the P8/E at this time, which acted as an entry-level model slotting in below the PL8 on the price list, while some places offered bikes without gearsets, identified by an 'H' suffix at the end of the model code.

The PX8 featured in the French brochure issued in the spring of 1969.

Model PA 10 E

Een echte PEUGEOT racefiets, zeer licht. Een prima amateurracefiets voor een lage prijs.
Frame en vork: gemaakt uit PEUGEOT buizen en NERVEX lugs. Voorvork met verchroomde uiteinden.
Stuur: racemodel, gemaakt van lichtmetaal.
Remmen: MAFAC Racer.
Zadel: kernleder.
Kettingbladen: SIMPLEX Competition.
Dérailleurs: SIMPLEX Criterium (10 versnellingen).
Naven: aluminium met uitvalassen.
Velgen: aluminium.
Zadelpen: aluminium.
Banden: tubes.
Framehoogten: 56, 58 en 60 cm.
Leverbaar in de kleuren: rood, wit en blauw BE.

Prijs, compleet met racepedalen, toeclips met riemen, bel en pomp

f. 348,–

Model PA 10 EH

Dezelfde fiets als bovenomschreven PA 10 E, maar dan zonder versnellingen. Dus voor de nieuweling.

Prijs f. 311,–

Model P 10

Complete racefiets met 10 versnellingen tegen een zeer lage prijs. Vorm gelijk aan PA 10 E, alleen iets eenvoudiger uitgevoerd.
Frame en vork: gemaakt uit PEUGEOT buizen.
Voorvork: gelakt.
Dérailleurs: SIMPLEX Prestige (10 versnellingen).
Remmen: ALTENBURGER Synchron.
Naven: met uitvalassen.
Banden: tubes.
Framehoogten: 56, 58 en 60 cm
Uitsluitend leverbaar in wit.

Prijs, compleet met racepedalen, toeclips met riemen, bel en pomp

f. 289,–

Model PX 10

De mooiste en lichtste racefiets van PEUGEOT.

Dit paradepaardje wordt zeer veel door de internationale profwielrenners gebruikt. Er werden al vele successen mee geboekt. Zoals overwinningen in wereldkampioenschappen op de weg, Tour de France, werelduurrecord en in vele klassiekers. De zogenaamde "gouden zit" van het PEUGEOT model PX 10 is gevonden en verwezenlijkt na lange jaren van proefnemingen.

Specificatie:
Frame en vork: speciaal raceframe met verchroomde vorkuiteinden. Buizen en vorkdelen zijn gemaakt uit Reynolds 531 buismateriaal.

Kettingwielen met cranks: Stronglight Competition 45 x 52 tands.

Balhoofdstel: Stronglight Competition.

Dérailleurs: SIMPLEX Criterium, 10 versnellingen.

Freewheels: CYCLO Competition, 5-voudig, 14–21 tands.

Remmen: MAFAC Course.

Naven: aluminium met uitvalassen.

Banden: zeer lichte tubes.

Zadel: BROOKS Professional.

Zadelpen: SIMPLEX Competition.

Stuur: uit lichtmetaal gemaakt.

Framehoogten: 56, 58 en 60 cm. Met een lange levertijd ook in andere gewenste hoogten.

Kleur: uitsluitend wit.

Prijs inclusief racepedalen, toeclips met riemen, pomp en bel

f. 650,–

Van de PA 10 E en de PX 10 E modellen kunnen ook de complete frames geleverd worden. Prijzen op aanvraag.

PEUGEOT = **synoniem voor resultaten: Sedert 1894 winnen amateurs en profs op de wegen en banen van Europa.**

The sporting bikes featured in the Dutch catalogue from 1969, which carried far more interesting pictures than the domestic one.

In racing, most of the headline riders were still with the team. The highlight of the 1969 season was Roger Pingeon's win on the Vuelta a España, the Frenchman holding on to beat Fagor rider Luis Ocaña by less than two minutes. Pingeon was second in the Tour de France, too – runner-up to Eddy Merckx (now with the Faema team, of course) in both the general classification and the green jersey competition; Désiré Letort finished the Tour in ninth. Another Peugeot-BP-Michelin man, Raymond Delisle (signed in 1965), was crowned the French national champion in August 1969, but otherwise, the decade seemed to fizzle out rather than exit with a bang. The equipe would return with a vengeance, though ...

Roger Pingeon (centre) looking pleased with himself after winning the 1969 Vuelta in Spain – one of the three Grand Tours of cycling, the others being the TdF and the Giro d'Italia, of course.

Pingeon holding off Merckx on the 1969 Tour de France. (Courtesy *L'Equipe*)

Charming picture used on the back of the 1969 UK brochure.

Delisle in his French champion colours on the 1969 TdF. (Courtesy *L'Equipe*)

4. THE SIZZLING SEVENTIES

By the time the seventies arrived, even though sales were booming again, many of the famous bicycle makers had fallen by the wayside, or were absorbed by stronger competition. Thankfully, Peugeot was in the latter group, with its successful Peugeot-BP-Michelin racing team keeping the marque firmly in the spotlight …

It was a strange situation, with some truly staggering numbers involved. If we take the US market as an example, 7,000,000 bicycles were sold in 1970, although the vast majority were kids' bikes, and only 200,000 were road-racers. It was therefore a difficult environment for those in the industry that specialised in sporting models. Indeed, few were able to weather the storm, and rivals were dwindling on an annual basis. Had the failed manufacturers managed to hold on, by 1972, they could have fought for a share of the 14,000,000 sales recorded in the US, with sports bikes accounting for over half these. It was a remarkable turnaround, reflected in the launch of new models, and a sudden surge of fresh catalogues in which to punt them.

Bernard Thévenet would play a key role in Peugeot's fortunes over the coming years.

Back to the start of the decade, though, and there simply wasn't the justification to keep changing model lines and graphics to attract buyers. In the sporting category, especially, it was good, solid products offered at sensible prices that kept enthusiastic customers lining up at the dealers, rather than edgy paintwork colours and tacky decals. As such, the same range was rolled out for home market buyers in 1970, including the H50, PL50 and PX50 randonneurs, the H8, PL8, PX8 and PX8L sports bikes, and the P10, PA10 and PX10 competition models. As before, the H8 and H50 were listed as part of the cheaper Hélium line-up.

In racing, Winfried Bölke had gone to a German team, but there were still a few hard hitters in the 23-man Peugeot equipe, and Bernard Thévenet was an important new signing. Jurgen Tschan had a convincing win on the Paris-Tours one-day event, and Raymond Delisle won the Puy de Dome and the Trophée d'Europe de la Montagne, beating none other than Eddy Merckx in the latter, so that has to go down in the history books as something special, too. Delisle was also Peugeot's top finisher in the 1970 Tour de France, in which the men in white claimed three stage victories. Ferdinand Bracke took the silverware in the Grand Prix de Wallonie revival, and Roger Pingeon was second in the Critérium du Dauphiné Libéré.

Although the range was carried over yet again for 1971, and the catalogues from this era are far from helpful, lacking dates and showing either old and/or awkwardly angled photography (or drawings that look nice but weren't updated), a little research throws up a few changes that may help with dating bikes. The main change was the head badge, which was similar to its predecessor but now based on a scutum-shaped shield rather than a heater-type one; this latest design was naturally repeated on the seat tube. In addition, the 'Peugeot' script on the down tube was now enclosed

Jurgen Tschan on his way to victory on the 1970 Paris-Tours race. (Courtesy *L'Equipe*)

in a block with parallel lines running off each side, although some models (such as the Hélium-badged bikes and the P10, PA10 and PX10) had shorter lines than those found on other bikes. The Hélium models also had new seat tube decals, bringing them closer to their Peugeot counterparts, but still without chequers in the design. Otherwise, the graphics were much the same as before across the board.

In competition, Jurgen Tschan was crowned the 1971 champion of Germany, and Jean-Pierre Danguillaume won the Grand Prix Ouest France in Plouay. In the Grand Tours, Bernard Thévenet had managed to win a stage of the Tour de France in the previous year, and did the same in 1971, along with Jean-Pierre Danguillaume, and new signing, Walter Godefroot (the green jersey winner in 1970, when the Belgian ace was with the Salvarani outfit). Thévenet ultimately finished the TdF in fourth, just under 15 minutes behind Merckx, with two more Peugeot riders in the top 20. While there was nothing to write home about in the Giro d'Italia, Ferdinand Bracke won the 1971 Vuelta a España after a calculated race, while another Peugeot rider, Wilfried David was second; Luis Ocaña, who'd won for the Bic team in the 1970 edition and would later go on to win the Tour de France, had to be content with third.

With the Beaulieu factory now covering 1.7-million square feet (155,000m^2) and employing around 1600 solely for the manufacturing of bicycles, plus a further 600 at Saint-Louis, annual production hovered around the 700,000 mark in the early seventies, and continued to rise on the back of a new boom. This sudden jump in volume created a few quality issues for a time, but they were duly brought under control, and a new 'Atelier Prestige' workshop was added at the main Beaulieu site for high-end and custom-made bikes in 1974, headed by the experienced Raoul Jeand'Heur and manned by just eight craftsmen. Interestingly, Raleigh opened its Specialist Bicycle Development Unit (SBDU) in 1974 as well, showing how upmarket sections of the industry had become, keeping it going until 1986. Another factory had been secured at Romilly-sur-Seine, to the east of Paris, too. Bought in 1972, it continued the work of the company's France Motor Cycles subsidiary (or

Action from the 1970 Tour de France, with a Peugeot course car at the head of the peloton. (Courtesy Wikimedia Commons: Jean-Pierre Bazard)

FMC) by making light motorcycles as well as bicycles for the Cycles Peugeot group.

As it happens, 1972 was to witness the first major overhaul of the Peugeot range in years, with the 'Nouveau Style' models leading the way. These were closely related to the smaller-wheeled 'Week-End' runabouts (by now offered in DA two-piece, PA folding and RA rigid guise), and were listed in both rigid (NS) and folding (PNS) lines, initially with two grades in each. There's actually quite a following for these 'Nouveau Style' bikes nowadays, with a number of dedicated clubs across the world.

The kids' range was also heavily revised at this time, while the ladies had less choice than before, with the PX45 being a victim of the cull, for instance; the PX8 variant was also reduced to a single grade in the French catalogues – a PX8L, although without another option, it was entered simply as the PX8 at this time. Saying that, the

Contemporary publicity material showing the P10, PR10 and PX10.

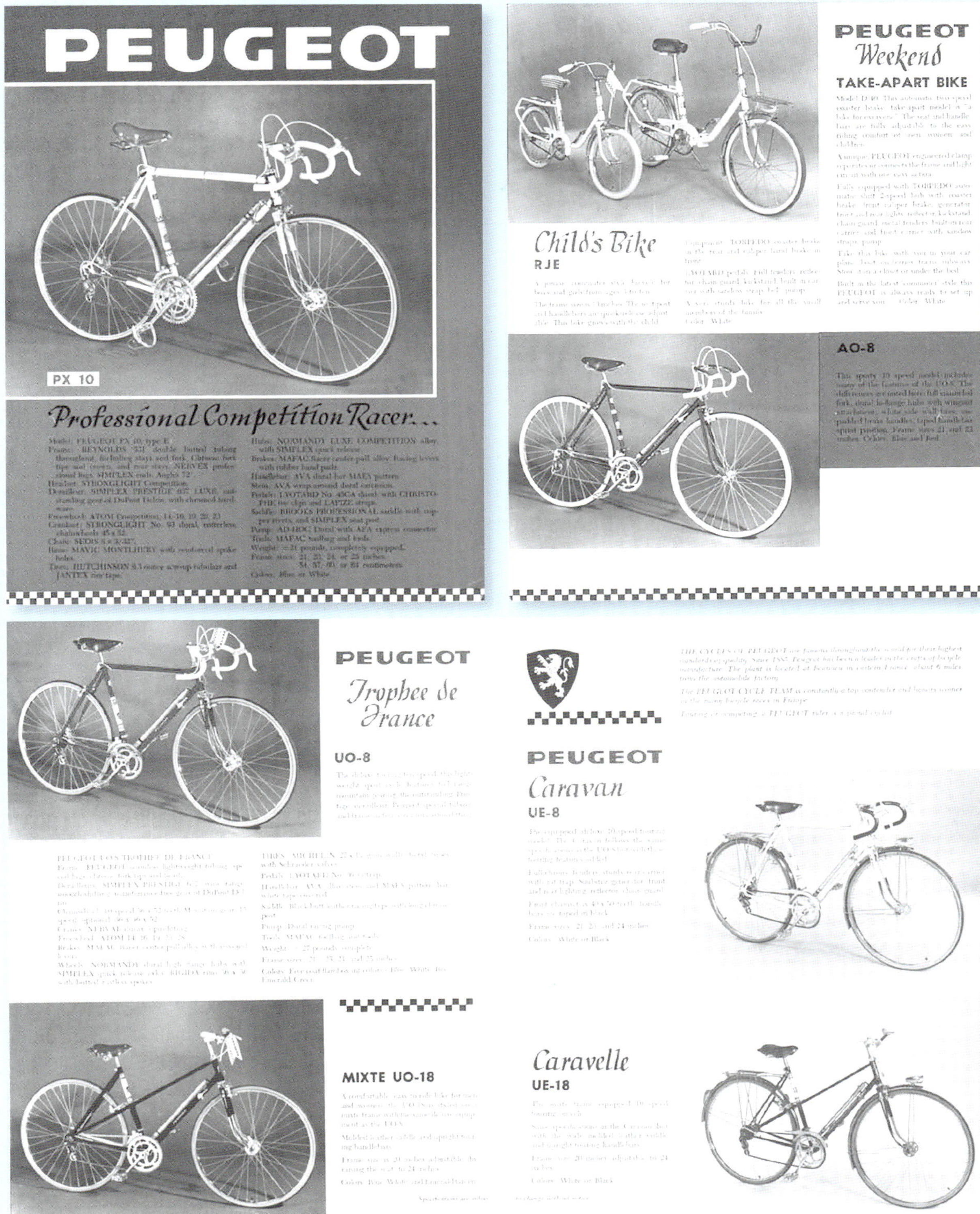

A four-page US brochure for the 1971 season. The UO- and AO-series bikes would have a strong following in the States.

Ferdinand Bracke in action on the 1971 Critérium du Dauphiné Libéré. The Belgian had a good year, winning the Vuelta in Spain, no less. (Courtesy *L'Equipe*)

H8 was now offered in four- and eight-speed trim like the PL50 and PL8, which was a lot more avant garde than the three-speed specification of yore.

Continuing the modernisation theme, the PX10 and PR10 were now built using plain Nervex 'DuBois' lugs rather than the gothic-style 'Professional' version. Sadly, the PA10 also lost its attractive Nervex lugs, adopting the Bocama items used on the P10 and PN10 at this time. However, domestic buyers could now get the PR10 competition model (previously export only), and the PN10 swelled the ranks of the road-racers still further, becoming the new entry-level bike in this category. Like the P10, the PN10 had budget Altenburger side-pull brakes, with things like cheaper rims helping to bring down the price further. All other home market sporting grades were carried over.

For the record, while the PA10, PR10 and PX10 were sold in white only in France, the PN10 was offered in White or Nasturtium Red, and the P10 in White or Peacock Blue. All five had the pair of lugs up front painted black, as expected, with colour-keyed ones elsewhere; decal sets were carried over from the 1971 season. A novel move was to paint the lugs securing the head tube black on lesser models, too – even the Hélium H8 and H50, so naturally the PL8, PL50 and PX8 were included in the update. In fact, virtually all the traditional bikes received this change in Europe.

As in France, the road-racer line-up was expanding in the States, too, with the PX10, UO8, AO8 and UO18 now augmented by PA10 and PR10 grades, as well as the G45 for younger riders. It seems like cheaper models had been abandoned at this stage in the proceedings, which would make sense from a marketing point of view, although they would ultimately make a comeback in the near future.

The Beaulieu factory is hardly recognisable compared with the image of the site in the first chapter. Many of the production methods were surprisingly similar to those illustrated in chapter two, though.

The new Romilly factory, which would assume greater importance as the years rolled by.

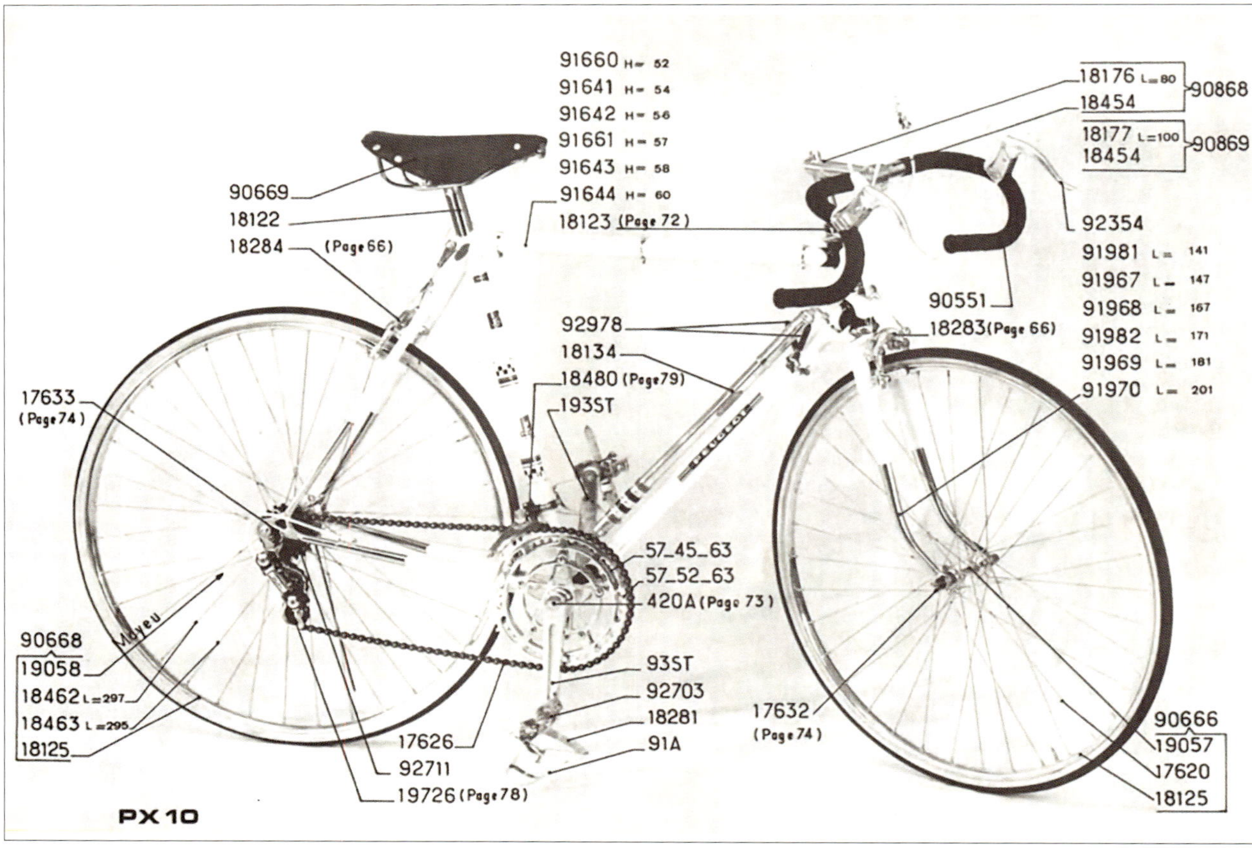

The PX10 as seen in the 1972 parts catalogue.

Oddly, it appears the UO8 and the other bikes not sold in France continued with colour-keyed head tube lugs.

Given the strong team Peugeot was blessed with, 1972 was a surprisingly quiet year. Godefroot beat Merckx to claim the Belgian national title, and Thévenet (coming ninth in the Tour de France, as Peugeot's top finisher) won the Tour de Romandie, but otherwise, there was little to celebrate.

A number of countries started receiving lesser versions of the top sports bikes for the 1973 season, making it necessary to add an 'L' suffix on several models. For instance, the domestic PX8 became the PX8L again in France and certain other markets for better clarification. Likewise, while places like Britain (where the limited range was now similar to the American line-up) and Spain sold a PA10 with fully-painted front forks, this dictated that the French model was given the

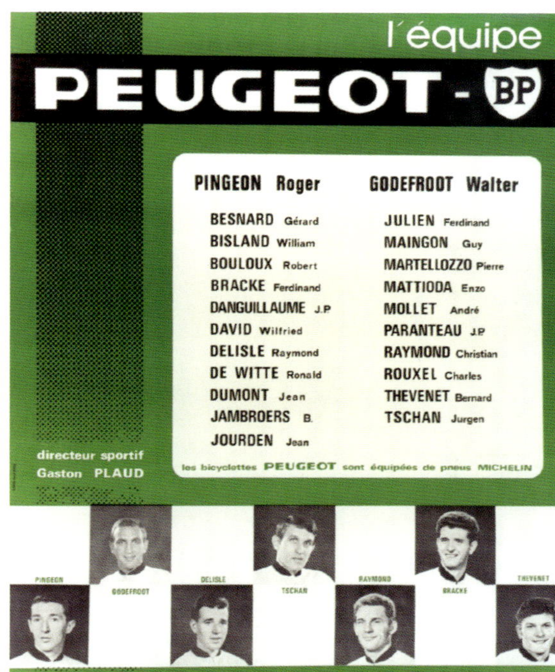

Poster showing the team line-up for 1972.

A domestic catalogue from February 1973.

PA10L moniker; the PR10 and PX10 followed suit, becoming the PR10L and PX10L, respectively, although the PN10 and P10 continued with their old designations. Incidentally, weights ranged from 10kg (22lb) for the PX10, up to around 11.5kg (25lb) for the cheaper road-racers.

Then, from February 1973, with bicycles firmly back in vogue, the range was given a big reshuffle. The 'Week-End' series limped on, although it was made largely redundant by the 'Nouveau Style' bikes by this time, with that particular range expanding rapidly. There were some changes in the G- and J-series kids lines, too, but more importantly, a general shift towards more sporting and lavish machinery. There were some minor changes on the colour schemes, too, but nothing dramatic, and more often than not simply a reduction in the number of shades on offer for each bike.

Anyway, the H8 morphed into the HA8 in the spring of 1973, with the H50 evolving into the HA50 at the same time; both became three-speed models only as a result, helping to keep the prices down. But even the

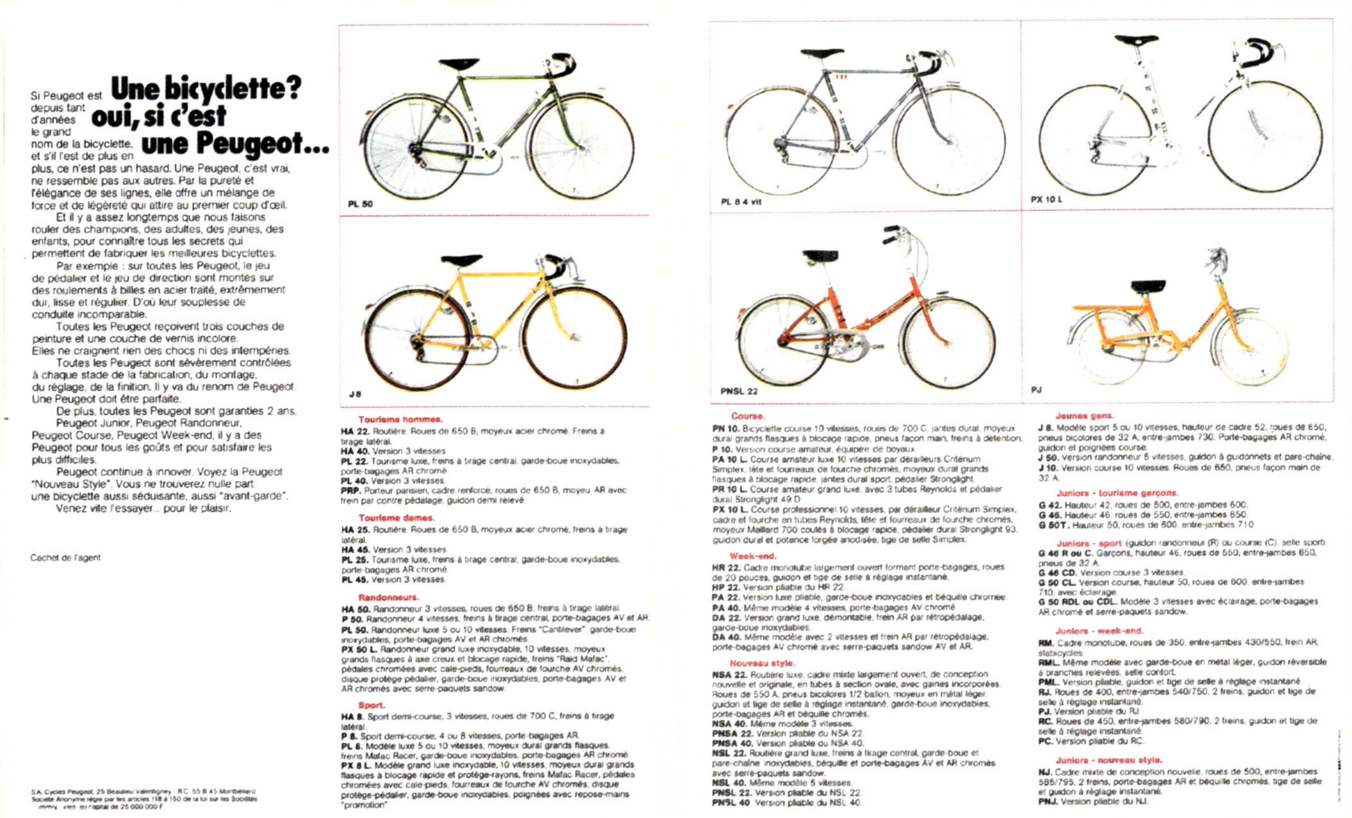

Une bicyclette? oui, si c'est une Peugeot...

Si Peugeot est depuis tant d'années le grand nom de la bicyclette, et s'il l'est de plus en plus, ce n'est pas un hasard. Une Peugeot, c'est vrai, ne ressemble pas aux autres. Par la pureté et l'élégance de ses lignes, elle offre un mélange de force et de légèreté qui attire au premier coup d'œil.

Et il y a assez longtemps que nous faisons rouler des champions, des adultes, des jeunes, des enfants, pour connaître tous les secrets qui permettent de fabriquer les meilleures bicyclettes.

Par exemple : sur toutes les Peugeot, le jeu de pédalier et le jeu de direction sont montés sur des roulements à billes en acier traité, extrêmement dur, lisse et régulier. D'où leur souplesse de conduite incomparable.

Toutes les Peugeot reçoivent trois couches de peinture et une couche de vernis incolore. Elles ne craignent rien des chocs ni des intempéries.

Toutes les Peugeot sont sévèrement contrôlées à chaque stade de la fabrication, du montage, du réglage, de la finition. Il y va du renom de Peugeot. Une Peugeot doit être parfaite.

De plus, toutes les Peugeot sont garanties 2 ans.

Peugeot Junior, Peugeot Randonneur, Peugeot Course, Peugeot Week-end, il y a des Peugeot pour tous les goûts et pour satisfaire les plus difficiles.

Peugeot continue à innover. Voyez la Peugeot "Nouveau Style". Vous ne trouverez nulle part une bicyclette aussi séduisante, aussi "avant-garde".

Venez vite l'essayer... pour le plaisir.

Cachet de l'agent

S.A. Cycles Peugeot, 25 Beaulieu Valentigney - R.C. 55 B 45 Montbéliard
Société Anonyme régie par les articles 118 à 150 de la loi sur les Sociétés [illegible] au capital de 25 000 000 F

PL 50

J 8

Tourisme hommes.

HA 22. Routière. Roues de 650 B, moyeux acier chromé. Freins à tirage latéral.
HA 40. Version 3 vitesses.
PL 22. Tourisme luxe, freins à tirage central, garde-boue inoxydables, porte-bagages AR chromé.
PL 40. Version 3 vitesses.
PRP. Porteur parisien, cadre renforcé, roues de 650 B, moyeu AR avec frein par contre pédalage, guidon demi relevé.

Tourisme dames.

HA 25. Routière. Roues de 650 B, moyeux acier chromé, freins à tirage latéral.
HA 45. Version 3 vitesses.
PL 25. Tourisme luxe, freins à tirage central, garde-boue inoxydables, porte-bagages AR chromé.
PL 45. Version 3 vitesses.

Randonneurs.

HA 50. Randonneur 3 vitesses, roues de 650 B, freins à tirage latéral.
P 50. Randonneur 4 vitesses, freins à tirage central, porte-bagages AV et AR.
PL 50. Randonneur luxe 5 ou 10 vitesses. Freins "Cantilever", garde-boue inoxydables, porte-bagages AV et AR chromés.
PX 50 L. Randonneur grand luxe inoxydable, 10 vitesses, moyeux grands flasques à axe creux et blocage rapide, freins "Raid Mafac", pédales chromées avec cale-pieds, fourreaux de fourche AV chromés, disque protège pédalier, garde-boue inoxydables, porte-bagages AV et AR chromés avec serre-paquets sandow.

Sport.

HA 8. Sport demi-course, 3 vitesses, roues de 700 C, freins à tirage latéral.
P 8. Sport demi-course, 4 ou 8 vitesses, porte-bagages AR.
PL 8. Modèle luxe 5 ou 10 vitesses, moyeux dural grands flasques, freins Mafac Racer, garde-boue inoxydables, porte-bagages AR chromé.
PX 8 L. Modèle grand luxe inoxydable, 10 vitesses, moyeux dural grands flasques à blocage rapide et protège-rayons, freins Mafac Racer, pédales chromées avec cale-pieds, fourreaux de fourche AV chromés, disque protège-pédalier, garde-boue inoxydables, poignées avec repose-mains "promotion".

PL 8 4 vit

PX 10 L

PNSL 22

PJ

Course.

PN 10. Bicyclette course 10 vitesses, roues de 700 C, jantes dural, moyeux dural grands flasques à blocage rapide, pneus façon main, freins à détention.
P 10. Version course amateur, équipée de boyaux.
PA 10 L. Course amateur luxe 10 vitesses par dérailleurs Critérium Simplex, tête et fourreaux de fourche chromés, moyeux dural grands flasques à blocage rapide, jantes dural sport, pédalier Stronglight.
PR 10 L. Course amateur grand luxe, avec 3 tubes Reynolds et pédalier dural Stronglight 49 D.
PX 10 L. Course professionnel 10 vitesses, par dérailleur Critérium Simplex, cadre et fourche en tubes Reynolds, tête et fourreaux de fourche chromés, moyeux Maillard 700 coulés à blocage rapide, pédalier dural Stronglight 93, guidon dural et potence forgée anodisée, tige de selle Simplex.

Week-end.

HR 22. Cadre monotube largement ouvert formant porte-bagages, roues de 20 pouces, guidon et tige de selle à réglage instantané.
HP 22. Version pliable du HR 22.
PA 22. Version luxe pliable, garde-boue inoxydables et béquille chromée.
PA 40. Même modèle 4 vitesses, porte-bagages AV chromé.
DA 22. Version grand luxe, démontable, frein AR par rétropédalage, garde-boue inoxydables.
DA 40. Même modèle avec 2 vitesses et frein AR par rétropédalage, porte-bagages AV chromé avec serre-paquets sandow AV et AR.

Nouveau style.

NSA 22. Routière luxe, cadre mixte largement ouvert, de conception nouvelle et originale, en tubes à section ovale, avec gaines incorporées. Roues de 550 A, pneus bicolores 1/2 ballon, moyeux en métal léger, guidon et tige de selle à réglage instantané, garde-boue inoxydables, porte-bagages AR et béquille chromés.
NSA 40. Même modèle 3 vitesses.
PNSA 22. Version pliable du NSA 22.
PNSA 40. Version pliable du NSA 40.
NSL 22. Routière grand luxe, freins à tirage central, garde-boue et pare-chaîne inoxydables, béquille et porte-bagages AV et AR chromés avec serre-paquets sandow.
NSL 40. Même modèle 5 vitesses.
PNSL 22. Version pliable du NSL 22.
PNSL 40 Version pliable du NSL 40.

Jeunes gens.

J 8. Modèle sport 5 ou 10 vitesses, hauteur de cadre 52, roues de 650, pneus bicolores de 32 A, entre-jambes 730. Porte-bagages AR chromé, guidon et poignées course.
J 50. Version randonneur 5 vitesses, guidon à guidonnets et pare-chaîne.
J 10. Version course 10 vitesses. Roues de 650, pneus façon main de 32 A.

Juniors - tourisme garçons.

G 42. Hauteur 42, roues de 500, entre-jambes 600.
G 46. Hauteur 46, roues de 550, entre-jambes 650.
G 50T. Hauteur 50, roues de 600, entre-jambes 710.

Juniors - sport (guidon randonneur (R) ou course (C), selle sport)

G 46 R ou C. Garçons, hauteur 46, roues de 550, entre-jambes 650, pneus de 32 A.
G 46 CD. Version course 3 vitesses.
G 50 CL. Version course, hauteur 50, roues de 600, entre-jambes 710, avec éclairage.
G 50 RDL ou CDL. Modèle 3 vitesses avec éclairage, porte-bagages AR chromé et serre-paquets sandow.

Juniors - week-end.

RM. Cadre monotube, roues de 350, entre-jambes 430/550, frein AR, stabicycles.
RML. Même modèle avec garde-boue en métal léger, guidon réversible à branches relevées, selle confort.
PML. Version pliable, guidon et tige de selle à réglage instantané.
RJ. Roues de 400, entre-jambes 540/750, 2 freins, guidon et tige de selle à réglage instantané.
PJ. Version pliable du RJ.
RC. Roues de 450, entre-jambes 580/790, 2 freins, guidon et tige de selle à réglage instantané.
PC. Version pliable du RC.

Juniors - nouveau style.

NJ. Cadre mixte de conception nouvelle, roues de 500, entre-jambes 585/795, 2 freins, porte-bagages AR et béquille chromés, tige de selle et guidon à réglage instantané.
PNJ. Version pliable du NJ.

The 1973 owners' handbook. The same girl and Nouveau Style bike were used on a number of publicity and reference items from the time.

Hélium bikes got a makeover, with fresh cranksets, and new badging that added a quality feel. The 'Hélium' name block now had longer lines running from it, virtually the full length of the down tube, the top tube coachlines were deleted, and the lugs became the same colour as the rest of the frame again. Otherwise, the HA8 sports bike and HA50 randonneur were much the same, with the seat tube and fork decals carried over.

For the record, the HA22, HA40, PL22 and PL40 touring bikes were still available, along with the equivalent ladies model (the HA25, HA45, PL25 and PL45). Moving up the ladder, there was a new P8 grade – a proper sporting machine with four or eight speeds, colour-keyed lugs, and new badging. Whilst similar to before, the 'Peugeot' name block on the down tube was given stronger lines running from it, chamfered at either end in order to finish horizontally in accordance with the angle of the metalwork. The top tube decal, not used on the pure racers, was also revised, becoming the single coachline previously found on both sides of the PL50 and PX50 models.

Spain had its own subtle variation on a theme, with some typical Latin exuberance added into the equation for good measure in these simpler times. Harmless though it may be, one wonders if such photography would nowadays get past the PC brigade?

Luis Ocaña leading Bernard Thévenet in the 1973 Dauphiné Libéré. The Spaniard would ultimately win the event, beating the Peugeot rider by just over a minute. (Courtesy *L'Equipe*)

The PL8 had the new down tube badge only (for some reason, the flashy top tube decal wasn't changed on this model), and continued with black lugs, but had five or ten speed options now, rather than four or eight. The PX8L had the same badging as the PL8s, and also retained the sporty black lugs on the head tube. The P50 was new as well, priced to fit in below the existing '50' randonneur line-up, which was also given mild revisions: in addition to the latest P8-type detailing combined with black lugs, the PL50 gained the same gearing enhancements as the PL8, while the PX50L got the new badging only.

Less sensitive to fashion trends, the pure road-racer models – the PN10, P10, PA10L, PR10L and PX10L – were carried over unchanged, with the same badging and black lugs. Some markets had fresh colour variations, but not all …

Considering that Walter Godefroot had already decided to move to the Flandria team and Roger Pingeon had defected to the German Rokado outfit, 1973 could

Bernard Thévenet (centre, in the colours of the French champion) sharing a lighter moment with Luis Ocaña (in yellow) and José Manuel Fuente on the 1973 Tour de France. These three men would fill the podium in Paris. (Courtesy *L'Equipe*)

have been a lot worse. Jean-Pierre Danguillaume won the Critérium National, Eric Leman won the Tour of Flanders in his first – and only – year with Peugeot, and the men in white filled the first four spots in the Tour l'Aude. As well as being crowned French national champion, Bernard Thévenet was third overall in the Vuelta, which was extremely competitive that year, with Merckx (Molteni) winning and Ocaña (Bic) second. A few weeks later, Ocaña duly won the Tour de France, with Thévenet claiming a magnificent second place; other Peugeot riders finished the 1973 event in tenth and 11th overall.

After overhauling the showroom bicycle range only a few months earlier, one can be forgiven for expecting very little in the way of change for the 1974 season. Indeed, the HA8, HA50, PL8, PL50, P8, P50, PX8L and PX50L were carried over unchanged. The PA10L and PR10L were also carried over once more. The only difference was the colour palette, with the PR10L now coming in imperial red or bamboo, in addition to the regular white shade. Oddly, while the PN10 and P10 were not featured in the 1974 master catalogue, they did appear in contemporary brochures and price lists, so they were definitely still available. Like the PA10L, they were listed with white or nasturtium red paintwork, although all three models had a unique third colour option: The PN10 had yellow, the P10 a champagne hue, and the PA10L, an attractive copper shade.

From a styling point of view, the 1974 PX10L was basically the same as the 1973 model for the start of the season, but now came with a more modern saddle and the lugs painted in the same hue as the frame colour, complete with coachlines on the lug edges – a unique feature.

An interesting newcomer for 1974 was the PA60, described as a 'Cyclotouriste' model, and duly joined by a more expensive version with Reynolds tubing and top-level components: the PX60. These were basically high-quality road-racers with lightweight mudguards, front and rear. The lugs were painted in the same colour as the frame tubing on the two '60' grades, but the decals were all-new, setting the pattern for years to come. Indeed, the

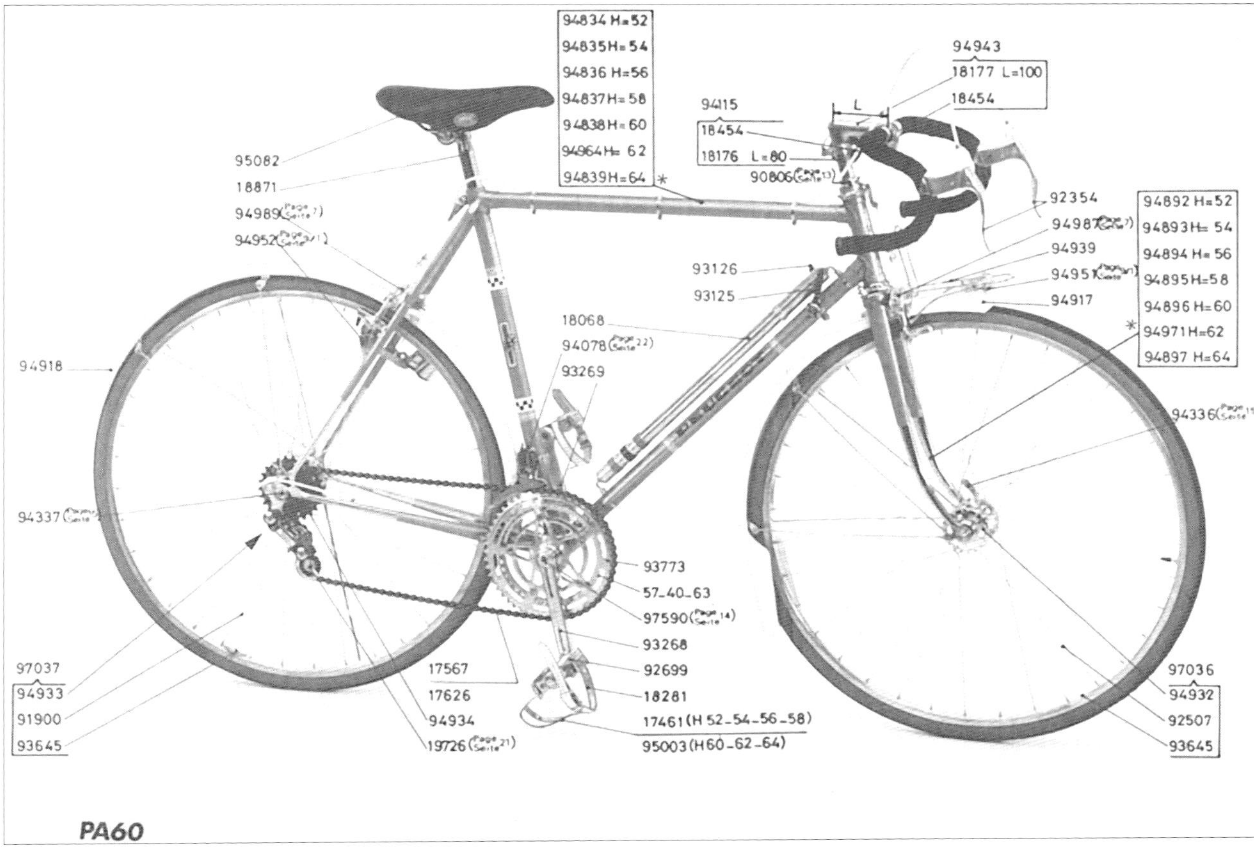

The PA60 model as it first appeared, illustrated here via the contemporary parts catalogue.

PX10 adopted the new '60' series-type badging (with strong 'Peugeot' script in block letters, framed by bands that were repeated on the seat tube to sit outside the chequer patterns and new lion logo) at some stage during the spring of 1974. By this time, even in France, the PX10L had become available in a wide range of colours, including traditional white, peacock blue, nasturtium red, imperial red, yellow, bamboo and violet.

The 'Atelier Prestige' shop that opened at Beaulieu in 1974.

Japanese brochure for the 1974 season.

The importers in the States were making the most of the cycling boom, with an extensive range offered for 1974. Full-size drop-handle bikes included the UE8 tourer with mudguards, carrier and lighting, the entry-level AO8 racer, the AE8, sitting between the UE8 and AO8, the UO8, the mixte-framed UO18C, the P10, PA10E, PR10L, PX10E, and the PX10LE, which was a replica of the latest works bike, with forged Maillard '700' hubs replacing the 'Normandy Super Competition' ones from the same company, a new, albeit similar braking system (a lighter MAFAC 'Competition' setup instead of a 'Racer' one), a Philippe handlebar, and a different saddle; there was also a UX10, which was a PX10E with different tyres. The extra effort would pay off, though, for US sales increased to roughly 430,000 units that year – almost three times the sales volume recorded in 1971.

Even Japan was getting in on the act, with Yamaha serving as an importer at this time, although Honda would take on the brand in later years. This is perhaps ironic, given that Peugeot was in the process of expanding its scooter and motorcycle ranges (with models like

The J10 model shown in an advert from the time.

the '100'-series cyclomoteur range, the GT10, and the SX5 sports bike waiting in the wings), but a business opportunity is just that, and European bicycles were hot property in a booming leisure market. Most of the 16-strong model line-up was sports orientated, with the top spec PX10E model commanding 250,000 yen for 1974 – a huge amount when one considers one could buy a Suzuki GT250B motorcycle in Japan for just 8000 yen more!

In the 1974 racing season, other than André Mollet moving on, there were no major changes to the Peugeot team line-up. Victories came on the Critérium National and Tour of Catalunya for Bernard Thévenet, while the Grand Prix du Midi Libre went to Jean-Pierre Danguillaume; the latter also won a couple of stages on the Tour de France, and was Peugeot's top finisher in the Vuelta, too, coming seventh overall. Given the amount of money being spent on the squad, though, it was not an amazing year, and this relative lack of success may have been the reason ex-racer Maurice de Muer was brought in to manage the Peugeot-BP-Michelin team for 1975 …

In the background, Peugeot acquired a 38 per cent share in Citroën in 1974, increasing to 90 per cent in the spring of 1976, when Citroën was as good as bankrupt. This led to the formation of what would become known as the PSA Group, with Peugeot very much in charge, and several brands collected over the years hived off to allow a greater level of product streamlining.

Poster showing the works racing team for 1974.

Bernard Thévenet on the 1974 TdF. He was forced to abandon the race this year, but would be back … (Courtesy *L'Equipe*)

Jean-Pierre Danguillaume on the 1974 Tour de France. He was 13th overall on the Tour, but managed to win a couple of stages along the way. (Courtesy *L'Equipe*)

THE CLASSIC COMPONENT SUPPLIERS: DRIVETRAINS

Chainwheels and cranks were ordered from Stronglight in the main when it came to the 'Golden Era', with alloy items on the top stuff, and steel on the lesser models. Some of the designs, such as the elegant 49D, literally stayed in production for decades. As well as the groupsets from Campagnolo and Shimano, Solida and Peyrard enter the story later on. This is where the web of intrigue kicks in, for the Solida brand was marketed by a firm founded by Achille Haubtmann in 1906, which duly bought the company that owned Stronglight in the early 1970s (bringing it to Saint Etienne in the process) after a failed attempt to buy Ets Peyrard de l'Horme.

Pedals were bought in from numerous places over the years, but the classic setup combines Lyotard pedals (made by Pierre Lyotard's company until its demise in the late-1980s) with Christophe toe-clips and straps, named after the French cyclist who invented them, Eugène Christophe.

Moyne (and sometimes Prior) freewheels were used on the top-end road-racers in the early 1950s, with Maillard and Atom items soon taking their place. As it happens, Maillard also made 'Normandy' branded hubs and bought out the company behind the Atom hubs, although Sachs ultimately acquired Maillard in 1987. Notwithstanding, unless imported groupsets were specified, these would remain the French brands that Peugeot relied on throughout the classic era.

Chain was almost exclusively sourced from Sedis. This famous chain company was officially founded in June 1946, but is actually Peugeot's own chain firm, making 'Chaîne Peugeot' since the turn of the century at Valentigney, duly separated to become a subsidiary. Also sold under the Yellorex name, Sedis was the choice of virtually all

The iconic Stronglight 49D crankset – a true French masterpiece.

A Maillard freewheel pictured in the 1977 Spidel brochure. It was also available in duralumin, but the cost increased four-fold for those seeking the best.

professional racing teams in the classic years. The last bicycle chains were made in 1999, which is well beyond the core subject of this book.

One of Peugeot's key suppliers for many years was Simplex, who fought off competion from Huret, Super Champion and Cyclo to lead the field in the French derailleur industry in the years immediately before WWII, with cable-operated devices already available for the front and rear by that time. Its founder-cum-designer, Lucien Juy, had actually invented several derailleurs before this, offering an early one to the Alcyon team back in 1928 (which the riders refused to use, as it happens), and helping Antonin Magne take the World Championship in 1936. But it was the postwar 'Tour de France' rear derailleur (often combined with a simple 'Compétition' lever-operated item up front) that truly established the brand, which wasn't really bettered until the parallelogram-type Campagnolo 'Gran Sport' was introduced in 1951, although the Huret 'Competition' model deserves a special mention as another worthy rival. Even then, with factories in Dijon and Milan, Simplex continued to dominate the scene, making more derailleurs than all the other companies combined for most of the decade!

While many racing teams chose rapidly-evolving Campagnolo components in the sixties and seventies (when Japan's Shimano and SunTour were just starting to make their presence felt), Peugeot stood firmly by Simplex. An attempt was made via the Spidel name to offer top notch groupsets (Simplex, Stronglight, MAFAC and Maillard parts), but a move to Delrin plastics in the 'Prestige' line had already damaged Simplex's reputation in many quarters.

Peugeot's insistence on using domestically-sourced components for its top-end bikes was ultimately its undoing. Although they have a special place in the hearts of enthusiasts, other nations, especially Japan, were catching

Superb Sedis advert from the 1950s.

up and overtaking the French in the technology stakes, introducing new systems at a pace the French component manufacturers could only dream of.

Still, Peugeot remained loyal, although Campagnolo, Shimano, Huret (later bought by Sachs) and Mavic components were starting to creep into catalogues by the latter half of the 1980s, as Simplex ultimately filed for bankruptcy. Sadly, the name disappeared once and for all in the mid-1990s. For the main eras covered by this book, however, Simplex was king for fans of the Peugeot brand ...

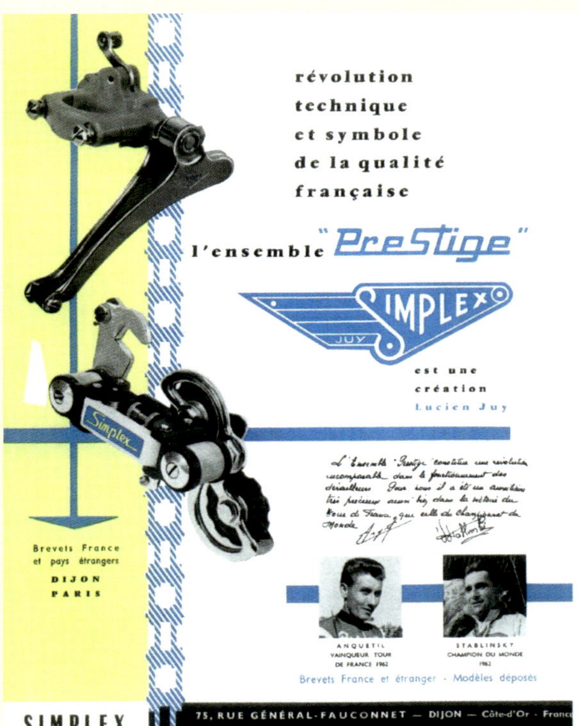

Simplex advertising from 1963.

There was little change for the 1975 domestic showroom models, with specifications and badging pretty much carried over, other than a new head badge that was gradually phased in over the year. Actually, it was similar to the 1971 version, but the traditional golden lion logo was now fully enclosed within a fresh red shield, and the 'Made in France' marking was gone. There were two types, as it happens, with certain lines (the PX60 being a good example) having a heavier two-piece version that was riveted to the head tube. With so many variations in down tube and seat tube decal sets, with debut timing often staggered according to model series and/or production aspects (using up old stock was the norm in almost all manufacturing environments before the escalation of just-in-time ordering), and then this head tube badge adding to the confusion, it's no wonder one sees so many people struggling to date bikes accurately now we find ourselves several decades further down the line.

Anyway, of the sporting models for 1975, the Hélium HA8 was cheapest, priced at 466FF, and joined by the HA50, as usual, for those wanting a little more comfort. The P50 was the entry-level Peugeot randonneur, commanding 540FF, with the PL50s slotting in between this and the 729FF PX50L. The two P8 variants kicked off the sports range, with prices starting at 514FF, augmenting the two PL8s and the 717FF PX8L. Then, there were the 1148FF PA60 and 1674FF PX60 grades, with the pure racers continuing as before, too: The PN10 and P10 were listed at a modest 691FF, with the PA10L and PR10L bracketed by these and the 1829FF PX10L.

Building on the introduction of the pair of '60' grades in the previous season, the push for prestige continued unabated. In addition to the PX22, PX25, PX40 and PX45 (luxury versions of the equivalent PL tourers), important newcomers for 1975 included the 3224FF PY10 and PY60 flagship models, and a ladies version of the PA60 – the PA65.

It's fascinating to watch the Peugeot range evolve in this period, as cycling became more of a hobby rather than a cheap form of transport for the masses. The PA60 had been introduced as a luxury version of the PA10L, with upgraded components, mudguards and lighting. The ten-speed PX60 tourer that followed was something rather special, with Reynolds tubing for

PEUGEOT MODELLEN '75

PEUGEOT PA 60

Deze exclusieve fiets met 10 versnellingen in 'gentleman' uitvoering heeft de lichte gang van een racefiets.

FOR GENTLEMEN
★ de lichtstlopende fiets
★ grote klasse
★ 10 versnellingen

Kleur:
Framehoogten: 58, 60 en 64 cm
Specificatie:
Frame en vork: superlichte Peugeot buizen met Simplex voorvorkeinden
Dérailleurs: voor: Simplex Super Competition; achter: Simplex Criterium
Kettingbladen met cranks: Stronglight Dural 49 D 40 x 50 tands, spieloos
Naven: Normandy Luxe Competition met uitvalassen
Freewheel: 14 x 17 x 19 x 22 x 26 tands
Bandenmaat: 28 x 1⅝ x 1⅜
Spatborden: Bluemel celluloid
Velgen: speciale versterkte lichtgewicht velgen
Zadel: Idéale 2001 lamsleer
Remmen: Mafac Racer gesmeed
Pedalen: racepedalen met toeclips en riemen (met reflectors)
Toebehoren: sportvoordragertje, speciale verlichting, bel, pomp en Mafac gereedschap
Gewicht: 13,0 kg

PEUGEOT PX 60 (afgebeeld op omslag)
Een met de hand gebouwde, goudkleurige prachtfiets in 'gentleman luxe' uitvoering met 10 versnellingen. Deze fiets is uitgevoerd als PA 60 met de volgende verfijningen.

Kleur:
Framehoogten: 58, 60 en 64 cm
Specificatie:
Frame en vork: uit Reynolds 531 buis en Nervex lugs
Balhoofdstel: Stronglight Competition
Dérailleurs: Simplex Super L.J.
Kettingbladen: Stronglight Competition 99 40 x 50 tands, spieloos **(1)**
Zadelpen: Simplex Competition
Stuur: Philippe Dural
Pedalen: lichtmetalen racepedalen
Gewicht: 10,7 kg

13

PEUGEOT PR 10

Lichte racefiets met 10 versnellingen voor de renner. Voordelig voor een fiets van deze klasse.

Kleur:
Framehoogten: 56, 58, 60 en 64 cm
Specificatie:
Frame en vork: frame van Reynolds 531 buizen en Nervex lugs, voorvork met verchroomde einden
Dérailleurs: voor: Simplex Prestige; achter: Simplex Criterium **(1)**
Kettingbladen met cranks: Stronglight 49 D, lichtmetaal, 45 x 52 tands, spieloos **(2)**
Naven: Normandy hogeflens-naven
Wielbevestiging: Simplex uitvalassen
Freewheel: 14 x 15 x 17 x 19 x 21 tands
Banden: tubes (desgewenst draadbanden 28 x 1⅝ x 1¼)
Velgen: lichtmetaal
Zadel: racemodel uit kernleder
Stuur: lichtmetaal
Remmen: Mafac Racer
Pedalen: racepedalen met toeclips en riemen (met reflectors)
Toebehoren: bel en pomp
Gewicht: 11,0 kg

VOOR RACERS
★ voor supertrimmers
★ voor coureurs
★ voor professionals

14

PEUGEOT PX 10 LE (niet afgebeeld)
Model Professional met 10 versnellingen (het werkpaard van de Peugeot profs!)

Kleur:
Framehoogten: 56, 58, 60 en 64 cm
Specificatie:
Frame en vork: speciaal raceframe met Nervex lugs, voor- en achtervork met verchroomde einden. Buizen en vorkdelen uit Reynolds 531 buis
Balhoofdstel: Stronglight Competition
Dérailleurs: Simplex Super L.J. **(1)**
Kettingbladen met cranks: Stronglight Competition 93, lichtmetaal, 45 x 52 tands **(2)**, spieloos
Naven: Maillard 700, speciaal gesmeed lichtmetaal
Freewheel: 14 x 15 x 17 x 19 x 21 tands
Banden: Wolber Transalpino tubes
Velgen: Mavic Monthléry
Wielbevestiging: uitvalassen
Zadel: Idéale 2001 lamsleer
Zadelpen: Simplex Competition
Stuur: Philippe **(3)**
Remmen: Mafac Competition **(3)**
Pedalen: Lyotard 45 CA met toeclips en riemen (met reflectors) **(4)**
Toebehoren: pomp Ad'Hoc Super 20, gereedschaptas en bel
Gewicht: 9,9 kg

PEUGEOT P 10 (niet afgebeeld)
Racefiets met 10 versnellingen voor de supertrimmer.

Kleur:
Framehoogten: 56, 58 en 60 cm
Specificatie:
Frame en vork: Peugeot buizen met Bocama lugs
Dérailleurs: Simplex Prestigo **(5)**
Kettingbladen: 46 x 50 tands **(6)**
Naven: Normandy naven met hoge flens
Wielbevestiging: Simplex uitvalassen
Freewheel: 16 x 17 x 18 x 19 x 21 tands
Banden: tubes (desgewenst draadbanden 28 x 1⅝ x 1¼)
Zadel: racemodel
Remmen: Altenburger Synchron **(7)**
Pedalen: racepedalen met toeclips en riemen (met reflectors)
Toebehoren: bel en pomp
Gewicht: 11,5 kg

15

The sporting models for the 1975 season, seen here in a Dutch catalogue. The bike on the cover is the PX60.

The PX50L from the 1975 brochure. Note the continuation of the older-style badging on models outside the '60' series.

the frame and forks, Nervex lugs, top Stronglight and Simplex components, MAFAC Racer brakes, lightweight handlebars, an Idéale saddle, mudguards, and Cibié lights. The PY10 was a prestige version of the PX10L, with 12 speeds and Simplex Super LJ derailleurs to distance the two, while the elegant PY60 was another Reynolds-framed sports bike, with decorative lugs, mudguards, lights and a luggage rack augmenting competition level components, such as MAFAC 2000 brakes, and Maillard 700 hubs.

While the PA60 came in white, champagne or imperial red, with the PX60 adding silver and bronze hues to these, the PY60 and PY10 were offered in white, silver, peacock blue, bronze, nasturtium red or black. The PY10 and PY60 had the established '60' series decals, but with rainbow bands acting as frames for the logos (like the face-lifted PX10L), in keeping with the pure sports image of the bike; the PX60 (and PA65, for that matter) had bands in red, white and blue, naturally intending to represent the French flag, and the PA60 had quieter gold bands with black coachlines.

In racing, perhaps the biggest news for 1975 was a change at the top, with Maurice de Muer taking over as DS. De Muer, who'd ridden for Peugeot in the forties and early-fifties, would breathe new life into the team. He was doubtless helped in his quest for victory by some useful signings, with Jean-Luc Molinéris, José Catieau and Jean-Luc Vandenbroucke pulling on fresh white

Scene from the 1975 Milan-San Remo race. (Courtesy *L'Equipe*)

Poster to mark the crowning of Régis Ovion as French champion.

jerseys that would actually only last one season due to an imminent change in sponsorship.

Under de Muer, a string of good results came thick and fast. Jean-Pierre Danguillaume came first in the Paris-Bourges race, and Bernard Thévenet, Raymond Deslisle, Patrick Béon, Jean-Luc Vandenbroucke and Rachel Dard each won similar one-day events – Deslisle three times, and Béon twice, as it happens. Thévenet was also the winner of the demanding Critérium du Dauphiné Libéré, while Jacques Esclassan claimed the silverware in the Critérium National.

Régis Ovion was also declared champion of France, but 1975 will always be remembered by Peugeot fans for the Tour de France. After a memorable head-to-head duel on stage 15 out of Nice, following orders from de Muer, Thévenet attacked Merckx at just the right moment on the Pra-Loup climb, and duly took the yellow jersey that day. Riding a silver PY10 with striking gold-coloured components (the latest weapon for the works team), the Frenchman duly held on over the next seven stages to take a fine win in front of a home crowd on the 20th July 1975 – fittingly, it was the first time the Tour had finished on the Champs-Elysées.

The domestic catalogues for 1976 were released in

Esclassan taking the Le Mans stage on the 1975 TdF race. (Courtesy *L'Equipe*)

Another poster from 1975; this one to commemorate Bernard Thévenet's victory on the Tour de France.

February, and were clearly marked with a year on the cover, showing a certain amount of confidence in the ability to sell a significant number of machines within a given period. As it happens, this had been the norm for decades, but as the cycling boom faltered, it became easier not to date them, and make them last. 1975 had seen a return to annual markings for the first time in many years as far as home market brochures were concerned, and the fact that this trend was continuing was a good sign, reflecting the health of the industry.

Anyway, there were new decal sets across the range for the 1976 season, including the head badge. Actually, it was basically the broad adoption of the first '60' series decals, with framing ring designs assigned to suit the bike's genre. Now universal, the new head badge design had began drifting through during the previous year, with two specific types available, as in 1975 – a sticker version, and an 'embossed' one.

Bikes like the PX8L gained the latest '60' style seat tube logos with rainbow bands, heavy block lettering on the down tube with subtle flashes either side, and familiar fork and top tube detailing. The PX40, meanwhile, was similar, but had gold framing bands on the seat tube and a single coachline on the top tube, and the PX50L was somewhere between the two, with rainbow bands and PX40-type badging elsewhere. Naturally, the more

Peugeot's rally campaign was still paying dividends. Interestingly, there was some distance from the bike team now, with Esso sponsorship usually seen on the cars (something that would be put right with BP's influence about to fall by the wayside), and brighter paintwork coming as the seventies unfolded. This 504, however, was the 1975 Safari Rally winner, which could still be linked with the cycling team colours.

Cover of a general catalogue from 1976. A fold-out poster was also produced using the same picture.

Cover (above) and product pages (opposite) from the sporting bike catalogue printed in April 1976. There was also a spread showing a race in progress, and a fairly plain back to make up eight pages.

expensive bikes continued pretty much unchanged, as these were the trailblazers for the latest graphics, and the 'Courses' range fell into line with these, with bands framing both the seat tube decals and the 'Peugeot' block lettering on the down tube, either in gold or red, white and blue depending on the grade.

Colours were actually the same as before on all but the PY models (with a classier satin black replacing the regular black hue on these), the PX10L (now coming in white, silver, peacock blue, nasturtium red or bamboo), the PR10L (silver added), and the PA65, which was given a fresh range of paintwork options.

As per the Week-End and Nouveau Style ranges, the Hélium line-up was exactly the same as it had been in 1975. Prices, though, would increase by as much as 25 per cent by the time the summer came along (the August 1976 price list states 586FF for the HA8 – a full 120FF up on the cost quoted in January 1975). Apart from the loss of the PL22, PL25, PL40 and PL45 (another sign of Peugeot's move upmarket), the tourers, randonneurs and cheaper sports bikes were all carried over, too. Again, only the pricing was changed, to cover the constant increases in French wages, with the PX8L going up from 717FF at the start of 1975 to 865FF over the course of the year. Notwithstanding, there were several changes afoot in the 'Gentlemen', 'Ladies' and 'Course' lines …

Taking them in the order listed above, the PY60 became the 3590FF PY60P. Apart from the paint change noted earlier, it was actually the same as before, but the 'P' suffix (for 'Prestige') allowed more gaps to be filled in other lines. The 994FF ten-speed P60 was a newcomer for the summer of 1976, slotting in below the PA60 via a 356FF saving. Indeed, it can almost be considered as its replacement, for although the PA60 continued in price lists, it was conspicuous by its absence in 1977 catalogues. The ladies also gained a new luxury bike in the shape of the PA55, which offered a decent saving on the cost of the PA65 it was listed alongside.

And so to the competition bikes, which is where things

PY 60 P

CYCLOTOURISME

Vous qui aimez les balades à bicyclette, les longues randonnées, enfourchez une bicyclette PEUGEOT.

Vous trouverez sur les modèles "Cyclotourisme" la même perfection technique que sur la bicyclette de Bernard THEVENET.

En côte, comme en plaine, pédaler c'est une joie avec une bicyclette PEUGEOT.

cyclotourisme gentlemen

PA 60

Cadre : tubes Peugeot, raccords Bocama, pattes forgées.

Fourche : tête 1/2 course, dessus chromé. Jambages chromés à mi-hauteur.

Moyeux dural, grands flasques, 36 trous, à blocage rapide. Jantes dural et pneus 700 × 28 C, façon boyaux. Garde-boue et fixation Bluemel's. Roue libre 5 vitesses : 14 × 17 × 19 × 22 × 26.

Pédalier : Stronglight dural 49 D, double plateau 40 × 50. Manivelles dural forgé à emmanchement carré. Pédales avec cale-pieds et courroies.

Dérailleurs : AV à parallélogramme Simplex. AR Simplex Critérium.

Éclairage : par génératrice sur la roue AR, projecteur rond fixé sur porte-sac, feu rouge AR fixé sur hauban.

Freins : Mafac Racer dural forgé à grand étrier. Poignée course avec repose-mains.

Selle Idéale 2001, cintre et potence en métal léger. Avertisseur en alliage léger. Porte-sac TA en fils chromés. Pompe type course à raccord rapide.

PX 60

Cadre : tubes Reynolds, raccords Nervex. Haubans et bases chromés à mi-hauteur. Pattes Simplex forgées.

Fourche : tubes Reynolds. Tête Nervex, dessus chromé. Jambages chromés à mi-hauteur. Pattes Simplex forgées.

Moyeux dural coulé, grands flasques, 36 trous, à blocage rapide. Jantes dural et pneus 700 × 28 C façon boyaux. Garde-boue et fixation Bluemel's. Roue libre 5 vitesses : 14 × 17 × 19 × 22 × 26.

Direction : Stronglight Compétition.

Pédalier : Stronglight dural 99. Double plateau 40 × 50. Manivelles dural forgé à emmanchement carré. Pédales type course avec cale-pieds et courroies.

Dérailleurs : AR Simplex Critérium. AV à parallélogramme Simplex.

Éclairage : par génératrice sur la roue AR. Projecteur rond fixé sur porte-sac. Feu rouge AR fixé sur hauban.

Freins : Mafac Racer dural forgé à grand étrier. Poignées course avec repose-mains.

Selle Idéale 2001. Tige de selle Simplex à chariot incorporé. Cintre en dural poli potence en dural forgé anodisé. Avertisseur en alliage léger. Porte-sac TA en fils chromés. Pompe type course à raccord rapide.

PA 65

PY 60 P

Cadre : entièrement fait main, tout en Reynolds avec haubans et bases chromés à mi-hauteur, raccords Nervex affinés et polis. Raccords de direction chromés. Hauteur au choix de l'utilisateur.

Fourche : tête Nervex, dessus chromés. Jambages chromés à mi-hauteur. Pattes Simplex forgées.

Moyeux petits ou grands flasques en dural forgé. Jantes dural étroites et pneus 700 × 28 C façon boyaux. Garde-boue et fixation Bluemel's. Rayons chromés ligaturés. Roue libre 5 vitesses de 13 à 28 dents, étagement au choix du client.

Direction : Stronglight Super Compétition.

Pédalier : dural Stronglight 99. Double ou triple plateau dural de 28 à 53 dents, étagement au choix du client. Manivelles dural forgé à emmanchement carré. Pédales Maillard 700 avec cale-pieds et courroies.

Dérailleurs : AV et AR Simplex Super LJ.

Freins : Mafac 2000 dural forgé anodisé.

Selle Idéale 2002 ou cuir traité. Tige de selle dural Simplex. Cintre course et potence en dural forgé anodisé aux mesures de l'utilisateur. Pompe type course à raccord rapide, corps aluminé gris mat.

Nota : sur le PY 60 P, les dérailleurs, freins, tige de selle, cintre et potence sont livrables en anodisation or ou argent, au choix de l'utilisateur.

cyclotourisme ladies

PA 55

Cadre : triangulé sport.

Fourche : tête 1/2 Course, dessus chromé. Jambages chromés à mi-hauteur.

Moyeux grands flasques. Jantes acier chromé et pneus 700 × 28 C. Garde-boue 1/2 Course acier inoxydable. Roue libre 5 vitesses : 14 × 17 × 19 × 21 × 24.

Pédalier : Double plateau acier chromé, 36 × 48.

Dérailleurs : AV et AR Simplex Prestige.

Éclairage : par génératrice sur la roue AR.

Freins : Mafac Racer avec poignées ville.

Cintre porteur plat acier chromé, potence métal léger. Avertisseur, porte-bagage AR chromé fixé au cadre.

PA 65

Cadre : allégé Peugeot triangulé sport. Pattes Simplex forgées. Raccord Bocama.

Fourche : tête 1/2 Course chromée. Jambages chromés à mi-hauteur. Pattes Simplex forgées.

Moyeux métal léger, grands flasques, 36 trous, à blocage rapide. Jantes en métal léger avec pneus 700 × 28 C façon boyaux. Garde-boue et fixation Bluemel's. Roue libre 5 vitesses : 14 × 17 × 20 × 24 × 28.

Pédalier : dural Stronglight 49 D, double plateau 38 × 48. Manivelles dural forgé à emmanchement carré. Pédales Lyotard en acier chromé avec mini-cale-pieds.

Dérailleurs : AV et AR Simplex Prestige.

Éclairage : par génératrice sur roue AR. Projecteur rond fixé sur porte-sac. Feu AR avec catadioptre.

Freins : Mafac Racer dural forgé à grand étrier. Poignées ville.

Selle capitonnée. Cintre porteur plat dural. Avertisseur en alliage léger. Porte-sac TA en fils chromés.

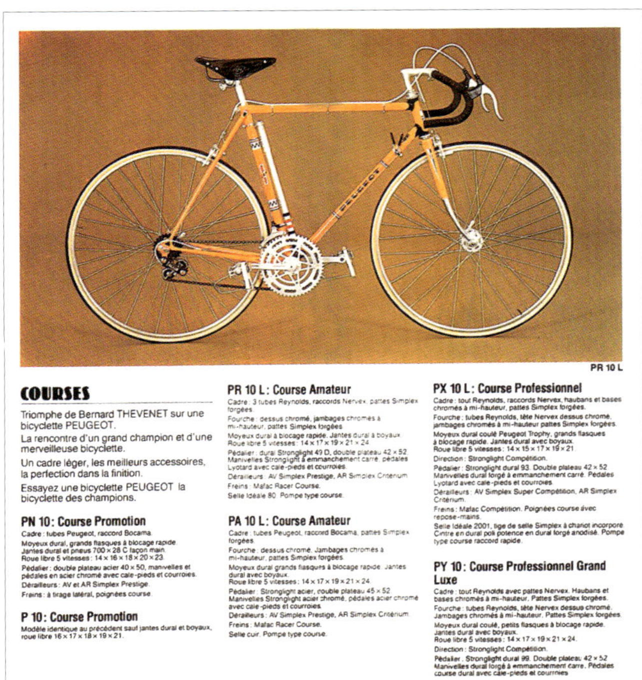

PR 10 L

COURSES

Triomphe de Bernard THEVENET sur une bicyclette PEUGEOT.

La rencontre d'un grand champion et d'une merveilleuse bicyclette.

Un cadre léger, les meilleurs accessoires, la perfection dans la finition.

Essayez une bicyclette PEUGEOT la bicyclette des champions.

PN 10 : Course Promotion

Cadre : tubes Peugeot, raccord Bocama.

Moyeux dural, grands flasques à blocage rapide. Jantes dural et pneus 700 × 28 C façon main. Roue libre 5 vitesses : 14 × 16 × 18 × 20 × 23.

Pédalier : double plateau acier 40 × 50, manivelles et pédales en acier chromé avec cale-pieds et courroies.

Dérailleurs : AV et AR Simplex Prestige.

Freins : à tirage latéral, poignées course.

P 10 : Course Promotion

Modèle identique au précédent sauf jantes dural et boyaux, roue libre 16 × 17 × 18 × 19 × 21.

PR 10 L : Course Amateur

Cadre : 3 tubes Reynolds, raccords Nervex, pattes Simplex forgées.

Fourche : dessus chromé, jambages chromés à mi-hauteur, pattes Simplex forgées.

Moyeux dural à blocage rapide. Jantes dural à boyaux. Roue libre 5 vitesses : 14 × 17 × 19 × 21 × 24.

Pédalier : dural Stronglight 49 D, double plateau 42 × 52. Manivelles Stronglight à emmanchement carré, pédales Lyotard avec cale-pieds et courroies.

Dérailleurs : AV Simplex Prestige, AR Simplex Critérium.

Freins : Mafac Racer Course.

Selle Idéale 80. Pompe type course.

PA 10 L : Course Amateur

Cadre : tubes Peugeot, raccord Bocama, pattes Simplex forgées.

Fourche : dessus chromé. Jambages chromés à mi-hauteur, pattes Simplex forgées.

Moyeux dural grands flasques à blocage rapide. Jantes dural avec boyaux. Roue libre 5 vitesses : 14 × 17 × 19 × 21 × 24.

Pédalier : Stronglight acier, double plateau 45 × 52. Manivelles Stronglight acier chromé, pédales acier chromé avec cale-pieds et courroies.

Dérailleurs : AV Simplex Prestige, AR Simplex Critérium.

Freins : Mafac Racer Course.

Selle cuir. Pompe type course.

PX 10 L : Course Professionnel

Cadre : tout Reynolds, raccords Nervex, haubans et bases chromés à mi-hauteur, pattes Simplex forgées.

Fourche : tubes Reynolds, tête Nervex dessus chromé, jambages chromés à mi-hauteur pattes Simplex forgées.

Moyeux dural coulé Peugeot Trophy, grands flasques à blocage rapide. Jantes dural avec boyaux. Roue libre 5 vitesses : 14 × 15 × 17 × 19 × 21.

Direction : Stronglight Compétition.

Pédalier : Stronglight dural 93. Double plateau 42 × 52. Manivelles dural forgé à emmanchement carré. Pédales Lyotard avec cale-pieds et courroies.

Dérailleurs : AV Simplex Super Compétition, AR Simplex Critérium.

Freins : Mafac Compétition. Poignées course avec repose-mains.

Selle Idéale 2001, tige de selle Simplex à chariot incorporé. Cintre en dural poli potence en dural forgé anodisé. Pompe type course raccord rapide.

PY 10 : Course Professionnel Grand Luxe

Cadre : tout Reynolds avec pattes Nervex. Haubans et bases chromés à mi-hauteur. Pattes Simplex forgées.

Fourche : tubes Reynolds, tête Nervex dessus chromé. Jambages chromés à mi-hauteur. Pattes Simplex forgées.

Moyeux dural coulé, petits flasques à blocage rapide. Jantes dural avec boyaux. Roue libre 5 vitesses : 14 × 17 × 19 × 21 × 24.

Direction : Stronglight Compétition.

Pédalier : Stronglight dural 99. Double plateau 42 × 52. Manivelles dural forgé à emmanchement carré. Pédales course dural avec cale-pieds et courroies.

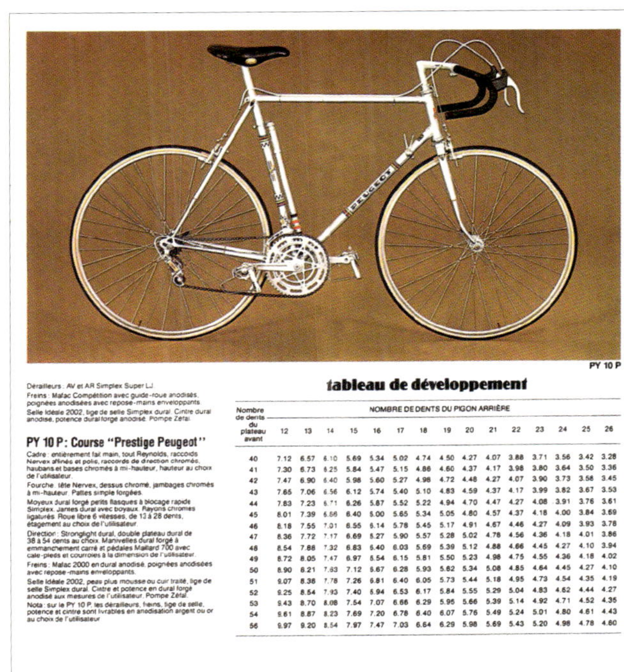

PY 10 P

Dérailleurs : AV et AR Simplex Super LJ.

Freins : Mafac Compétition avec guide-roue anodisés, poignées anodisées avec repose-mains enveloppants.

Selle Idéale 2002, tige de selle Simplex dural. Cintre dural anodisé, potence dural forgé anodisé. Pompe Zéfal.

PY 10 P : Course "Prestige Peugeot"

Cadre : entièrement fait main, tout Reynolds, raccords Nervex affinés et polis, raccords de direction chromés, haubans et bases chromés à mi-hauteur, hauteur au choix de l'utilisateur.

Fourche : tête Nervex, dessus chromé, jambages chromés à mi-hauteur. Pattes simple forgées.

Moyeux dural forgé petits flasques à blocage rapide Simplex. Jantes dural avec boyaux. Rayons chromés ligaturés. Roue libre 6 vitesses, de 13 à 28 dents, étagement au choix de l'utilisateur.

Direction : Stronglight dural, double plateau dural de 38 à 54 dents au choix. Manivelles dural forgé à emmanchement carré et pédales Maillard 700 avec cale-pieds et courroies à la dimension de l'utilisateur.

Freins : Mafac 2000 en dural anodisé, poignées anodisées avec repose-mains enveloppants.

Selle Idéale 2002, peau plus mousse ou cuir traité, tige de selle Simplex dural. Cintre et potence en dural forgé anodisé aux mesures de l'utilisateur. Pompe Zéfal.

Nota : sur le PY 10 P, les dérailleurs, freins, tige de selle, potence et cintre sont livrables en anodisation argent ou or au choix de l'utilisateur.

tableau de développement

Nombre de dents du plateau avant	NOMBRE DE DENTS DU PIGON ARRIÈRE														
	12	13	14	15	16	17	18	19	20	21	22	23	24	25	26
40	7.12	6.57	6.10	5.69	5.34	5.02	4.74	4.50	4.27	4.07	3.88	3.71	3.56	3.42	3.28
41	7.30	6.73	6.25	5.84	5.47	5.15	4.86	4.60	4.37	4.17	3.98	3.80	3.64	3.50	3.36
42	7.47	6.90	6.40	5.98	5.60	5.27	4.98	4.72	4.48	4.27	4.07	3.90	3.73	3.58	3.45
43	7.65	7.06	6.56	6.12	5.74	5.40	5.10	4.83	4.59	4.37	4.17	3.99	3.82	3.67	3.53
44	7.83	7.23	6.71	6.26	5.87	5.52	5.22	4.94	4.70	4.47	4.27	4.08	3.91	3.76	3.61
45	8.01	7.39	6.86	6.40	6.00	5.65	5.34	5.05	4.80	4.57	4.37	4.18	4.00	3.84	3.69
46	8.18	7.55	7.01	6.55	6.14	5.78	5.45	5.17	4.91	4.67	4.46	4.27	4.09	3.93	3.78
47	8.36	7.72	7.17	6.69	6.27	5.90	5.57	5.28	5.02	4.78	4.56	4.36	4.18	4.01	3.86
48	8.54	7.88	7.32	6.83	6.40	6.03	5.69	5.39	5.12	4.88	4.66	4.45	4.27	4.10	3.94
49	8.72	8.05	7.47	6.97	6.54	6.15	5.81	5.50	5.23	4.98	4.75	4.55	4.36	4.18	4.02
50	8.90	8.21	7.63	7.12	6.67	6.28	5.93	5.62	5.34	5.08	4.85	4.64	4.45	4.27	4.10
51	9.07	8.38	7.78	7.26	6.81	6.40	6.05	5.73	5.44	5.18	4.95	4.73	4.54	4.35	4.19
52	9.25	8.54	7.93	7.40	6.94	6.53	6.17	5.84	5.55	5.29	5.04	4.83	4.62	4.44	4.27
53	9.43	8.70	8.08	7.54	7.07	6.66	6.29	5.95	5.66	5.39	5.14	4.92	4.71	4.52	4.35
54	9.61	8.87	8.23	7.69	7.20	6.78	6.40	6.07	5.76	5.49	5.24	5.01	4.80	4.61	4.43
56	9.97	9.20	8.54	7.97	7.47	7.03	6.64	6.29	5.98	5.69	5.43	5.20	4.98	4.78	4.60

get complicated. At the start of the season, the PY10 was split into two grades – the PY10 and PY10P. The latter was basically last year's model, now priced at a whopping 3590FF, while the strict PY10 was offered with ten-speeds instead of 12, and three rather than six colour choices (white, silver or bronze). Other savings allowed the bike to be sold for 2657FF, which helped bridge a huge gap in pricing in the 'Course' category. Not long after, the

PN10 was joined by a PN10L version in the summer of 1976, priced at 870FF. This model would ultimately take the place of the PN10 in catalogues, allowing better distancing between grades, with the strict PN10 and P10 at 824FF, and the PA10L at 1030FF. The PR10L and PX10L continued, although the PRN10 – another new grade – was added at the same time that the PN10L arrived, which was the same as the PR10L, but fitted with lightweight Michelin Elan TS tyres. At 1345FF, the PRN10 was only a little more than the model on which it was based, but 744FF cheaper than the contemporary PX10L.

Export markets had a quite different line-up, often unique to each country. Cycles Peugeot (UK) Ltd, for instance, listed the PE41 tourer, the AO8 and AE8 sports bikes, the UE18 and PX45 for the ladies, the J10L for youngsters, and the PR10L/E and PX10L/E in the road-racer line-up. Holland, on the other hand, went with the PE41, PL8, PX8, UE18, PE46, J8, P8, UO8, P10, PR10 and PA60. America sat somewhere between the two. However, hot on the heels of Procycle Inc taking over Canadian imports, the formation of Cycles

Régis Ovion on the 1976 Tour de France. (Courtesy Wikimedia Commons: Réne Milanese)

Raymond Delisle pushing hard on the Tour de France. He rode in first for a little while, but was destined to finish the 1976 event in fourth. (Courtesy Wikimedia Commons: Réne Milanese)

Jean-Pierre Danguillaume fighting hard on the cobbles of the Paris-Roubaix in 1976. (Courtesy *L'Equipe*)

Peugeot (USA) Inc in January 1976 (headquartered on East Alondra Boulevard in Gardena, California) meant a new distribution system for the USA, too. As it happens, the Canadians went a stage further, and managed to secure manufacturing rights as well, although the North American side of the story was still far from over.

In racing, the long-standing relationship with BP as co-sponsor came, replaced by Esso. Naturally, this meant fresh team jerseys, although only the sleeve logos were changed, and the men wearing them were virtually the same as they had been in 1975 – Francis Campaner was new to the squad, but his best years were already behind him.

All eyes were on the Peugeot-Esso-Michelin team. With Eddy Merckx on the sidelines through injury, Bernard Thévenet must have been a hot favourite to win the 1976 Tour de France. Sadly, he fell ill halfway through the event, although his team-mate, Raymond Delisle, was in yellow for a couple of days, and

Poster showing Guy Sibille in his French championship jersey.

ultimately finished in fourth overall, just over 12 minutes down on the winner.

In the smaller races, at least, the Peugeot equipe managed to justify the high expectations with an excellent season. Peugeot's fourth consecutive Critérium National came courtesy of Patrick Béon, Jean-Luc Vandenbroucke won the Etoile des Espoirs and GP de Fourmies, and Jean-Luc Molinéris took the flag in the

THE SPORTING RIVALS

GITANE (FRA)

One of Peugeot's greatest rivals in the sixties and seventies, the Gitane brand originates from Machecoul, close to Nantes, when Marcel Brunelière starting making his own bicycles back in 1930. Gitane moved into professional racing just after the war, and came to the fore when the mighty St. Raphaël team dropped Helyett machinery in favour of Gitane bikes fitted with Campagnolo components for the 1963 season; Jacques Anquetil duly won the Tour de France and Vuelta a España that year, and repeated his TdF success in the 1964 edition, when the Giro d'Italia also fell to the Frenchman, proving it was no fluke. As if to rub salt into Helyett's wound, the company was forced to merge with Gitane in 1966.

Some time after Brunelière retired and sold up, Renault started buying into Gitane's parent company, Micmo (a shortened version of Manufacture Industrielle de Cycles et Motorcycles SA), duly becoming the owner in 1976, by which time Gitane was flying high thanks to Lucien Van Impe. When Renault decided to join the racing scene in 1978 to try and steal Peugeot's limelight, Gitane bikes were naturally the weapons of choice. They won the Tour de France first time out thanks to Bernard Hinault, and made it a double in 1979. Raleigh took cycling's biggest prize in 1980, but Hinault came back to win again in 1981 and 1982, before Laurent Fignon's own double in 1983 and 1984.

After encouraging all sorts of innovations, especially in the field of time trial bikes, Renault withdrew its support at the end of 1985, but the team continued under the Système U banner for a little while. Ultimately, though, the writing was on the wall after Renault sold Micmo, and the Gitane brand became part of the Cycleurope Group in 1992 in order to survive. It still exists, although the current line-up is hardly suitable for a Tour winner.

The Gitane name proudly displayed on a Renault-Elf team card featuring Greg LeMond.

RALEIGH (UK)

The Raleigh brand dates back to the early part of 1885, with its roots in Nottingham. Frank Bowden bought into the company soon after, and duly guided it into a position as the world's largest bicycle manufacturer by the outbreak of the Great War. Motorcycles and the odd car were built, too, but never in large numbers. Raleigh continued to be a leading light in the British cycle industry after WWII, building a million units annually at the start of the 1950s, but started to struggle as the decade continued.

The TI Group (owner of Reynolds Tube and several metal and engineering enterprises, including large Birmingham-

Raleigh advertising showing the team's iconic racing colours.

Paris-Bourges one-day event. Jacques Esclassan and Jean-Pierre Danguillaume also clocked up wins, Guy Sibille was crowned champion of France, while Thévenet was simply on fire. The highlight of his season was another win on the Critérium du Dauphiné Libéré, but there were so many strong results, it's hardly surprising he'd been so fancied in the Tour. Like Arnie in the movies, though, he'd be back …

based bicycle makers like Phillips and Hercules) bought out Raleigh in 1960, the latter also owning the Humber, Rudge, Triumph, BSA, Sunbeam and Carlton bicycle brands (cars and motorcycles were a different matter altogether) by this stage in the proceedings, as well as some smaller marques, the Sturmey-Archer name and the famous Brooks saddle firm.

Although there were oddities like mopeds, the Moulton and the Schwinn Sting-Ray-inspired but hugely-successful Chopper, Raleigh will always be remembered by enthusiasts for its racing bikes, with the TI Raleigh team building on the success of riders like Reg Harris, who made his name after the Second World War. Even building a Tour de France winner (Britain's first) couldn't stop the seemingly inevitable, though, and Raleigh was ultimately sold to Derby International of Luxembourg in 1987. The company has gone through several changes of hands since, but still produces bicycles of note to this day …

MOTOBECANE (FRA)

Founded in 1923, Motobécane was originally a successful motorbike manufacturer, but the Paris-based marque's bicycles were equally famous. Known for their quality in the sixties and seventies, a Motobecane-branded model (there is no accent on the newer bicycle markings) carried Luis Ocaña of the Bic team to victory in the 1973 Tour de France. Notwithstanding, the company filed for bankruptcy in 1981, duly selling off the motorcycle side of the business to Yamaha, and making its last bicycles in 1984.

BOTTECCHIA (ITA)

Coming to the fore thanks to its links with the Molteni team in the sixties, the Bottecchia brand is named after Italy's first Tour de France winner, Ottavio Bottecchia. Not long after Bottecchia bikes started being produced by Teodoro Carnielli, Bottecchia died in rather mysterious circumstances. At least his name lived on thanks to Carnielli, and later through his sons. The company was sold in 1998 to Cicli Esperia (which had built bikes for Bianchi, and also owns the rights to the Legnano name), moving south a little to Cavarzere in the process, where it remains to this day.

Beautiful piece of Colnago publicity material.

COLNAGO (ITA)

There is a great deal of romance attached to the Colnago name, with the story beginning when a very young Ernesto Colnago started work at the Gloria cycle company. He eventually opened a small workshop in Cambiago in 1954, and became friends with Firenzo Magni, an unsung hero from the classic era of top Italian riders, who took him on as his race mechanic. Within a few years, Colnago was making complete racing bikes for Eddy Merckx, which naturally led to greater things. The rest, as they say, is history, and before long, the 'ace of clubs' trademark associated with Colnago bicycles would become known the world over. The brand would later link up with Ferrari, giving straight front forks a start in life, and picked up numerous race victories with a range of innovative machines. Despite its long history, Colnago remained under family management until very recently.

Peugeot had accounted for 37 per cent of the 1,900,000 bicycles made in France during 1976, over half of the country's bike exports, and captured some 45 per cent of France's total moped production. As President of Cycles Peugeot, Bertrand Peugeot felt there was still room for improvement, though, and the domestic catalogues released in January and February 1977 continued to show a relentless desire to offer as wide a range of bicycles as possible.

Most of the range was exactly the same, with the same colouring and badging. Although the 12-speed PY10P was still featured in the catalogues, according to the price list issued in the middle of February, the PY10P became the PY10CP at this time (with painted forks, custom paint options, and the chance to specify an 18-speed setup), and while the PA60 and PN10 were missing from the brochure pages, they were still mentioned in the price lists anyway, probably due to there being a few examples left over in stock.

And then there were three newcomers – all in the sporting and road-racer categories. The PR60 was basically a replacement for the PA60, listed at the same price and with the same colour options, but with Reynolds tubing employed on the new model. The PS10

Cover and selected pages (opposite) from a French brochure dated February 1977.

Bike production at Romilly.

PX 40, PX 45 : Pour ceux qui préfèrent le tourisme à la compétition.

Les modèles "tourisme" de la gamme cycles Peugeot sont des bicyclettes à tout faire. Elles ont un sens pratique très développé, un dévouement sans limite, une disponibilité constante et sans faille.

Que vous alliez faire vos courses ou que vous partiez en promenade touristique avec des amis, elle vous servira fidèlement toujours et partout car ce sont des Peugeot.

PR 60, PA 65 : L'art du raffinement.

Elaborées, jusque dans les moindres détails, ces bicyclettes sont réservées aux vrais cyclotouristes.

Routières dans l'âme, elles conviennent aux amateurs passionnés, aux spécialistes des grandes randonnées qui aiment se mesurer avec la route, aux sportifs qui cultivent le plaisir de l'effort physique et recherchent la perfection.

PRN 10 : La bicyclette d'entraînement et ses pneus révolutionnaires.

Une bicyclette exceptionnelle par la qualité de sa fabrication ; exceptionnelle également à cause des pneus révolutionnaires dont elle est la seule à être équipée. Ces pneus possèdent toutes les qualités des boyaux, alliées à celles du pneu : ultra-légers, ils sont pourtant très résistants et faciles à réparer.

Pneu.

Aussi léger et souple qu'un boyau, le pneu extra-léger Michelin Elan TS possède la résistance d'un pneu classique.

PY 10 : Pour être dans la course.

La démonstration n'est plus à faire : les meilleures bicyclettes de course sont signées Cycles Peugeot. Les 1800 coureurs amateurs et l'équipe de professionnels Peugeot remportent depuis des années les plus grandes compétitions internationales.

Véritables bancs d'essais, les courses nous permettent de vous offrir un matériel de haute technicité parfaitement fiable.

Pédalier.

Pédalier dural forgé anodisé Stronglight 105 Bis avec double plateau dural anodisé perforé 42 x 52.

The Peugeot team making good progress on the 1977 TdF. (Courtesy *L'Equipe*)

was another gap filler, sitting in-between the PRN10 and PX10L in the line-up, and coming with a Reynolds frame finished in either silver or bronze. The 2850FF PY10C was the last of the three, bridging the gap between the strict PY10 and the newly-renamed PY10CP, with the same restricted colouring as the former, but the 12-speed setup of the latter.

After the huge jumps experienced over the previous 24 months, there was thankfully not much difference in pricing for 1977. Indeed, the HA8 went up by just 8FF, the PX8L by an equally reasonable 13FF, and even the flagship PY60P (with ten- or 15 speeds) was only 51FF more expensive than before.

A great poster proclaiming Peugeot's success on the 1977 Tour de France, both in the overall standings and the green jersey competition.

Another poster from the time; this one showing Jacques Esclassan wearing his green jersey in the 1977 edition of the TdF.

A fitting cover for the 1978 catalogue after a good solid year in competition during the 1977 season.

The UO10 was an important new model for America, having a lighter Stronglight TS crankset than the UO8, as well as alloy rims, but otherwise, most of the range was familiar enough. It was duly joined by the UO9 in the following season, giving three steps on the ladder in the States, although this particular model was not so common elsewhere; Britain listed the UO10 only, for instance.

In racing, there were a number of changes in the team, with the most surprising being the loss of Raymond Delisle, who'd been with Peugeot for many years. With just one more season in his legs, he decided to spend it with the Miko-Mercier team.

The Tour de France was once again the highlight of the season. Dietrich Thurau (TI-Raleigh) was in yellow for two weeks, but Bernard Thévenet took the lead at the end of day 15, and never looked back. Thévenet duly claimed Peugeot's tenth and final TdF victory on 24th July 1977. Another Peugeot man, Michel Laurent, came seventh overall, ahead of a gaggle of Miko riders, including Delisle, and Jacques Esclassan claimed the green jersey for the Peugeot-Esso-Michelin equipe.

This stunning success did tend to overshadow what had been a brilliant season, with 12 other big wins in France, and a win in Spain for Thévenet on the Escalada a Montjuïc. But ask anyone in the street, even those who don't follow racing, to name the first bicycle competition that springs to mind, and we all know what the answer will be in nine out of ten cases …

The domestic brochures for 1978 were printed up in January, and most of the range and badging looked familiar. The 'Week-End' series was discontinued in adult sizes, but the 'Nouveau Style' was revised to suit, with certain new models having fresh down tube decals that would act as a trailblazer for 1979. A new 'Ville' range (VL/VX) was launched alongside an updated 'Porteur' (PRP) bike, and the TH8 tandem was a real oddity. Peugeot tandems had been around for a long time, but this was the first catalogue entry for such a contraption in many, many years.

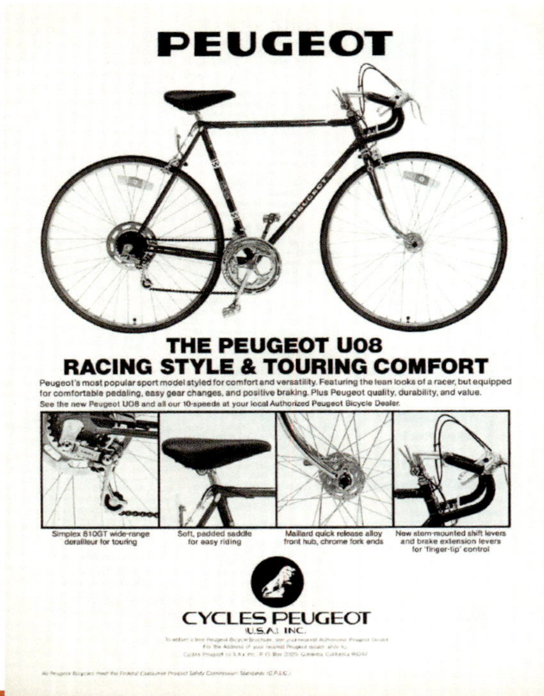

With so many changes in the line-up over the last few seasons, it's worth listing the range as it stood in 1978, starting with the models that were carried over. All the regular 'Hélium' grades continued, with the HA22/HA25, HA40/HA45, HA50 and HA8 being rolled out for service once more. In the cheaper Peugeot lines, there was the PX22/PX25 and PX40/PX45 tourers, the P50, PL50 5V/10V and PX50L randonneurs, and P8 4V/8V, PL8 5V/10V and PX8L sports bikes. Then, thanks to the continuous push upmarket, things start getting more complicated …

In the 'Gentleman' line, the P60 was carried over, augmented by a new PR60L grade that replaced the PR60 and PX60; the PY60P was dropped. Interestingly, extra effort was pumped into the 'Lady' line instead, which

American advertising from 1978.

The Peugeot racing team for 1978.

Michel Laurent, winner of the 1978 Flèche Wallonne.

Gregor Braun after being crowned champion of Germany. This picture was actually taken in early 1979, judging by the bike livery.

provided an ideal opportunity to nurture a niche market in luxury bikes for the fairer sex. While the PA55 was continued, the PA65 was replaced by two new grades – the P65 and the PR65 – to give more choice and smaller steps in the gaps in pricing .

In the all-important 'Course' range, the strict PY10 was dropped, but all other existing grades were carried over, giving us the PN10L, the P10, PA10L, PR10L, PRN10, PS10, PX10L, PY10C and PY10CP. One would have thought that was more than enough to satisfy every need, but no! For 1978, enthusiasts gained the PXN10L, PRN13 and PSN10 models. The PXN10L was actually the same as the PX10L, but with Michelin Elan TS tyres, and the same was true of the PS10/PSN10 relationship. The PRN13, meanwhile, was a PRN10 with a triple front crankset rather than a double one. As such, it was the only bike offered with 15 speeds – the two PY10 grades had 12 (18 optional), and all the other road-racers still had ten.

It should be noted that certain models, like the PY10s, began using individual derailleur levers at this time. The raised diamond section on the frame (used for location purposes on paired levers) was still visible for a while, until single levers became the norm, and as a result, eventually, it was changed to a square seating piece only.

There was some serious money in racing circles now, with a 4,000,000FF annual budget being called for to run a decent team. Nonetheless, Peugeot's biggest rival in the world of automobiles, Renault, duly got in on the act. Contemporary Renault motorsport included Le Mans and F1 programmes, with rallying through Alpine, and, owning the parent company behind Gitane bikes, seeing the promotional benefits of cycle racing, the next move was obvious.

Belgian rider Roger Rosiers joined Peugeot-Esso-Michelin to replace Jurgen Tschan, who retired, but otherwise there was little change in the team line-up.

Selected pages from a 1979 domestic brochure.

In addition to numerous stage wins for Peugeot over the year, Régis Ovion won the Paris-Bourges, Michel Laurent claimed the Flèche Wallonne, Tour de Corse, Critérium des As and Tour du Vaucluse, Yves Hézard took the GP de Fourmies and Ronde de Seignelay, and Gregor Braun won a one-day event in his native Germany; Braun was also crowned champion of Germany that year.

Apart from a couple of stage wins on the Tour de France, there was little to take back from the Grand Tours in 1978, though. Bernard Hinault had come to the fore, winning both the Vuelta and the Tour de France, and sadly for the newly-formed Renault-Gitane team. Hinault would repeat his TdF success in 1979, 1981, 1982 and 1985, proving he was the new man to beat now Merckx had left the arena …

In the background, the PSA Group's purchase of Chrysler Europe in 1978 ultimately led to a revival of the Talbot marque and, for a little while at least, a number of bicycles were built using the Talbot moniker in due course, with the name even appearing in racing circles.

Le PY 10 CP.
Le vélo de compétition par excellence.
Ultra-léger. Equipements Spidel.

Cadre Reynolds 5/10e fait main. Hauteurs de 50 à 64, cm par cm. Raccords longues pointes. Haubans AR Reynolds biconiques. Base AR droite chromée. Guides-gaine de frein AR brasés. Guides-câbles de dérailleurs AV et AR brasés sur boîte de pédalier. Fourche Reynolds 5/10e épaules basses chromée. Jantes dural Super Champion 700 C. Chaîne Sedis. Cintre course dural, potence dural forgée anodisée à expandeur noyé Atax. Selle course Idéale 2002. Cale-pieds, courroies, pompe type "Z" Poutrait-Morin. Et tous les équipements Spidel : Pattes AR de cadre forgées avec butées à vis. Pattes de fourche forgées. Jeu de direction compétition S7. Pédalier 105 bis anodisé, perforé, plateaux 42 x 52. Roue libre 700, 6 vitesses 13 x 14 x 15 x 17 x 19 x 21. Dérailleurs SLJA 302 à l'AV et SLJ 5500 CP à l'AR. Moyeux 700 petits flasques à blocage rapide. Tige de selle dural à chariot incorporé. Freins compétition à tirage central, poignées perforées course avec repose-mains caoutchouc. Pédales dural course 700.

Le PX 8 M.
Le vélo de prédilection des sportifs et des amateurs de grande randonnée.

Cadre à raccords, nouveau gabarit. Hauteurs 54 - 57 - 60. Jambages de fourche chromés à mi-hauteur. Roues de 700 C. Moyeux Maillard grands flasques à blocage rapide. Guidon type course. Potence à expandeur noyé. Direction indéréglable Peugeot. Freins Mafac à tirage central. Pédalier dural à emmanchement carré. Pédales chromées avec cale-pieds et courroies. Porte-bagages AR chromé. Garde-boue inox. Eclairage.

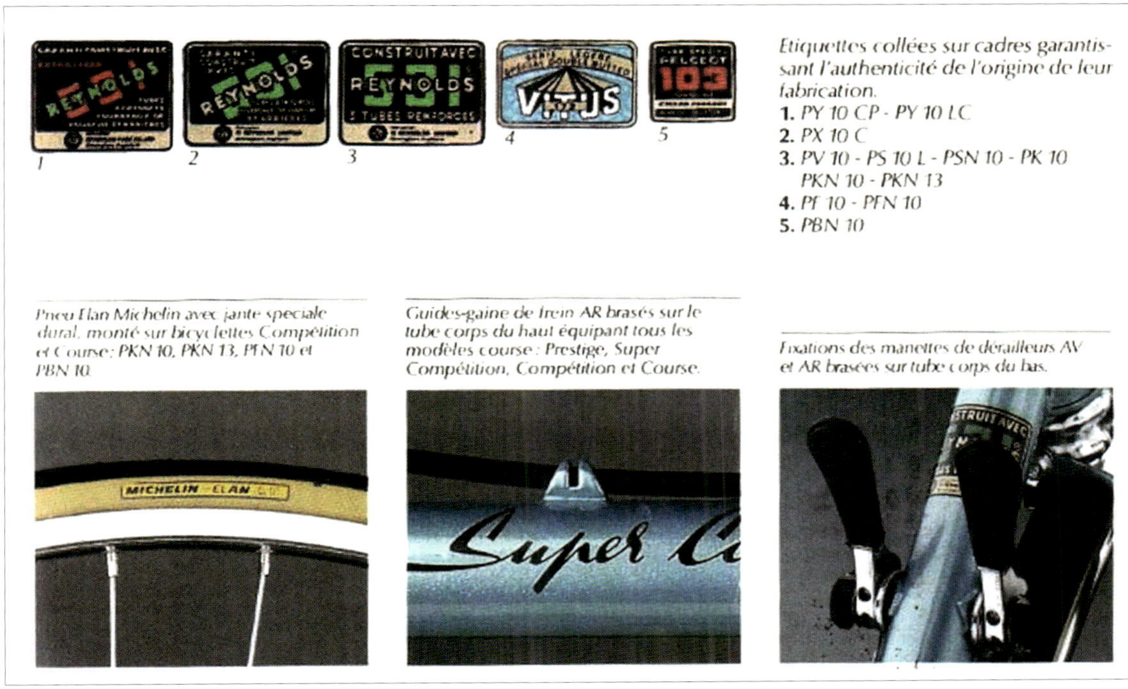

Etiquettes collées sur cadres garantissant l'authenticité de l'origine de leur fabrication.
1. *PY 10 CP - PY 10 LC*
2. *PX 10 C*
3. *PV 10 - PS 10 L - PSN 10 - PK 10 PKN 10 - PKN 13*
4. *PF 10 - PFN 10*
5. *PBN 10*

Pneu Elan Michelin avec jante speciale dural, monté sur bicyclettes Compétition et Course: PKN 10, PKN 13, PFN 10 et PBN 10.

Guides-gaine de frein AR brasés sur le tube corps du haut équipant tous les modèles course : Prestige, Super Compétition, Compétition et Course.

Fixations des manettes de dérailleurs AV et AR brasées sur tube corps du bas.

Detail from a different 1979 catalogue.

Component lines and gearing variations had increased somewhat over the last few seasons, mirrored by the growth of the model range, and giving buyers a greater level of choice according to their budget and/or specific requirements. But despite all the fine-tuning of recent years, the Peugeot line-up was given another major overhaul for 1979. Indeed, the domestic catalogues from January that year (as was becoming the norm, there was a proper one for cycling enthusiasts, and a more general Cycles Peugeot version that included scooters and suchlike) showed off a new range, with all-new badging, and a number of technical changes that will help date frames in the future.

First, the general changes. The head badge was similar, but modified on the vast majority of bikes to become a squarer, more compact silver design, with two types fielded again – a simple decal and a cast version. The Peugeot lettering on the down tube was made larger, and the framing bands were deleted. The existing seat tube lion logo was modernised, and sat higher up than before, atop graduated chequer graphics. Again, the framing bands were dropped, giving the bikes a much cleaner look. Some models had line markings on the trailing edge of the top tube (such as 'Prestige Peugeot' and 'Super Competition'), and others had new chequer-style fork badges, too, although the latter was only found on the cheaper grades as a rule. Also new for 1979 was the way the rear brake cables were held in place on the top tube: The former jubilee-type clamps were replaced on all the road-racers and 'Prestige' models (plus other selected grades) by three welded guides. It's also fair to say that pre-prepared down tube mounts for bottle holders were becoming more common, at last spreading from the top stuff down.

The France-only 'Hélium' range was gradually being brushed under the carpet at this stage in the proceedings. Indeed, the H10 (a basic ten-speed road-racer) was the only model featured in the 1979 catalogue. A few other grades did make it in production, however, with the HA8 becoming the H8 (still with three speeds), and the HA25 evolving into the H25M – the latter being what the Japanese delightfully term a 'Mama-Chari,' or mother's chariot! New entry-level models included the PH22, PH25, PH40 and PH45, with the 'H' in the code giving a clue as to the origins, and these took the place of the PX22 in the Peugeot line-up.

PROFI-RENNRAD „PRESTIGE PEUGEOT“ PY 10/CP · Straße · 12 Gänge · 27″

Von Spezialisten in Einzelanfertigung hergestellt und montiert. Dieses Rennrad wird von der PEUGEOT-Profi-Rennmannschaft gefahren.

Rennrahmen:	Alle Rohre, einschl. Hinterbau = REYNOLDS 531-5/10, NUR Unterrohr 7/10 – wegen der Stabilität. NERVEX-Muffen, geschmiedete SIMPLEX-Ausfallenden mit Stellschrauben, Hinterbaustrebe rechts ganz verchromt, links halb verchromt, Anlötteile für Flaschenhalter und Schalthebel, Spezial-Tretlagergehäuse mit angelöteten Kabelführungen
Renngabel:	REYNOLDS-Rohre 531-5/10, verchromt, Gabelkopf SUPER-VITUS, SIMPLEX-Ausfaller
Steuersatz:	STRONGLIGHT SUPER COMPETITION
Antrieb:	LM-Tretlager STRONGLIGHT 105 Bis, Tretlagerachse Mod. 650 – Titan, Fünfarm-Kurbeln L = 170 mm, DD-Blätter 42 × 53 Zähne – gelocht, silber eloxiert, LM-Tretlagerschalen
Zahnkranz:	6-fach, MAILLARD 700, DURAL (Kränze und Körper), 13 × 14 × 15 × 17 × 19 × 21 Zähne
Kette:	SEDISCOLOR, silber, 1/2 × 3/32″, 108 Gl.
Schaltung:	SIMPLEX, hinten – vorne
Naben:	Niederflansch, MAILLARD 700, DURAL geschmiedet mit Schnellspann-Verschlüssen
Felgen:	Extra leichte LM-Felgen PELLET-Record du Monde
Reifen:	Schlauchreifen CLEMENT-Criterium 290 gr
Lenkerbügel:	Rennlenker (DURAL) PHILIPPE-Professionnel, silber eloxiert
Vorbau:	LM-Vorbau PHILIPPE-PEUGEOT geschmiedet, mit Inbus-Innenklemme, silber eloxiert
Bremsen:	MAFAC-COMPETITION, mit gelochten Bremsgriffen MAFAC LS, silber eloxiert, Handschutz PARA
Sattel:	Rennsattel IDEALE 2002, Titan-Untergestell
Sattelstütze:	SIMPLEX SLJ 4164, DURAL, gerillt, silber eloxiert
Pedale:	MAILLARD 700, DURAL, komplett mit extra leichten CHRISTOPHE-Fußhaken und LAPIZE-Rennriemen aus der Serie „Z“
Pumpe:	PM-Pumpe „Z“, silber, extra leicht
Gewicht:	ca. 9–9,5 kg
Rahmenhöhen:	52, 54, 56, 58, 60, 62 und 64 cm
Farbe:	perlmutt-weiß (BK)

*) Konstruktions-, Ausstattungs- und Farbänderungen behalten wir uns vor. Ersatzteil-Probleme gibt es nicht, denn PEUGEOT unterhält in der Bundesrepublik Deutschland ein umfangreiches Zentral-Ersatzteillager.

Peugeot-Modell PY 10/CP

The PY10CP page from the contemporary German brochure.

The PX25 was continued, as were the PX40 and PX45, although the latter pair became known as the PX40M and PX45M at this time. The P50 morphed into the PH50, the PL50 into the PL50M (again offered with five or ten speeds), and the PX50L became the PX50M. Continuing the upmarket trend, the P8 4V and 8V evolved into the PH8M 5V and 10V, while the PL8 was still sold with five or ten speeds, but as the PL8M for 1979; the PX8L was given the PX8M moniker.

In the 'Gentleman' and 'Lady' lines, the P60 became known as the P60M, and the PR60L as the PK60, both with ten speeds. The PA55 was carried over with the same designation, while the P65 gained an 'M' suffix, and the PR65 became the PK65.

As if things weren't complicated enough, the 'Course' range had an even bigger makeover. The H10 we've already mentioned, and the next rung on the ladder was occupied by another newcomer, the PBN10. This had Peugeot 103 tubing, Bocama lugs, ten speeds, Weinmann 506 brakes and painted forks. The P10 was replaced by the PF10, and the closely related PN10L by the PFN10. This had a Vitus 172 frame, Bocama lugs, ten speeds, Weinmann 506 brakes and half-chromed forks; as before, the 'N' version added Michelin Elan TS tyres into the equation.

The PA10L was dropped, but the three PR/PRN models were continued in upgraded form. The PR10L became the PK10, with a Reynolds 531 frame (but not the forks), Nervex lugs, 12 speeds, and MAFAC 'Competition' brakes. The PKN10 built on this via Elan TS tyres, and PKN13 one stage further again by sporting 18 speeds. The PS10, with a Reynolds frame and forks (with chromed ends) became the PS10L, gaining an extra two speeds in the process; the Elan TS-shod sister model, also with MAFAC brakes, kept the old PSN10 designation, despite the gearing update.

The PV10 was another debutante, with Reynolds tubing and Nervex lugs, half-chromed forks, 12 speeds, and Weinmann 605 brakes. While the PXN10L grade fell by the wayside, the PX10L became the PX10C with Reynolds tubing throughout, and an otherwise similar spec to the PV10. The PY10C became the PY10LC, with fully chromed forks and chainstay ends, 12 speeds and top class Spidel grouped components, and the hand-built PY10CP (oddly, the name remained unchanged, despite the cosmetic upgrade) built on this with a host of options, including 14V, 18V and 21V gearsets.

While Germany and Holland probably offered the biggest range outside France, North America was still an important market. The US listed the UO10, PKN10E and PXN10LE in the pure road-racer lines at this time, while Canada was unique in that it was now building all the bikes except the PK12 and PX12 on home territory via the Vélo Sport arm of Procycle Inc (run by Raymond and Roger Dutil, and part of the Pro Velo group of companies). Eventually, the Canadians would start exporting certain bikes south of the border, too, to augment shipments of French-made imports.

With Jean-Pierre Danguillaume retiring from the peloton, there were quite a few changes in the racing team. The arrival of rookie Pascal Simon would be significant, as would that of the Dutch rider Hennie Kuiper, although almost half of the squad for 1979 was new to wearing Peugeot's white shirts. Perhaps this explains the relative lack of success that year. Jean-Luc Vandenbroucke took the honours in the GP de Fourmies, Jacques Esclassan won the GP de Monaco, and Gregor Braun the Tour d'Indre-et-Loire. Michel Laurent claimed the Tour Méditerranéen and the GP de Lugano time trial event, and was fourth overall in the Giro d'Italia. New signing Hennie Kuiper was an excellent fourth in the Tour de France, but Hinault stole the limelight for Renault-Gitane again. Given the budgets involved, the men back at head office had a right to expect more from the equipe …

Hennie Kuiper made a strong impression at Peugeot straight away …

5. EIGHTIES APEX

By the end of the seventies, the cycling boom had started to peter out, while cycle racing was now an extremely expensive business, adding to the manufacturers' financial woes. Market niches were called for, like Raleigh's Chopper line and BMX bikes. Instead, in the main, Peugeot doggedly relied on its traditional customer base, hoping innovation would see the company through to better times.

After the major overhaul of the Peugeot bicycle range for 1979, it's hardly surprising that few changes were outlined for the 1980 season – after all, with annual production hovering at around the 850,000 mark, given the business climate, it was a pretty good indicator that the French giant was on the right track, so to speak.

The tourers and randonneurs were basically carried over, with an 'M' suffix duly added on certain models, and a little simplification. The Hélium H8 sports bike was still listed, too, almost as a footnote, and priced at 745FF. It was put in with the two PH8M grades, the two PL8M models, and the 1310FF PX8M, all continued from 1979. New for 1980 were three variants for the ladies – the five-speed PH18M, the ten-speed PL18M, and the ten-speed PX18M. Also worth a mention are the tandems, now available in male-male and male-female guise.

In the 'Gentleman' and 'Lady' ranges, the grades were reshuffled to give the P60M (ten speeds), a new PF60 grade with Vitus 172 tubing and 18 speeds, and the top 1920FF PK60 model with a Reynolds frame. The latter, at 10FF more than the PF60, was not featured in the catalogues, but was in the price lists, meaning there must have been stock still on hand. The PA55 was gone, and the PK65 found itself in the same position as the PK60; ladies looking for luxury therefore had the P65M and the new PF65 to choose from for 1980.

In the 'Course' line-up, the Hélium H10 continued for the time being, priced at 749FF, and was joined by a new

Cover of the 1980 road-racer catalogue.

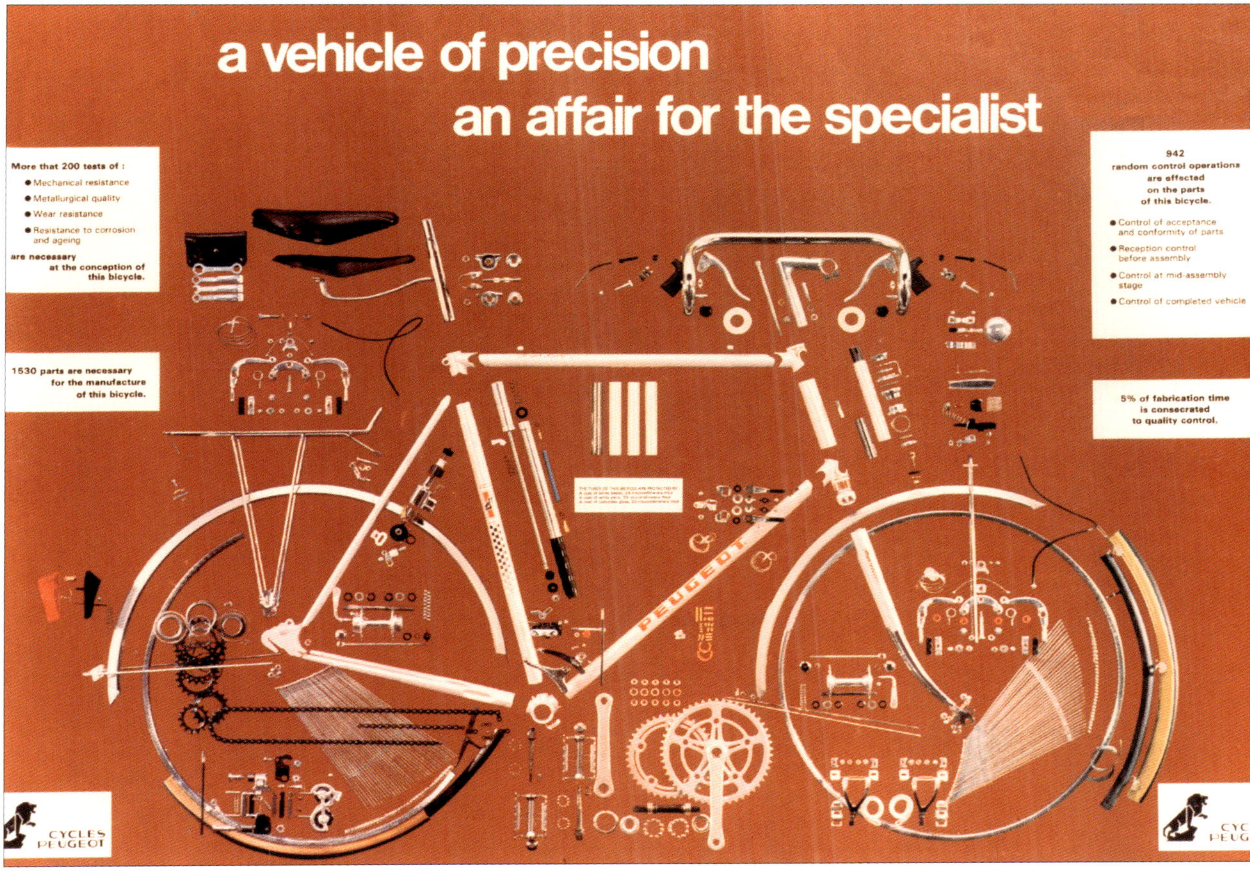

Fascinating advert showing the parts that go into making a top class bicycle. Naturally, components differed from bike to bike, but one gets the general idea of what was involved …

ten-speed PH10 model positioned just above it, badged as a Peugeot, tipping the scales at 12.5kg (27.5lb) and costing 216FF more. The 1325FF PBN10, along with the 1660FF PF10 and PFN10, were much the same as before, and the 1978FF PK10 and its PKN10 and PKN13 sister models were basically carried over, too.

While the PS10L and PSN10 grades were dropped, the PV10 gained a Stronglight 104 Bis crankset and a fully-chromed front fork, but was otherwise similar to before, with a painted back-end. At the same time, the PX10C became the 2980FF PX10S, with a Stronglight 106 crankset and all-chrome forks justifying the new suffix added to the model code.

The PY10LC became the PY10S thanks to a different Spidel 106 crankset and Spidel LS2 brakes, but, priced at 4690FF, it remained a 12-speed model. The PY10CP, meanwhile, transformed into the PRO10, with even more interesting options available for 1980: With the right budget, one could specify Reynolds 753 tubing, a titanium crankset, a seven-cog setup at the rear, and an exotic titanium/leather saddle.

As before, export markets often had unique models that used their own codes. The PRO10 was also offered in CFX frameset guise in Britain and America, for instance, sometimes listed alongside the PY10CP just to add to the confusion, although there was some integration of the domestic and export ranges – a little more than before, at least. For 1980, Britain listed bikes like the PH8, PL8, UO9, PX8/PX18, PFN, PKN and PX10 Professional. Germany went down a similar path, but added more of the pure racers, while buyers in the US were offered the PH8, UO8/UO18, UO9/UO19, UO10, PKN10E, PFN10E, PXN10E and PY10CP, as well as the CFX frame.

Another advert from the time, this one for the PRO10.

The team line-up for 1980.

There were a few changes in the works racing team for 1980, with the arrival of Robert Millar and Aussie rider Phil Anderson going some way towards making up for the loss of Bernard Thévenet, Gregor Braun, Jean-Luc Vandenbroucke and Jacques Esclassan in the squad.

Hennie Kuiper was a noble second in the Tour de France, less than seven minutes down on Joop Zoetemelk of the TI-Raleigh team. Sadly, that was all the Peugeot-Esso-Michelin equipe could take away from the Grand Tour arena. There were a couple of big wins worthy of note, however, including a victory for Michel Laurent on the Critérium National, and another for Gilbert Duclos-Lassalle on the Paris-Nice. In addition, Duclos-Lassalle won the Etoile des Espoirs and three other smaller

Gilbert Duclos-Lassalle keeping an eye on Francesco Moser on the 1980 Paris-Robaix. (Courtesy *L'Equipe*)

Hennie Kuiper in the thick of it during the 1980 Tour de France. (Courtesy *L'Equipe*)

Kuiper on the 1980 TdF again: he finished the event in second. Next to him are top climber Raymond Martin (Miko-Mercier) and Joop Zoetemelk (Raleigh), who held on to the yellow jersey into Paris. (Courtesy *L'Equipe*)

Below left: A poster for the Trophée Peugeot series, which continued to generate interest amongst amateur riders, although the pros would soon be joining the lower ranks in the battle for honours. The same artwork had been around for years, by the way.

Below: Peugeot even offered something for dedicated followers of fashion.

Above: Jean-Réne Bernaudeau getting the inside line on Bernard Hinault during the second day on the 1981 TdF. Bernaudeau won several big races for Peugeot that year, but had to be content with sixth in this event. (Courtesy *L'Equipe*)

Stephen Roche on his way to victory on the 1981 Paris-Nice. (Courtesy *L'Equipe*)

French races, and Laurent took the Tour du Vaucluse. Of the other team members, Yves Hézard won the Paris-Bourges, Jacques Bossis took the GP de Fourmies and GP de la Ville de Nogent-sur-Oise trophies, Marcel Tinazzi won the Tour l'Aude, Roger Legeay the GP de Mauléon-Moulins, Pascal Simon the Tour du Haut Var, and Régis Délepine won the Circuit d'Indre event. All in all, a fine display of in-depth talent, and the kind of season that would normally keep sponsors happy …

None of the 'Hélium' bikes were mentioned in the 1981 brochures, recently split into racers, tourers and junior categories. It made sense to streamline things from a production point of view, and splitting the range brochures also doubtless saved money in the long-

THE CLASSIC COMPONENT SUPPLIERS: WHEELS & RELATED PARTS

The iconic Mavic logo, this one from 1973.

The most important name in this section is that of Mavic. Founded in 1889 by Léon and Laurent Vielle, the EMR company soon branched out into bicycle components under the guidance of Henri Gormand. A stronger link with the industry came about when Gormand bought out Mavic (Manufacture d'Articles Vélocipédiques Idoux et Chanel), as he was interested in a mudguard they had created.

Mavic would later make hubs and branded groupsets (some employed by Peugeot), but, for most of us, the Mavic name conjures up an image of alloy wheel rims, with the lightweight 'Dura' model making its debut back in 1934, at a time when wooden rims were still considered the norm on racing machinery. It evolved into a thing of beauty, culminating in the Module E rim of 1975 (when Bruno Gormand, son of Henri, was in charge), designed to take Michelin's contemporary high-pressure Elan tyre.

On the subject of tyres, one look at the racing team sponsors tells us a lot. Wolber (later absorbed by Mavic) was followed by Dunlop, then Englebert, and finally Michelin. Certainly, other tyre makes were used, and for a time, bikes were fitted with Peugeot-branded rubber, doubtless bought in from suppliers other than the current team sponsors. Some of the older tyre manufacturers like Clément and Hutchinson were also involved in racing, so have a certain amount of romance attached to their names – the latter was being fitted on some 'Course' grades into the 1980s.

As for hubs, Maillard is the brand that springs to mind during the classic era. Maurice Maillard founded the company in Incheville just before the Great War, often using the 'Normandy' name in reverence

A recent but nonetheless charming advert for Michelin tyres.

to his idyllic location. By 1971, with Pierre Maillard (Maurice's son) at the helm, with the takeover of Atom and so on, as well as joint-marketing ventures with the likes of Perrin & Courson, Maillard had five factories and over 1500 employees, but the end of the US bike boom hit hard at a time when a huge amount was being invested in the development of the combined 'Hélicomatic' rear hub and freewheel.

Naturally, Maillard took part in the Spidel groupset project, but it was sold not long after that failed to Fichtel & Sachs (the German giant later being known simply as Sachs), who at least allowed the name to continue for a while, albeit in Sachs-Maillard form on many products. Of course, further down the line, the bicycle component section of the Sachs business was duly sold to SRAM of America.

Rounding things off, quick-release mechanisms (or skewers) were usually sourced from Simplex or Atom, while lightweight pumps were bought in from the likes of Batam and AFA, with Poutrait-Morin becoming Peugeot's main supplier in the early-1980s.

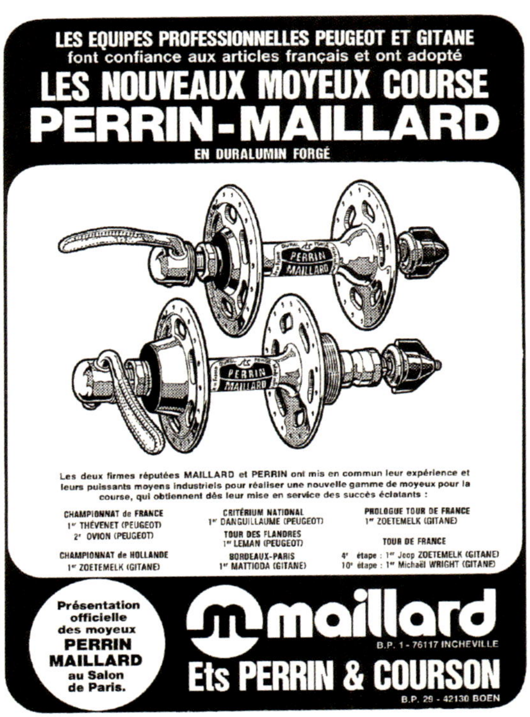

A domestic Maillard hubs advert from the summer of 1973.

term. After all, a customer looking for a PK10 or something of that ilk wasn't going to be in the market for a PH22M, and even less likely to want an M23S kids bike. Interestingly, there was another brochure for BMX bikes, which was also quite rightfully considered a different subject.

In addition to the 'Hélium' range being axed, the 'Nouveau Style' bikes were updated for 1981, and the touring range was further simplified, with some of the five-speed models being dropped. On saying that, the PX50M became the PX50S, and the PH8S was added to augment the two existing PH8M grades.

As for the top-end sporting machines, compared with some years, there wasn't that much to talk about given the major changes for 1979 and the fine-tuning that followed in 1980. The PH10 was joined by a PH15 mixte version for the ladies (also with Peugeot 103 tubing, ten speed gearing and Weinmann brakes), the PBN10, PF10 and PFN10 became 12-speed models, the PKN13 was replaced by the PFN13, the PV10 was replaced by a cheaper 12-speed PSV10 grade with Vitus tubes and Nervex lugs instead of a Reynolds/Nervex combination, and the Maillard 'Hélicomatic' rear hub was added to the spec sheet on all models up to the PX10S, which had Maillard 'Trophy' hubs; the PY10S and PRO10 had Spidel '700' hubs.

The Americans lost the UO8, UO18 and PY10CP at this stage, although the PBN10 was added, along with three PH variants (the PH15 being the sporty one). The Canadians had a massive range by comparison, as did the Germans. Indeed, the 1981 German road-racer line-up alone included the PH10E, PBM10E, PF10E, PFN10E, PK10E, PK13E, PKN10E, PV10E, PVN10E, PX10E, PXN10E and PY10LCD models, covering all budgets and weights that ranged from 12.5kg (27.5lb) to just 9kg (20lb) at the top end of the pyramid. It's hard to imagine, but the Peugeot brand was sold in around 70 countries by this time!

In racing, Maurice de Muer was now assisted by Roland Berland, and there were no less than six changes in the squad: Jean-René Bernaudeau was a big signing, defecting from the Renault team, as was the Irishman, Stephen Roche. Bernaudeau duly won the Grand Prix du Midi-Libre, GP de Monaco and Route du Sud, and Roche took the Paris-Nice, the Tour de Corse, the Tour d'Indre-et-Loire, and the Etoile des Espoirs. While the team came back from the Grand Tours empty-handed (Bernaudeau was sixth in the Tour de France, with Phil Anderson tenth, after wearing yellow for a day – the first Aussie ever to do so), nine other Peugeot riders recorded a win apiece over the season, so it was another decent year for the men in white.

A rather special badge to mark a special occasion. While mass production didn't begin until 1886, which can cause confusion, there's no doubt that 100 years had passed since the first Peugeot bike was made.

Cover and selected pages (opposite) from the 1982 French catalogue. Note that while the text says the bike illustrated is a PY10S, it's actually a PRO10 model.

Things had moved fairly slowly on the technology front for some time, with a series of evolutionary rather than revolutionary changes. In 1982, though, to celebrate Peugeot's cycling centenary, the company not only produced a handful of limited editions (the Z40/Z45, Z8/Z18 and Z10, with special head badges based on those from around the time of the Great War), it completely overhauled the range, and introduced the PX10DU bike with a duralumin frame at the same time.

Aluminium alloy bikes were hardly a new idea, as patents exist from the thirties, but they were certainly rare at the time, and worthy of the excitement enthusiasts greeted the PX10DU model with. Made with Vitus Duralinox 979 tubing, the lugs were actually bonded in place rather than welded or brazed, and gave the buyer a significant saving of more than a kilo (2lb). While the frame was prone to flex more than a top steel one, there were some events on rougher surfaces where pro riders actually welcomed the damping effect this caused, and for hobby cyclists, where comfort is always an added bonus, the PX10DU really was an excellent choice.

Before we get too carried away with a specific model, though, we need to chart the general changes, for they came thick and fast in the 1980s – folks having trouble dating bikes from the previous decade will find they have to be careful in this one, too. Some years are thankfully crystal clear, but certainly not all of them, and if one looks at the German catalogues for 1982, for instance, it features a strange mix of new and old, with only a handful of bikes displaying the latest styling revisions. It was the same story in America!

Anyway, officially, the main cosmetic change for

VELOS COURSE : CARACTERISTIQUES COMMUNES.

Tous les vélos du PRO 10 au PF 10 sont montés avec : Haubans AR biconiques – Pattes AR SIMPLEX avec butée à vis – Guide-gaines, guide-câbles, supports de manettes de dérailleurs, écrous de porte-bidon et repos de chaîne brasés – Chaîne étroite SEDISPORT – Roue libre 6 vitesses – Jantes dural – Pédales Dural avec cale-pieds et courroies.

PRO 10.

Cadre et fourche tout REYNOLDS 531 5/10, fabriqué en atelier spécial selon méthode artisanale – Cotes à la demande dans les hauteurs 50 à 64 – Direction SPIDEL D8 – Les autres caractéristiques figurent dans le tableau pages 22 et 23.
Options à la demande. Consultez votre concessionnaire.

PY 10 S.

(Photo ci-contre). Cadre tout REYNOLDS 531 5/10, raccords NERVEX, haubans REYNOLDS – Bases et haubans chromés – Hauteurs 52, 54, 56, 58, 60, 62, 64 cm – Fourche REYNOLDS chromée, épaules basses – Direction SPIDEL – Les autres caractéristiques figurent dans le tableau pages 22 et 23.

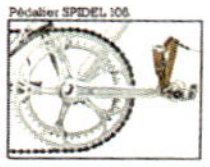

Pédalier SPIDEL 106.

PX 10 DU.

(Photo ci-contre). Cadre duralinox VITUS 979 – Hauteurs 52, 54, 56, 58, 60, 62, 64 cm – Fourche duralinox – Direction dural – Les autres caractéristiques figurent dans le tableau pages 22 et 23.

Jambage de fourche.

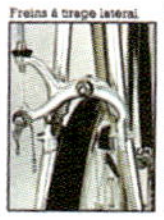

Freins à tirage latéral.

Selle et tige de selle. Raccords.

PX 10 S.

Cadre tout REYNOLDS 7/10, raccords NERVEX – Hauteurs 52, 54, 56, 58, 60, 62 cm – Fourche REYNOLDS chromée, tête forgée épaules basses – Direction LIGHTRACE – Les autres caractéristiques figurent dans le tableau pages 22 et 23.

PSV 10 S.

Cadre SUPER VITUS 980, raccords NERVEX – Hauteurs 52, 54, 56, 58, 60, 62, 64 cm – Fourche SUPER VITUS chromée – Les autres caractéristiques figurent dans le tableau pages 22 et 23.

Freins à tirage latéral.

Selle et tige de selle.

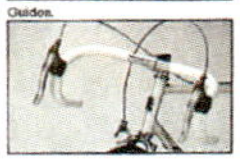

Guidon.

PF 10 S.

(Photo ci-contre). Cadre trois tubes VITUS, raccords NERVEX – Hauteurs 52, 54, 56, 58, 60, 62, 64 cm – Jambages de fourche chromés, tête de fourche épaules basses – Les autres caractéristiques figurent dans le tableau pages 22 et 23.

PFN 10 S.

Même modèle que le PF 10 S avec pneus MICHELIN Élan et jantes adaptées – Les autres caractéristiques figurent dans le tableau pages 22 et 23.

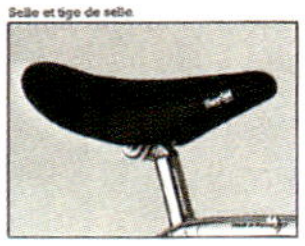

Selle et tige de selle.

PF 10.

(Photo ci-contre). Cadre trois tubes VITUS, raccords BOCAMA – Hauteurs 52, 54, 56, 58, 60, 62, 64 cm – Jambages de fourche chromés, tête de fourche épaules basses – Les autres caractéristiques figurent dans le tableau pages 22 et 23.

PFN 10.

Même modèle que le PF 10, avec pneus MICHELIN Élan et jantes adaptées – Les autres caractéristiques figurent dans le tableau pages 22 et 23.

PFN 13.

Même modèle que le PFN 10, avec pédalier dural triple plateau 52 x 42 x 32 – Les autres caractéristiques figurent dans le tableau pages 22 et 23.

PBN 10 S.

Cadre tubes PEUGEOT, raccords BOCAMA – Hauteurs 52, 54, 56, 58, 60, 62, 64 cm – Les autres caractéristiques figurent dans le tableau pages

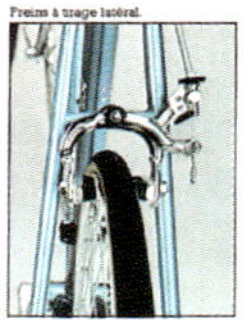

Freins à tirage latéral.

Selle et tige de selle.

Guidon.

PH 15 :

Cadre sport dame, 3 tubes, soudo-brasé sans raccord – Hauteurs 50, 53, 57 cm – Guidon course – Roues de 700 c – Blocages rapides – Roue libre 5 vitesses – Pédalier dural 48 x 36 – Pédales avec mini cale-pieds – Dérailleur SIMPLEX – Freins à tirage latéral – Poignée avec double levier – Selle sport.

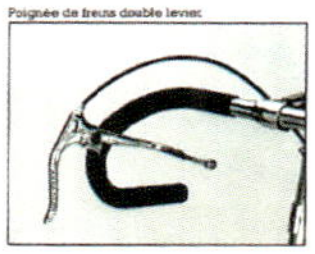

Poignée de freins double levier.

PH 10 S.

(Photo ci-contre). Cadre soudo-brasé sans raccord – Hauteurs 50, 54, 57, 60 cm – Les autres caractéristiques figurent dans le tableau pages 22 et 23.

P 10

Cadre soudo-brasé sans raccord - hauteur : 57 cm - roues de 700 c - blocages rapides - pédalier acier double plateau 42 x 52 - roue libre 5 vitesses, 14 à 24 dents.

PX 18 S.

Cadre mixte – Hauteurs 50, 53, 57 cm – Fourche chromée à mi-hauteur – Guidon dural type Helvetia – Roues de 700 C, jantes dural, moyeux dural à blocages rapides – Pédalier dural, couple dural 48 x 36, pédales dural avec mini cale-pieds – Roue libre 5 vitesses – Dérailleurs SIMPLEX – Freins à tirage central – Selle sport – Garde-boue – Porte-bagages AR étroit – Éclairage.

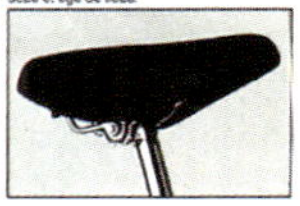

Selle et tige de selle.

PX 8 S.

(Photo ci-contre). Cadre homme – Hauteurs 54, 57, 60 cm – Guidon dural – Roues de 700 C, jantes dural blocages rapides – Pédalier dural 50 x 40, pédales dural, cale-pieds, courroies – Roue libre 5 vitesses – Dérailleurs SIMPLEX – Freins dural à tirage central – Garde-boue – Porte-bagages AR - Éclairage.

PH 8 S.

Cadre sans raccord – Hauteurs 54, 57, 60 cm – Guidon type course – Roues de 700 C – Pédalier dural, couple dural 50 x 40 – Roue libre 5 vitesses – Dérailleurs SIMPLEX – Freins dural à tirage latéral – Selle demi-course – Garde-boue – Porte-bagages AR – Éclairage.

PH 8 M.

Même modèle que le PH 8 S, avec pédalier acier et couple acier. **Existe également en version 5 vitesses, hauteurs 54 et 57 cm : PH 8M 5V.**

P 8.

Cadre sans raccord – Hauteur 54 cm – Guidon type course – Roues de 700 C – Pédalier acier – Roue libre 5 vitesses – Dérailleur SIMPLEX - Freins à tirage latéral – Selle sport - Garde-boue – Porte-bagages AR - Éclairage.

PH 18 S.

(Photo ci-contre). Cadre triangulé. Hauteurs 50, 53, 57 cm – Guidon type Helvetia – Roues de 700, à blocages rapides – Pédalier dural, couple dural 48 x 36, petit garde-chaîne, pédales acier avec catadioptres – Roue libre 5 vitesses – Dérailleurs SIMPLEX – Freins à tirage latéral – Garde-boue – Porte-bagages AR – Éclairage.

Pédalier dural.

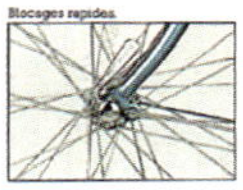

Blocages rapides.

P 18.

Cadre mixte sans raccord. Hauteur 50 cm – Guidon type Helvetia – Roues de 700 – Pédalier acier – Petit garde-chaîne – Roue libre 5 vitesses – Freins à tirage latéral – Garde-boue – Porte-bagages AR – Éclairage.

A Japanese flyer making the most of Peugeot's racing success and the new, supremely elegant PX10DU model.

1982 was a distinct move towards simplicity. The head badge became the lion rampant adopted on Peugeot cars in the mid-1970s and already used on Cycles Peugeot's commercial documents for some time. The logo was repeated on the seat tube (again via relief badges, but smaller than the head one), and the top tube was used to distinguish model ranges: The more expensive road-racer grades had block lettering on an oblong plate, with larger lettering and the backing plate deleted on the mid-range PF/PFN models; in addition, the seat tube lion became a decal. A chequer pattern was then introduced on the entry-level bikes, augmenting the block lettering found on the PF/PFN series. Apart from the mixte machines, these general changes would be applied to each model group – at least the ones that interest us – and according to rank …

Apart from the latest graphics, the randonneurs and tourers were all pretty familiar with domestic buyers, with the PX40M dropped and only the ladies getting new models in this category (replacements for the PX45M and PH25M, plus one new grade). In the sporty line, the P60M and P65M were axed, but the P8 was new, as was the P18 sister model. These took the place of the PL8M and PL18M, while the PH18M, PX8M and PX18M grades became the PH18S, PX8S and PX18S, respectively.

In the 'Course' line-up, the P10 was added as a new entry-level bike, with the PH10 becoming the PH10S, but still augmenting the PH15 for ladies. The PBN10 became the PBN10S, and while the PF10, PFN10 and PFN13 grades were carried over, they were now joined

Cover of the Dutch catalogue from 1982, with a truly varied selection of machines shown.

by the PF10S and PFN10S, which were basically the same, except the newcomers had MAFAC brakes and enhanced wheel and hub specifications. In reality, they were the direct replacements for the PK10 and PKN10, which were no longer listed.

Moving further up the ladder, the PSV10 evolved into the PSV10S, with upgraded derailleurs; the PX10S was much the same other than the new badging, and then there was the PX10DU. The frame construction was different, of course, and the polished finish on the latter not only looked attractive, it saved weight, too. After all, the lack of paint is what gave birth to the legend of the

Bernaudeau getting a welcome soaking from an enthusiastic spectator during the 1982 TdF. (Courtesy *L'Equipe*)

Below: The Peugeot team for the 1982 Tour de France, with (l-r) the DS, Maurice de Muer, then the racers, namely Bernard Bourreau, Patrick Perret, Phil Anderson, André Chalmel, Frédéric Brun, Gilbert Duclos-Lassalle, Jean-Réne Bernaudeau, Hubert Linard, and Pascal Simon; Michel Laurent was the tenth member, but isn't in the shot. (Courtesy *L'Equipe*)

Phil Anderson wearing yellow on the 1982 Tour de France. (Courtesy *L'Equipe*)

Mercedes-Benz 'Silver Arrows' – ultimately, anything that can save weight in racing is welcomed with open arms, as long as it doesn't affect a component's integrity. It also had different brakes (the Weinmann Carrera 400 type) compared with its other PX10 stablemate.

The PY10S and PRO10 models were basically carried over, with new Spidel LSX brakes and the latest badging separating them from their predecessors. The PRO10 also had a Spidel 107 crankset for 1982, with the filled-in spoke ends and cranks said to help aid aerodynamic efficiency.

To talk about export markets is only going to cause confusion, and there's enough of that already. Let's just say it was a transition period, with the old and new model mix combined with old and new graphics, the latter seemingly chosen at random. Unique decals could also be found, such as those on the UK-spec PH12, along with bikes not sold in France, like the PZ10 listed in Germany. It is worth mentioning, however, that Cycles Peugeot SA and Procycle Inc signed an agreement that strengthened Peugeot's activities in North America. In addition, some months earlier, from April 1982, Honda had taken over Japanese distribution – the trading arm of the manuafcturing company having previously handled the Raleigh brand. As it happens, the pair would later co-operate in the scooter arena, the Japanese maker supplying Peugeot with engines for the SC50/80.

1982 saw Esso's place as the works racing team's sub-sponsor taken by Shell, thus giving birth to the Peugeot-Shell-Michelin equipe. This naturally meant new jerseys, although the design was actually similar to that of the late-sixties, but with the Shell logo on the sleeves rather than the BP one. There were few changes in the list of men wearing this latest shirt, though, with the arrival of Sean Yates being the biggest news.

For a centenary year and with a new sponsor to impress (especially seeing as professional riders were now earning far more than before), it could have been a better season. Michel Laurent won the 1982 Critérium du Dauphiné Libéré, plus two other races, Jean-René

Bernaudeau took the honours on the GP du Midi-Libre, and Francis Castaing, Gilbert Duclos-Lasalle and Patrick Perret each won a race apiece. There was no joy in the Grand Tours, with Bernard Hinault of the Renault-Elf team winning both the Giro d'Italia and the Tour de France. It should be noted that Phil Anderson came fifth in the TdF, though, winning a stage, and wearing the prized yellow jersey for no less than ten days; his achievement was duly honoured in the French brochure issued for the 1983 season. As it happens, this was the highlight of Maurice de Muer's final year as DS for the team.

While BMX bikes were given more prominence in the 1983 domestic catalogue, they were still limited in number compared to traditional bicycles. Indeed, the elegant VX and VL range was enhanced (it was the VX's three-speed Sturmey-Archer hub that distanced it from its VL brethren, incidentally), and while most of the other lines were carried over, a small amount were revised, plus four additional models were added, including the PH60 and PH65. The PF60 gained the decals similar to those first seen on the British market's PH12 at this stage, with a strong coachline that went across the top tube (broken for the Peugeot name in block lettering), continuing down the side of the head tube, and then along the down tube, with both ends fading out about halfway through the frame. The PF60 didn't actually have the head tube section, but was otherwise the same. The main reason for bringing it up is that variations on the theme would be used for certain domestic 'Course' models for 1983, too.

With regard to the road-racers, it's easier to start with the grades that didn't change, for the range was given several important additions. Models carried over included the PSV10S and PX10S (although even they came with a different crankset, with CLB brakes added on the latter), the PX10DU (albeit with new derailleurs), and the PY10S and PRO10 (both with different brakes sourced from Weinmann). And now the fun really begins …

Cover and selected pages from the domestic 1983 master catalogue.

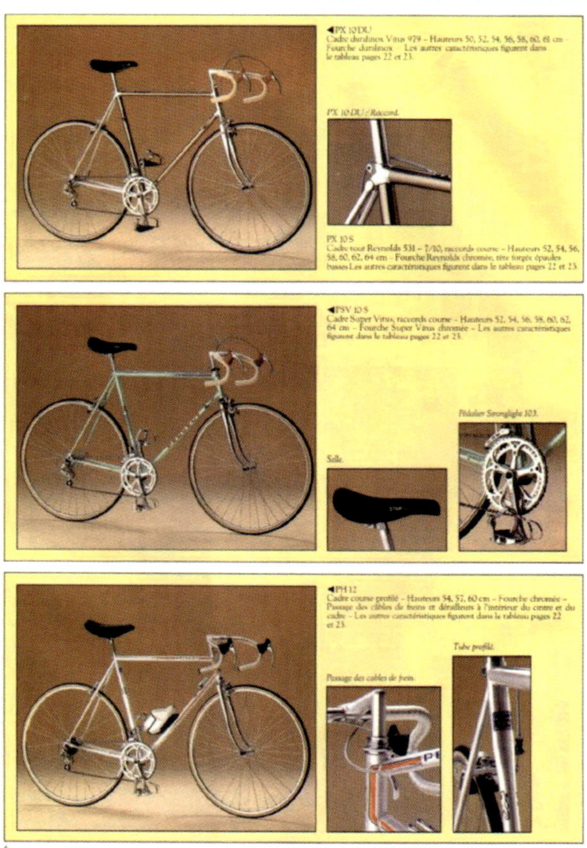

PY 10 FC ▶
Cadre 3 tubes fibre de carbone – Hauteurs 50, 52, 54, 56, 58, 60, 61 cm – Fourche, bases, haubans et raccords en duralinox Vitus 979 – Les autres caractéristiques figurent dans le tableau pages 22 et 23.

PY 10 FC : Dérailleur AR Simplex.

PRO 10
Cadre et fourche tout Reynolds 531 – 5/10, fabriqué en atelier spécial selon méthode artisanale – Cotes à la demande dans les hauteurs 50 à 64 – Les autres caractéristiques figurent dans le tableau pages 22 et 23 – Options à la demande, consultez votre concessionnaire.

PY 10 S ▶
Cadre tout Reynolds 531 – 5/10, raccords course – Chromage fonctionnel des bases et haubans – Hauteurs 52, 54, 55, 56, 57, 58, 59, 60, 62, 64 cm – Fourche Reynolds chromée, épaules basses. Les autres caractéristiques figurent dans le tableau pages 22 et 23.

PZ 10
Cadre tout Reynolds 7/10 – Hauteurs 52, 54, 56, 58, 60, 62, 64 cm Chromage fonctionnel des bases et haubans – Équipements Campagnolo "Record et super Record" – Les autres caractéristiques figurent dans le tableau pages 22 et 23.

PZ 10 : Frein AR Campagnolo.

PZ 10 : Pédalier Campagnolo.

◀ F 12
Cadre course profilé brasé sans raccord – Hauteurs 54, 57, 60 cm – Passage des câbles de freins dans le guidon et le cadre – Les autres caractéristiques figurent dans le tableau pages 22 et 23.

Poignée de frein.

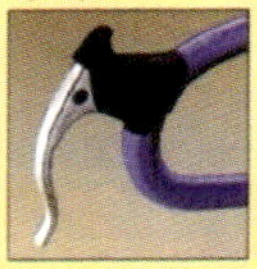

Pédalier.

◀ PH 15 T
Cadre sport dame, 3 tubes brasés sans raccord – Hauteurs 50, 53, 57 cm – Guidon plat type Helvetia – Roues de 700 C, jantes dural, pneus noir et blanc BIB TS 700 x 20 C – Blocages rapides – Roue libre 6 vitesses – Pédalier dural 48 x 36 – Pédales dural avec mini cale-pieds – Dérailleurs Simplex – Freins dural à tirage latéral – Selle sport – Petits garde-boue Esge.

Guidon plat.

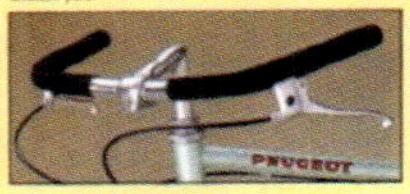

◀ F 10 S
Cadre course brasé sans raccord – Hauteurs 54, 57 cm – Pédalier en fibre de verre armée avec pare-chaîne circulaire – Manivelles dural – Les autres caractéristiques figurent dans le tableau pages 22 et 23.

F 10 S : Pédalier fibre de verre armée Solida 2000.

F 10 L
Cadre brasé sans raccord – Hauteurs 54, 57 cm – Roues de 700 C Les autres caractéristiques figurent dans le tableau pages 22 et 23.

PF 10 L ▶
Cadre 3 tubes Vitus – Hauteurs 52, 54, 56, 58, 60, 62, 64 cm – Jambages de fourche chromés – Modèle à boyaux Les autres caractéristiques figurent dans le tableau pages 22 et 23.

PFN 10 L
Même modèle que le PF 10 L avec pneus Michelin BIB TS 20 et jantes adaptées.

PF 10 M
Cadre 3 tubes Vitus – Hauteurs 52, 54, 56, 58, 60, 62, 64 cm – Jambages de fourche chromés – Tête de fourche épaules basses – Modèle à boyaux – les autres caractéristiques figurent dans le tableau pages 22 et 23.

PFN 10 M
Même modèle que le PF 10 M avec pneus Michelin BIB TS 20 et jantes adaptées.

PBN 15 ▶
Cadre tubes Peugeot 103 – Jambages de fourche chromés Pédalier dural triple plateau Les autres caractéristiques figurent dans le tableau pages 22 et 23.

Roue libre Maillard Hélicomatic.

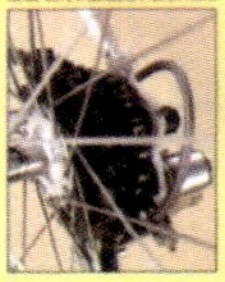

Triple plateau Stronglight.

PH 10 SL ▶
Cadre brasé sans raccord – Hauteurs 50, 54, 57, 60 cm Les autres caractéristiques figurent dans le tableau pages 22 et 23.

PH 10 C : Calculateur *intégré dans la potence.*

PH 10 M
Cadre brasé sans raccord – Hauteurs 50, 54, 57, 60 cm Les autres caractéristiques figurent dans le tableau pages 22 et 23.

PH 10 C
Même modèle que le PH 10 M avec calculateur 3 fonctions intégré dans la potence assurant : 1) la distance parcourue ; 2) le temps mis ; 3) la vitesse instantanée – Passage des cordons dans un jambage de fourche – Les autres caractéristiques figurent dans le tableau pages 22 et 23.

PX 8 L ▶
Cadre homme – Hauteurs 54, 57, 60 cm – Fourche demi-chromée – Guidon dural – Roues de 700 C – Jantes dural – Blocages rapides – Pédalier dural 40 x 50 – Pédales dural, cale-pieds, courroies – Roue libre 5 vitesses – Dérailleurs Simplex – Freins dural à tirage central – Garde-boue et porte-bagages AR Esge – Éclairage.

PH 8 S
Cadre sans raccord – Hauteurs 54, 57, 60 cm – Guidon type course – Roues de 700 C – Pédalier dural, couple dural 40 x 50 – Roue libre 5 vitesses – Dérailleurs Simplex – Freins dural à tirage latéral – Selle demi-course – Garde-boue – Porte-bagages AR – Éclairage

PH 8 M
Même modèle que le PH 8 S, avec pédalier acier et couple acier.
Existe également en version 5 vitesses, hauteurs 54 et 57 cm : PH 8 M 5 V.

P 8
Cadre sans raccord – Hauteur 54 cm – Guidon type course – Roues de 700 C – Pédalier acier – Roue libre 5 vitesses – Freins à tirage latéral – Selle sport – Garde-boue – Porte-bagages AR – Éclairage.

PH 18 M
Cadre triangulé – Hauteurs 50, 53, 57 cm – Guidon type Helvetia – Roues de 700 – Pédalier acier 36 x 48 avec carter de chaîne – Pédales acier – Roue libre 5 vitesses – Freins dural à tirage latéral – Garde-boue – Porte-bagages AR – Éclairage.

P 18 L ▶
Cadre mixte sans raccord – Hauteur 50 cm – Roues de 700 – Pédalier 36 x 48 acier – Roue libre 5 vitesses – Freins – Porte-bagages AR – Éclairage.

TANDEMS TM 8
Cadre Homme/Femme – Guidon AV type course, guidon AR plat – Roues 700 C, pneus 37-622 – Transmission AV : pédalier dural Stronglight, 32 dents à gauche – Transmission AR : pédalier Stronglight 52 x 42 – Pédales avec cale-pieds – Dérailleurs Simplex – Freins AV Cantilever – Freins AR à tambour Maillard (Ø 90) et Cantilever spécial – Poignées de freins course – Selle confortable – Porte-bagages AR – Éclairage. Existe également version Homme/Femme : TH 8.

PX 50 S ▶
Cadre homme – Hauteurs 54, 57, 60 cm – Guidon course dural, Roues de 700, jantes dural, blocages rapides – Pédalier dural triple plateau 30 x 40 x 50, pédales acier, cale-pieds, courroies – Roue libre 5 vitesses Maillard Hélicomatic 14 à 24 – Dérailleurs Simplex – Freins à tirage central poignées à double levier – Porte-bagages AV et AR – Garde-boue – Éclairage.

PL 50 M
Cadre homme – Hauteurs 54, 57, 60 cm – Roues de 700 – Pédalier acier 36 x 48 – Roue libre 5 vitesses – Dérailleurs Simplex – Freins à tirage latéral, poignées à double levier – Porte-bagages AV et AR – Garde-boue – Éclairage.

PH 50 M
Cadre homme sans raccord – Hauteurs 54, 57 cm – Roues de 650 B – Pédalier acier – Roue libre 3 vitesses – Dérailleur Simplex – Freins à tirage latéral, poignées à double levier – Porte-bagages AR – Garde-boue – Éclairage.

The P10 was divided into the P10L and P10S grades for 1983, with a different crankset distinguishing them, and now coming with a choice of Huret or Simplex derailleurs. The PH10S became the PH10SL, with the grade further broken down into the PH10M and PH10C, with different hubs; the thing separating the PH10M and PH10C was the novel three-function trip computer fitted on the latter. It's easier to say that the old PF-series of five bikes disappeared at this stage, for their replacements were either indirect or heavily revised, with a change in suffix helping identify four of them. The PFN13 morphed into the PBN13, now with Peugeot frame tubes rather than Vitus ones. The other grades were the PF10M, PFN10M, PF10L and PFN10L, with the brakes (Weinmann 506s on the 'M' models, and higher class 605s on the 'L' grades), derailleurs and standard saddles defining the two groups.

Cover of the Canadian brochure from 1983. Interestingly, delivery on French-built models was quoted at 16 weeks.

The PBN10S was dropped, replaced by the P12 and PH12. These were similar to the old model, as they had Peugeot frames, and were given different derailleurs and brake sets to create two new grades. Although it had already been sold in certain export markets, the PZ10 was a newcomer to France that sat in amongst the PX10s, with Reynolds tubes for the frame, but fitted out with Campagnolo 'Record' components that were all the rage thanks to Hinault's TdF victories. At least the option was there now (one that was chosen by the short-lived ANC racing team from Britain, as it happens).

The detailing was something of a minefield. The P12 and PH12 gained the UK PH12-inspired graphics (in full, with the head tube section included), while the PH10s and the PB and PF variants followed the latest French PF60-type pattern, and the P10 models had the same top tube decal design, but without any of the other pieces lower down. The PSV10S, PZ10 and PY10S, meanwhile, basically brought back 1981-style badging combined with a shortened version of the latest top tube decal. There was also a gradual move towards a no-nonsense decal replacing the chunky head badge on certain models – something that would basically become the norm by the start of the next season, with the plain outline following the same lines as the silver edging of the earlier badge.

Advertising for the carbon-tubed PY10FC. The earliest models were basically free of graphics.

Peugeot has never been afraid to innovate, and the company's racing cars from either side of the Great War show this has long been the case. The final newcomer

Above: The Peugeot works team for the 1983 season.

Pascal Simon in yellow on the 1983 Tour de France. (Courtesy *L'Equipe*)

Stephen Roche in action during the 1983 edition of the TdF. (Courtesy *L'Equipe*)

Gilbert Duclos-Lassalle taking a break, and then en route to victory on the 1983 Bordeaux-Paris race. Note the special time trial bike used for some of the stages. (Courtesy *L'Equipe*)

for 1983 – the PY10FC – proves it beyond any doubt. Ernesto Colnago has often said in interviews that Colnago made the first carbonfibre bikes, although

Opposite and overleaf: English language version of the 1984 main catalogue, with this being the 'Course' section.

"Alone, with the whistling sound of the racing tyres, the noise of the free wheel, a feeling of happiness, of well-being and, in the end, always the miracle of having managed to do better than before."

PEUGEOT-SHELL-MICHELIN team's bicycle.

PY10FC Frame: tubes Peugeot carbon fibre, available in sizes 19 1/2, 20 1/2, 21, 22, 23, 23 1/2, and 24 in. Duralinox 979 forks, seat and chain stays and lugs. Further details in the chart on page 22 and 23. A carbon fibre frame is also available at your dealer's in sizes 19 1/2, 20 1/2, 21, 22, 23, 23 1/2 and 24 in.

SIMPLEX SLJA 522 derailleur and MAILLARD 700 freewheel.

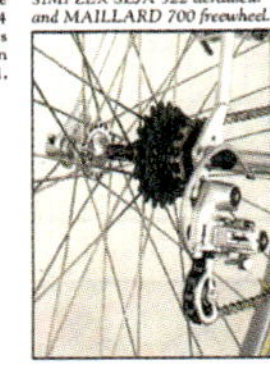

STRONGLIGHT 107 crank-set.

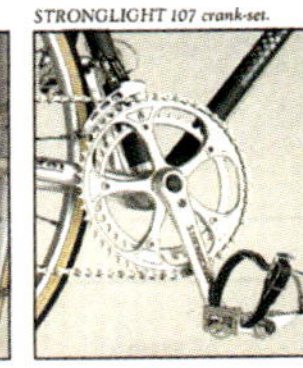

WEINMANN Carrera 400 brake.

PRO10 Frame and forks: REYNOLDS 531 - 5/10. Available in sizes 19 1/2 to 25 in. New seat stays/seat tube connection. Further details in the chart on page 22 and 23. Ask your local dealer for optional extras.

PY10LS Frame: REYNOLDS 531 throughout - 5/10. Available in sizes 20 1/2, 21, 21 1/2, 22, 22 1/2, 23, 23 1/2, 24 1/2 and 25. REYNOLDS chromed forks with sloping crown. New seat stays/seat tube connection. Further details in the chart on page 22 and 23.

PZ10 Frame: REYNOLDS 531 throughout - 7/10. Available in sizes 20 1/2, 21, 22, 23, 23 1/2, 24 1/2 and 25. REYNOLDS chromed forks. Further details in the chart on page 22 and 23.

New seat stays/ seat tube connection.

Shifters on brazed-on mounting.

PGN10 Frame: tubes REYNOLDS 501, chromed forks. New seat stays/seat tube connection. Available in sizes 20 1/2, 21, 22, 23, 23 1/2, 24 1/2 and 25 in.

A MODEL IS ALSO AVAILABLE WITH TUBULAR TYRES: PG10.

Further details in the chart on page 22 and 23.

REYNOLDS 501 tubes.

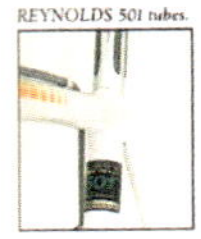

WEINMANN brake.

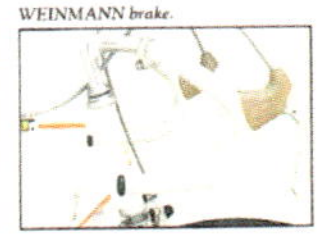

PX10DU Frame and forks: Duralinox 979 throughout. Available in sizes 19 1/2, 20 1/2, 21, 22, 23, 23 1/2 and 24 in. Further details in the chart on page 22 and 23.

A Duralinox frame is also available at your dealer's in sizes 19 1/2, 20 1/2, 21, 22, 23, 23 1/2 and 24 in.

PX10LS Frame: REYNOLDS 531 throughout - 5/10. Available in sizes 20 1/2, 21, 22, 23, 23 1/2, 24 1/2 and 25. REYNOLDS chromed forks. New seat stays/seat tube connection. Further details in the chart on page 22 and 23.

STRONGLIGHT 106 crank-set.

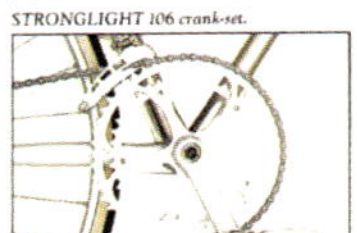

PH12 Aerodynamic seamless racing frame, all tubes PEUGEOT Carbolite, chromed forks. Available in sizes 21, 22 1/2 and 23 1/2 in. Brake cable housed in handlebars and gear cable housed in frame tube. Further details in chart on page 22 and 23.

Streamlined tube.

Feed-through of brake cables.

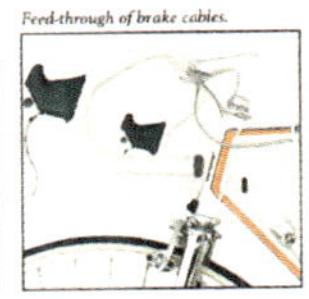

PSV10L Frame: Super Vitus throughout chromed forks. New seat stays/seat tube connection. Available in sizes 20 1/2, 21, 22, 23, 23 1/2, 24 1/2 and 25 in. Further details in the chart on page 22 and 23.

PH13 Frame: PEUGEOT Carbolite seamless tubes, chromed forks. Available in sizes 19 1/2, 21, 22 1/2, 23 1/2 in. New seat stays/seat tube connection. Further details in chart on page 22 and 23.

SOLIDA 5371 crank-set.

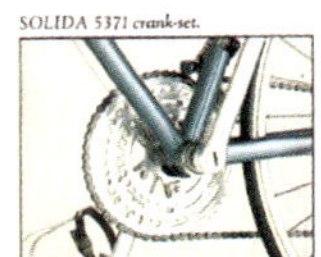

New seat stays/ seat tube connection.

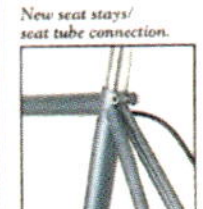

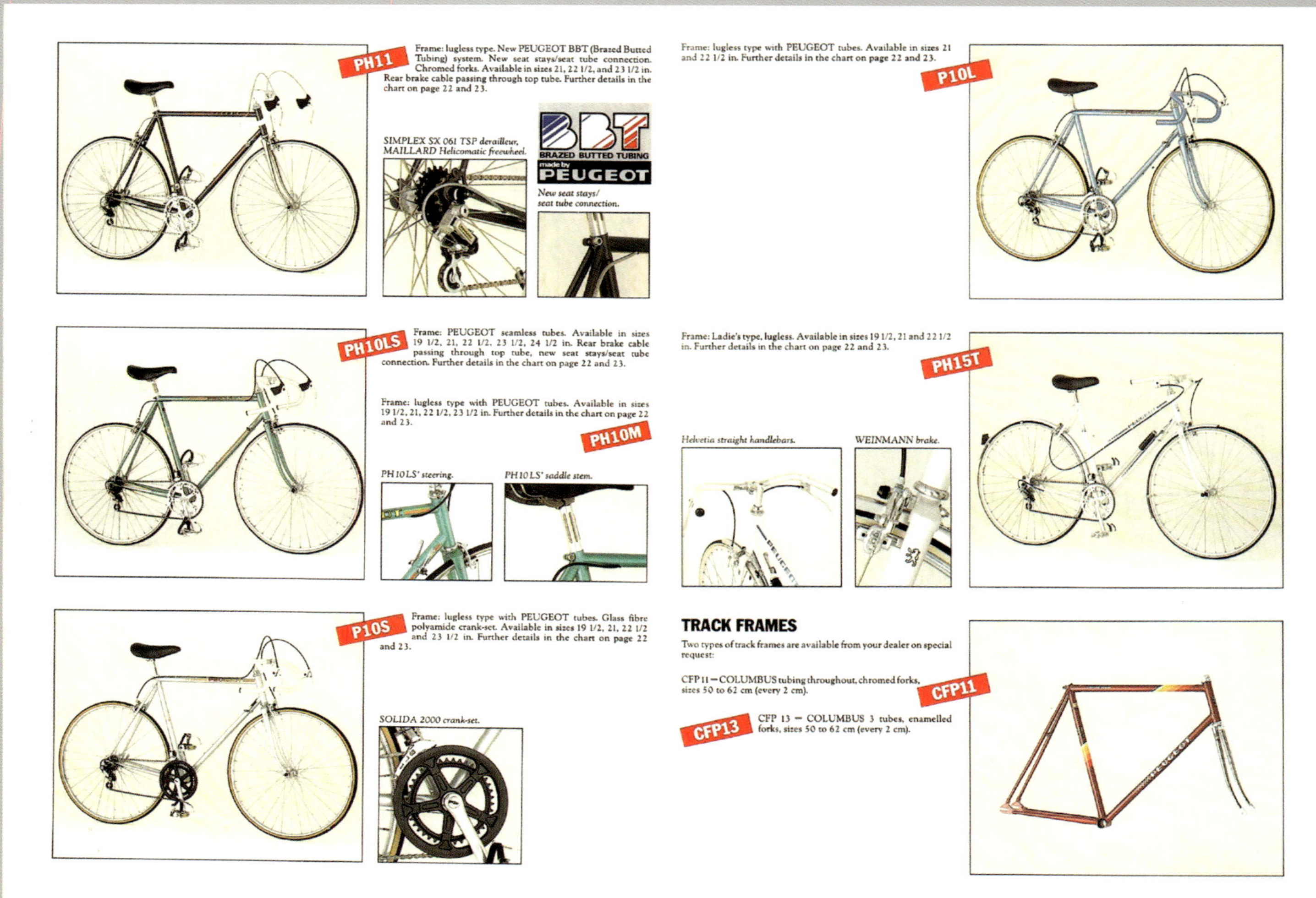

PH11

Frame: lugless type. New PEUGEOT BBT (Brazed Butted Tubing) system. New seat stays/seat tube connection. Chromed forks. Available in sizes 21, 22 1/2, and 23 1/2 in. Rear brake cable passing through top tube. Further details in the chart on page 22 and 23.

SIMPLEX SX 061 TSP derailleur, MAILLARD Helicomatic freewheel.

New seat stays/ seat tube connection.

PH10LS

Frame: PEUGEOT seamless tubes. Available in sizes 19 1/2, 21, 22 1/2, 23 1/2, 24 1/2 in. Rear brake cable passing through top tube, new seat stays/seat tube connection. Further details in the chart on page 22 and 23.

Frame: lugless type with PEUGEOT tubes. Available in sizes 19 1/2, 21, 22 1/2, 23 1/2 in. Further details in the chart on page 22 and 23.

PH10M

PH10LS' steering.

PH10LS' saddle stem.

P10S

Frame: lugless type with PEUGEOT tubes. Glass fibre polyamide crank-set. Available in sizes 19 1/2, 21, 22 1/2 and 23 1/2 in. Further details in the chart on page 22 and 23.

SOLIDA 2000 crank-set.

Frame: lugless type with PEUGEOT tubes. Available in sizes 21 and 22 1/2 in. Further details in the chart on page 22 and 23.

P10L

Frame: Ladie's type, lugless. Available in sizes 19 1/2, 21 and 22 1/2 in. Further details in the chart on page 22 and 23.

PH15T

Helvetia straight handlebars.

WEINMANN brake.

TRACK FRAMES

Two types of track frames are available from your dealer on special request:

CFP 11 – COLUMBUS tubing throughout, chromed forks, sizes 50 to 62 cm (every 2 cm).

CFP11

CFP13

CFP 13 – COLUMBUS 3 tubes, enamelled forks, sizes 50 to 62 cm (every 2 cm).

Raleigh had built a carbonfibre prototype back in 1971! Whoever built the first will always be a hazy subject, for production models and prototypes are two different things, as are limited runs, and partial- and full-carbon frames. What is absolutely certain, however, is that Peugeot's first carbonfibre bicycle was launched in time for the 1983 season, and that makes it one of the earliest examples of the breed to be offered to the public, whichever way one looks at it.

Back then, carbonfibre really was space age technology – significantly lighter than steel, yet stronger and stiffer, and fiercely expensive as a result. For the PY10FC, it was found in the three main tubes only, with the rest of the frame being the same as that of the PX10DU, so made of Duralinox 979 light alloy. A Stronglight 107 titanium crankset was employed, along with top-of-the-range Simplex derailleurs and Weinmann 'Carrera 400' brakes – as a set, the PY10FC tipped the scales at just 8.6kg (19lb), which was quite remarkable. As such, not surprisingly, it was a costly bike, priced around 60 per cent higher than the PX10DU, which itself could hardly be classed as a bargain basement model! The colouring on the early examples was very staid, with the natural carbonfibre finish of the tubes highlighted by the polished alloy sections attached to them; badging was kept to an absolute minimum, with just a nod to the material and tiny 'Peugeot' script on the top tube. The works bikes, however, were soon given more dramatic graphics that would ultimately be adopted on the showroom models for the 1984 season.

Meanwhile, those works bikes were being put to use in a gruelling season that witnessed a new generation come to the fore. There were quite a few changes to the Peugeot-Shell-Michelin team, with Jean-René

Dedicated brochure for the PH11 model.

Bernaudeau moving to the Wolber-Spidel outfit being the biggest revelation, and Roland Berland becoming the new DS, ably assisted by Roger Legeay. Australian Allan Peiper was signed as a rookie, which would later prove to be a good move.

The Tour de France had been cruel. Pascal Simon had been in yellow for seven days, but, hurt from a fall, Laurent Fignon of Renault kept eating away at his lead, and had the yellow jersey when it really mattered; poor Simon had retired on the Chapelle Blanche. Few would have thought it possible, but this would prove to be the last time a Peugeot man would wear the iconic maillot jaune.

At least Stephen Roche won the Tour de Romandie (it would be many years before a Peugeot rider would win that one again), the Etoile des Espoirs, GP de Wallonie and Paris-Bourges, Gilbert Duclos-Lassalle won the Bordeaux-Paris, GP de Fourmies and Route du Sud, and Phil Anderson took the silverware in the Tour l'Aude and Amstel Gold Race; Anderson was also Peugeot's top finisher in the Tour de France again, coming home in ninth in the 1983 edition.

Before leaving 1983, it's worth a quick look at the export markets, for things had basically started to settle again by this time, both in terms of badging and the model mix. In America, buyers looking for a road-racer were given the choice between a PF60, UO14, P6, P8, PH10S, PH12, PB14, PFN10, PSV10, PX10, PZ10D and PY10FC – many of these bikes having a familiar ring to them. For a change, Germany's line-up was actually quite similar to the domestic range, too, and even Japan had like for like grades, with Honda adding a 'J' suffix onto the regular model codes.

For 1984, the most striking thing was the colouring used for some of the latest domestic showroom models, with angled red, orange, yellow and white stripes on the

The Peugeot squad for 1984, with team car and descriptions of the top bikes available to the public featured as well. As it happens, Peugeots were still being used for Tour de France course car duty at this time, although Fiat moved in to claim the honour as the Eighties drew to a close.

top and seat tubes, and 'Peugeot' in heavy block lettering on the down tube, augmented by a subtle chequer pattern. The factory racers had already used it during the 1983 season, and, in fact, it had been around long before that, having first been seen on Peugeot's BMX bikes. As a works replica, this colour scheme was duly adopted on the 9800FF PY10FC, complete with a white decal for the head badge, but it was also found on the PRO10, PY10LS, PZ10, PX10LS and PSV10L grades. Most of the other models came with badging that was now familiar to followers of Peugeot lore – at least those living in France!

The PY10S became the PY10LS for 1984 (priced at 6447FF), but like the PRO10 and PY10FC positioned above it, as well as the 6121FF PZ10 below it in the pecking order, the only difference compared to the 1983 model was in the graphics. The same was basically true of the PX10S, although in becoming the PX10SL, it did at least inherit some new brakes (Weinmann 405s); the 5892FF PX10DU was carried over unchanged. In addition, in its transition from PSV10S to PSV10L, the Stronglight crankset was replaced with a Peyrard one, and the brakes from the latest PX10SL were adopted.

Last season's graphics were still evident on the PH12, which was carried over, and similar decals were used on two newcomers – the PG10 and PGN10. These replaced the PF10M, PFN10M, PF10L and PFN10L grades in the line-up, and featured Reynolds 501 Cr-Mo tubing (not 531, which is Mn-Mo), chromed front forks, a Peyrard 3020 crankset, Simplex derailleurs and Weinmann 506 brakes; as before, the 'N' signified the fitment of Michelin TS tyres.

The 1833FF PH13 was new, replacing the PBN13, with Peugeot 'Carbolite' 103 tubes, painted forks,

Above: Robert Millar staying ahead of Laurent Fignon (Renault-Elf) whilst proudly wearing the jersey for the top climber in the 1984 Tour de France. (Courtesy *L'Equipe*)

Left: French advert for the new PH501 grade.

a Solida crankset and CLB brakes keeping the price in check. There was also a PH11 version, which replaced the P12, and had different Simplex derailleurs to those fitted to the PH13. It also had two chainrings up front, rather than the triple-plate setup associated with the '13' grades.

The PH10SL became the PH10LS, although it was basically the same, as was the PH10M, P10L and P10S. Incidentally, the PH10C sister model to the PH10M was not in the catalogue, but it did appear in price lists, so it was still available. In a similar price range, the 1634FF PH15T was a basic debutante aimed at the ladies.

A fascinating addition for 1984 was a Columbus frameset, offered in CFP11 and CFP13 guise. The former used Italian tubing throughout, and came with chrome-plated forks, while the latter had Columbus tubes for the three main frame sections

Pascal Simon holding a PY10FC aloft in a piece of US advertising.

Accessories catalogue from 1985.

The Peugeot-Shell-Michelin team for the 1985 season.

and painted forks. Finished in a deep red with PY10FC-type stripes, as it happens, the option was only listed for this one season, but collectors should be aware of its existence.

Outside the pukka road-racers, very little had changed. The P8 transformed into the 1259FF P8L, the PH60 and PH65 became available with optional trip computers, and the PF60 and PF65 were replaced by the PCA10 and PCA15, respectively. That was it, other than the fact that BMX models were breeding, and the PMBF1 opened up the new mountain bike niche, with all-terrain bicycles (or ATBs) being the latest craze.

Midway through the 1984 season, the PX10SH had been introduced at 4626FF, giving buyers the option of Shimano components, the PH15T was joined by the 1322FF P15 and 1899FF PH15FB road-racers (the PH11FB was also added, with the 'FB' suffix signalling Forban-designed brake cables), the PH12 and PG10 had been dropped, a couple of other old favourites in the shape of the PX8L and PX18L had also fallen by the wayside, the PVD02 and PVD05 had become the latest entry-level tourers, the luxurious PX80 made its debut (ultimately replacing the PX50S in the 1985 catalogue), and the pair of tandems had made a comeback in updated form. It was a busy period, although things were thankfully set to become far simpler in the near future …

Export markets had by and large fallen into line with domestic models. Even America was using similar codes to those seen in France, although some bikes had gained names at this stage, with the UO14 (the last of the 'UO' series) giving way to the 'Le Vagabond'. In Europe, an interesting variant was the PX10DU sold in England, which sported the stripes of the other top road-racers; it retained its original appearance in France, as had been the norm elsewhere before. Incidentally, for some reason, the PX10DU was not listed in German or Dutch catalogues that year.

In racing, without Phil Anderson and Stephen Roche onboard, 1984 was to prove a disappointing season. Granted, Hubert Linard won the Bordeaux-Paris and Paris-Camembert, Allan Peiper the Tour de l'Oise and Tour of Sweden, Gilbert Duclos-Lassalle the Etoile des Espoirs, Pascal Simon the Route du Sud, Dominique Garde the GP du Midi-Libre, and team newcomer Dag-Otto Lauritzen was crowned champion of Norway. It could have been worse, for sure, but the relative

Isabelle Nicoloso – the 1985 World Champion in the ladies category.

lack of success in the Grand Tours (other than a fine performance from Robert Millar in the Tour de France, earning him the polkadot jersey and fourth overall) did not go unnoticed.

Although there were several changes, the 1985 'Course' line-up was in fact much the same as that seen at the tail-end of the previous season as far as the domestic market was concerned, both in looks and content. The PY10LS was renamed the PY10M, and the PSV10L became the PSV10M after inheriting Modolo brakes; the PSN10M was the same bike fitted with Michelin TS tyres. The PGN10 became the PGN10M thanks to Huret derailleurs replacing the former Simplex items, and the iconic stripes formally reserved for the top bikes filtered down through the ranks (only the three P10s and the pair of ladies bikes had to do without them).

The PH10M, PH12, PX10LS and PZ10 models were all dropped, although the PH501 and P10LS grades were new to the range. The PH501 was a lesser version of the PGN10M, with the '501' designation pointing towards the use of Reynolds 501 chro-moly (chromium-molybdenum) tubing for the frame. The P10LS, meanwhile, was like the P10L and P10S sister models, but with Michelin rubber. One could also buy a carbon frame only via the CFY10C product code.

Finished with familiar badging, the regular bikes outside the 'Ville' and 'Course' line-up were reshuffled completely for 1985, with the range being reduced slightly to 18 models; at the same time, the 'Nouveau Style' line was left with just two grades in it. In reality, in the context of this book, there was nothing really noteworthy in the clean-out, but the reduction in numbers (largely made possible through replacements that covered more ground) at least forged more space for the VTT1, which duly joined the PMBF1 in the mountain bike category.

About the only thing worth noting from the export markets was that America continued to punt the PZ10, with Campagnolo 'Super Record' components. Things were quiet on the racing front, too. Reigning Aussie champion Peter Besanko joined the works outfit, which witnessed quite a few changes for 1985, as it happens. Team leader Robert Millar was a superb second in the Vuelta a España (losing out by just a few seconds, in a race that many say the Scot should have won had it not been for the overwhelming desire of the Spaniards to have a native on the top spot of the podium), but, even as Peugeot's top finisher, he could only claim 11th place on the Tour de France that year. While Millar did win the Tour of Catalunya, and newcomer Ronan Pensec took the spoils in the Etoile des Espoirs, there was little else to write home about. Not surprisingly, this lack of success meant that Roland Berland's tenure as Directeur Sportif was destined to be a short one.

The 1986 domestic line-up was quite similar to that of the previous year, although the adoption of model names – something already seen in several export markets, its introduction doubtless due to the confusion caused by similar and constantly changing model codes – was starting to filter through in France, too. In addition, the striped decals previously associated with the top road-race bikes were now used throughout the 'Course' line.

There was little change in the regular machinery, just an expansion of the 'PV' series, and the PL60 and PL65 joining the fray as indirect replacements for the pair of PH50s and the PH22M. Sporting tasteful gold stripes (slightly different to the 'Course' graphics) and gold down tube lettering without the chequers, the new 'Force 8' PLs were actually the first bikes to feature Peugeot's strong yet light 'HLE' tubing, which was an inhouse-developed alloy of manganese, niobium, aluminium, carbon and titanium. The PXR80 was also new – a PX80 with racy paintwork.

The PX10DU and PSN10M grades were dropped from French catalogues, although there were several newcomers to take their place and further swell the numbers in the 'Course' line-up. The PGN10T was for triathlon types, with heavier stripes distancing it from its stablemates, while the PH20M was for the budget conscious, slotting in below the PH501, and featuring Peugeot 'Carbolite' 103 tubing. The PH513 was a PH501 with Simplex derailleurs instead of Huret items, and the PH153T was a PH15T with a triple chainring

Cover of the US brochure for 1986.

THE SPORTING RIVALS

ORBEA (ESP)

Like its Spanish rival BH, Orbea was founded by three brothers – Juan Manuel, Mateo and Casimiro Orbea. Orbea Hermonos originally dealt in guns, but one section of the sprawling business empire turned to bicycles in 1930. In the 1960s, the family sold out to a worker co-operative, and a new factory was ultimately built in Mallabia, where the company remains to this day. For decades, it has been hard to imagine a professional peloton without at least one team using Orbea bikes in it ...

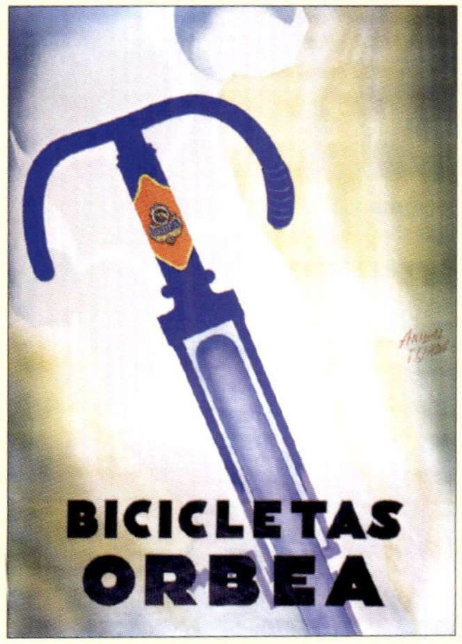

An attractive prewar Orbea poster.

EDDY MERCKX (BEL)

Named after the famous racer with other 500 wins to his credit, the Eddy Merckx brand is steeped in history. When he was racing – and winning – Merckx often had special frames built, back then by the likes of Masi and Colnago, and even during his time at Peugeot. After retiring in 1978, it was only natural that he set up his own bike company, initially with technical advice coming from De Rosa. The road-racers he built were much more than a mere marketing ploy, as their competition results clearly show. Although Merckx stepped back from the company a few years ago, it still exists, building a variety of machines to suit all tastes.

CONCORDE (HOL)

This was a real pan-European effort, with a Belgian importer joining a Dutch company in the creation of a Dutch bike using Italian frames and components. The brand came to the fore in the 1980s, and garnered a huge amount of success in the latter half of the decade courtesy of the PDM team.

LOOK (FRA)

Look started life as a French sports equipment manufacturer founded by Jean Beyl in 1951. Its clipless bike pedals were all the rage for a time, but the company's influence was far deeper after its new owner, Bernard Tapie, founded the La Vie Claire cycling team in 1983, built around Bernard Hinault after the latter had a fall-out with the Renault equipe. Under Tapie, Look was influential in bringing carbonfibre into the game, with TVT employed to create the KG86 frame, which duly took Greg LeMond to victory on the 1986 Tour de France. The Look brand has been associated with carbonfibre bikes ever since, and continues to supply the pro peloton to this day, fighting off competition from a string of other newer brands like Cervélo, Trek, Cannondale, Specialized (S-Works), Ridley and Scott.

The La Vie Claire (or Look) team for 1984, with Bernard Hinault leading the pack.

PINARELLO (ITA)

Cicli Pinarello was founded by Giovanni Pinarello, who used to ride for the famous Atala factory team in his first years as a pro, in 1953. He already had experience in the manufacturing field, having worked for a time at Paglianti, and the business soon took off, allowing him to create a works team as the 1960s arrived. Fame finally arrived in 1975, when Fausto Bertoglio won the Giro d'Italia on a Pinarello, with Giovanni Battaglin securing the brand's legendary status not long after. Miguel Indurain kept Pinarello in the spotlight with a gaggle of Tour de France wins, and the proud name continues to be associated with Grand Tour winners.

A Pinarello catalogue from the classic era.

The 'Gold' special edition featured on the cover of the German catalogue for 1986. In the background is another limited edition, this one being the 'Jubile' model, which failed to ignite the same kind of enthusiasm as the black and gold bike.

Roger Legeay in his younger days, before his Peugeot era, first as a rider and then as DS.

Below: Ronan Pensec keeping up a good pace on the 1986 TdF. (Courtesy *L'Equipe*)

setup at the front rather than a double one.

Finally, the 'Gold' special edition was basically a black PGN10M with PL60/PL65 stripes and gold-coloured forks and detailing. It was an attractive package, and one can often see the model up for sale on today's various auction sites. The stock PGN10M continued alongside it, incidentally, joined by a new PG10SH grade with Shimano components.

By the way, a new head badge was phased in during the year. Actually, it was basically the same, as it had the familiar lion logo, but now 'Peugeot' script was added beneath it in block letters. Its use seems hit and miss at first, but in time, this would become the norm across the range.

Looking abroad, America offered some interesting models, with the PZ continuing alongside an exotic new PX model based on the CFP11 frameset with Columbus tubing. It doesn't appear to have been offered elsewhere, and was only listed in the States for one more year.

Peugeot was flying high in the rally arena in the mid-1980s, with the Group B version of the 205 (seen here in a contemporary Michelin advert) giving the French maker the WRC title in 1985 and 1986. It would be a while before they would dominate the scene again, but they would in due course (along with sister brand Citroën), and also left their mark in WSPC and F1 racing.

There were some huge changes in the racing team for the 1986 season, with Roger Legeay moving up the ladder to become the latest DS, Robert Millar going to the Panasonic outfit amid a flurry of transfers, and new, albeit similar, jerseys to show that Michelin had withdrawn its support. Interestingly, the 'Velo Talbot' logo was added to the factory shirts at this time, although fate would see to it that the design was destined to last just one season.

Ronan Pensec was the top Peugeot-Shell rider in the Tour de France, finishing the 1986 event in sixth overall, almost 26 minutes down on the dominant La Vie Claire pairing at the head of the field, mounted on Look-badged carbonfibre bikes made by the TVT concern (the first but certainly not the last TdF win for a carbon frame). There were some good results in the smaller graded races, though, with Gilbert Duclos-Lassalle winning three, new face Gilbert Glaus taking two (including the Bordeaux-Paris classic), and Pascal Simon, Jan Koba, Didier Garcia, Bruno Wojtinek and Jérôme Simon each claiming one victory apiece.

However, despite a much better collection of silverware compared to 1985, the boss of Cycles Peugeot, William Desazars de Montgailhard, revealed that the racing budget had already been exceeded well before the season ended, and with finances tight due to a lack of suitable sponsorship, the factory could no longer afford to support a full works team. As such, the Peugeot equipe would officially be disbanded at the end of 1986. It was a sad moment, bringing literally decades of history to an abrupt end, but perhaps inevitable given the huge amounts of money involved in top class cycling thanks to wages and the cost of logistics.

Under the long-running PSA Group leadership of Jacques Calvet, fans of the French marque would be dealt another blow during 1987. As noted earlier, Cycles Peugeot had been obliged to make car components and other products to survive in the past, but now Calvet passed an order that would see a formal merger between Cycles Peugeot and AOP (Peugeot's steel and tooling division), giving birth to the ECIA subsidiary, which

Advertising for the new A-series range, which featured aluminium frames.

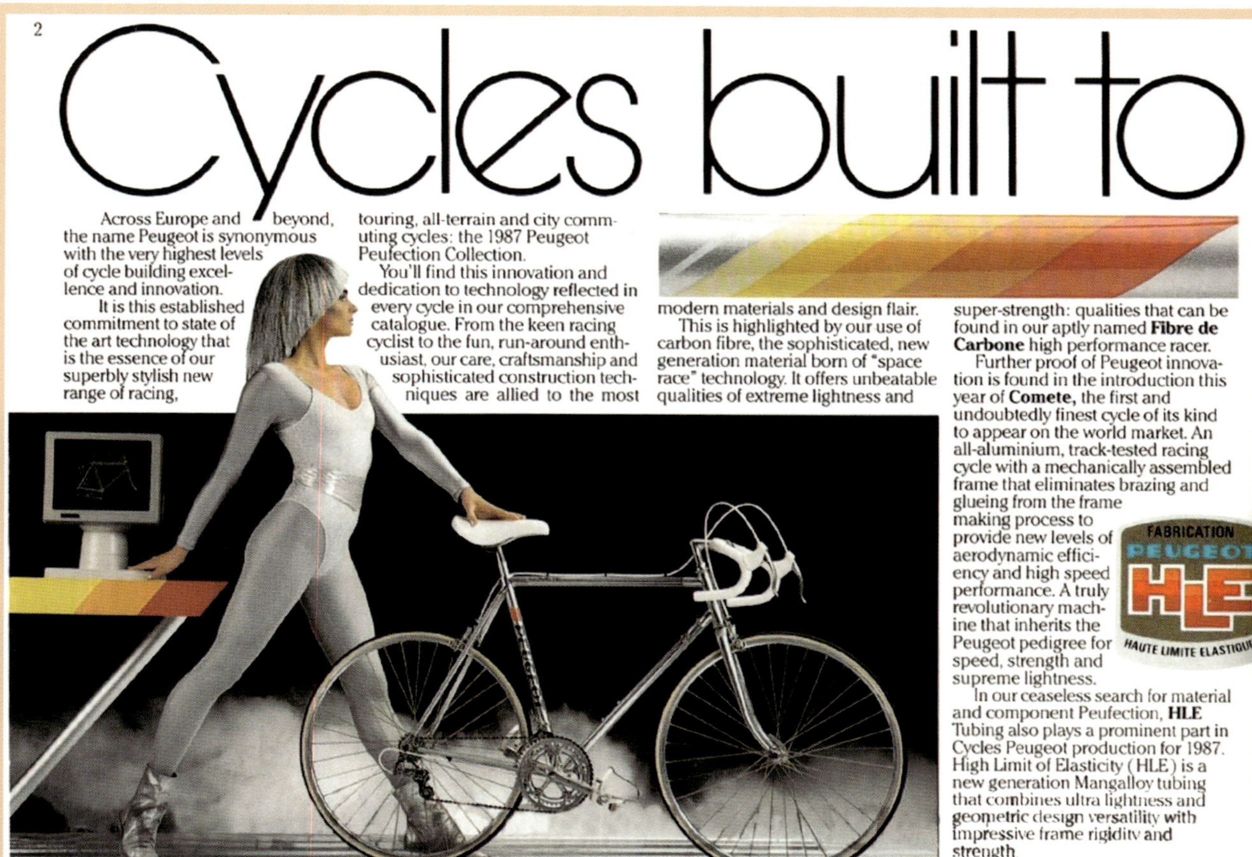

The cover and striking introduction pages from the UK brochure for 1987.

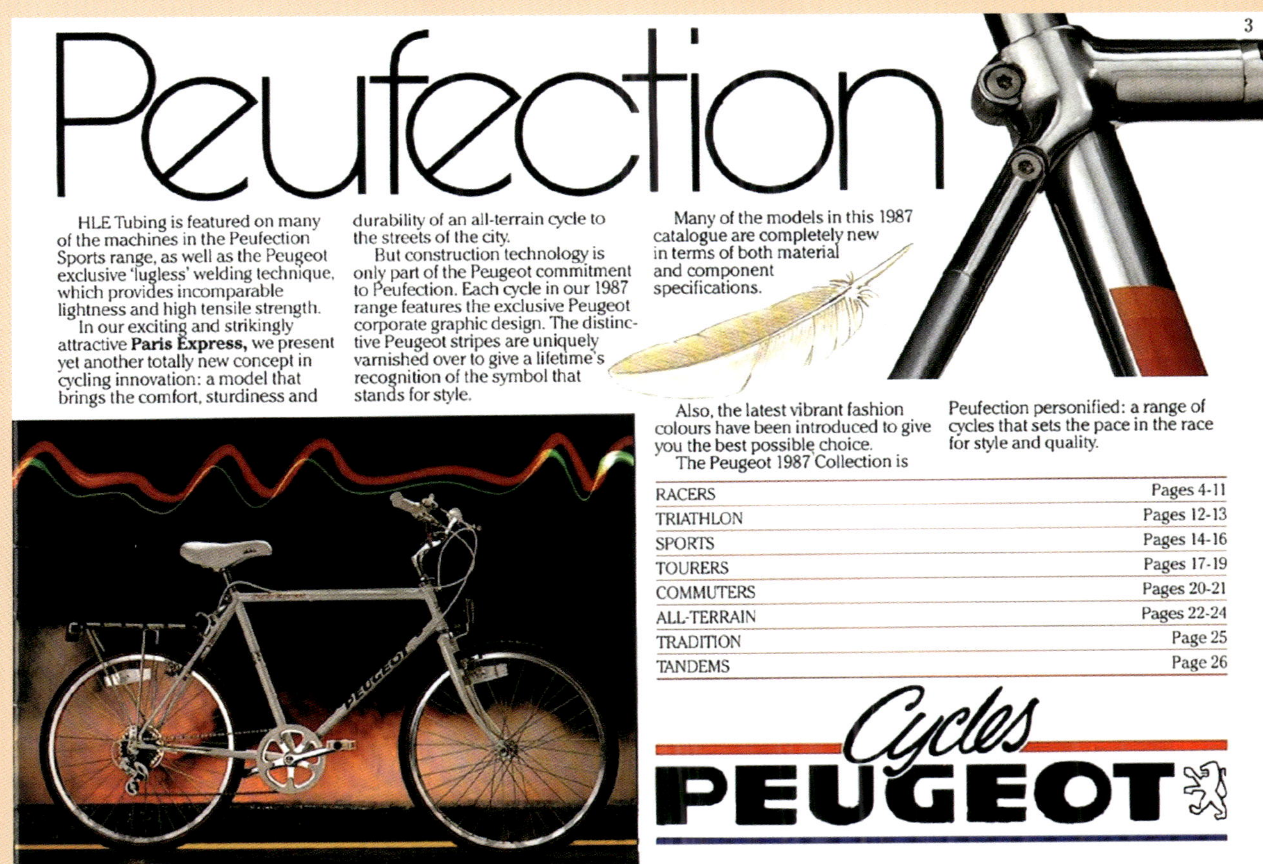

3

Peufection

HLE Tubing is featured on many of the machines in the Peufection Sports range, as well as the Peugeot exclusive 'lugless' welding technique, which provides incomparable lightness and high tensile strength.

In our exciting and strikingly attractive **Paris Express,** we present yet another totally new concept in cycling innovation: a model that brings the comfort, sturdiness and durability of an all-terrain cycle to the streets of the city.

But construction technology is only part of the Peugeot commitment to Peufection. Each cycle in our 1987 range features the exclusive Peugeot corporate graphic design. The distinctive Peugeot stripes are uniquely varnished over to give a lifetime's recognition of the symbol that stands for style.

Many of the models in this 1987 catalogue are completely new in terms of both material and component specifications.

Also, the latest vibrant fashion colours have been introduced to give you the best possible choice.

The Peugeot 1987 Collection is Peufection personified: a range of cycles that sets the pace in the race for style and quality.

Cycles PEUGEOT

would be recognised first and foremost as an equipment supplier.

Thankfully, the bikes were allowed to continue, built at the Romilly factory, where the head office was now registered (the time-honoured Valentigney address was no longer used, with the motorcycle side of the Peugeot business inheriting the Beaulieu site), although catalogues and suchlike now featured the Peugeot corporate logo with the word 'Cycles' added underneath, more as a description of a product line rather than a distinct enterprise. Peugeot Cycles was formed as a new concern to keep things tidy on paper, however, although one could still find the old Cycles Peugeot moniker in a number of foreign markets, where it was easier to leave existing distribution arrangements in place. With hindsight, looking at the big picture, it was obvious that with the cycling boom coming to an end and a shrewd businessman like Calvet at the top, the bicycle section suddenly found itself living on borrowed time.

Ironically, given the backroom wrangling that must have been going on as the new catalogues were being printed, 1987 was to be quite a year for new bikes. About half-a-dozen grades fell by the wayside in the regular, less profitable lines, with striped decals spreading further throughout the range – even finding their way onto 'Ville' models. The increase in the number of VTT all-terrain bikes available was also noticeable, as this was the market niche where sales were growing fast.

Meanwhile, with cycling enthusiasts firmly in mind, a big thing was made of the PX10DU's ultimate replacement – the 'A'-series road-racers, which featured aluminium alloy 5086 'Aviatube' combined with special lugs developed by Cegedur-Pechiney that eliminated the need for brazing and/or bonding joints. Tipping the scales at around 2kg (4.5lb) including the forks, the frame was not only light, but the purely mechanical construction techniques employed kept it stiff and also simplified the manufacturing process, helping to keep costs in check.

Three 'A'-series grades were offered initially in France, with the A300 'Cosmic' being the cheapest (with a Peyrard crankset, Simplex derailleurs and CLB brakes), the A400 'Comète' next in the pecking order (Stronglight cranks, Huret shifters and Weinmann brakes), and the A500 'Galaxie' as the flagship, featuring the latest Shimano 105 components. Not surprisingly, new graphics were used on these newcomers, with horizontal lines down most of the front-end of the frame, and large slanted 'Peugeot' lettering on the seat tube.

Other than the PY10FC and the ladies models, which were carried over, the road-racers were given a major reshuffle. The PRO10 and PSV10M were axed, while the PY10M became the similar-looking PY10P, the PX10SH became the PX SIS (with Shimano 600 SIS components), the PG10SH the PG SIS, the new PJ10B slotted in-between the PX SIS and PG SIS, and the PGN10T morphed into the PG10T.

The PGN10M was replaced by the PGN10P, with painted forks being adopted on the 'Gold' sister model, which was offered once more, but not brought out again for the 1988 season; the closely-related PG10PB was also put forward at this time, coming with two-tone paintwork, and the new PC10 had a similar spec, too, with a lesser crankset setting it apart. The P10L, P10S and P10LS were squeezed into new PE10S1 and PE10LS grades, and the use of 'HLE' tubing transformed the PH20M into the PHE20, the PH13 into the PHE13, and the former PH10LS and PH11 grades into the PHE10.

Export markets adopted a confusing mix of model code numbers for 1987, and while some models tie-up via their official name, many simply don't. The Galaxie, for instance, was the same in all markets, while the P4 was called the 'Sports 5' or 'Sports 10' in Britain, and the 'Corbier' in the US; it didn't exist in France. Bikes like the PE10LS came with the 'Aubisque' moniker in France and the 'Aspin' one in the UK, while the PE10S1 'Avoriaz' shared its name in the States, but was called a P8!

Anyway, time for the interesting oddities. Germany was still listing the PRO10, and also offered separate CFX10 (Reynolds 531) and CFG10 (Reynolds 501) framesets, the latter with two-tone colouring. Both Britain and the US had a PZ in their catalogues, with the PX10 name still proudly displayed in both of them as well; the UK listed the PZ SIS 'Perthus' with Shimano components, while American buyers had the PZ10, fitted with the Campagnolo 'Super Record' groupset. To finish, the 'Perthus' name was later adopted for a model in the domestic range, yet it was a completely different bike, as was the 'Perthus Pro' that came out in England in 1988. It's that minefield again.

In the meantime, the 1987 racing season was a subdued one for Peugeot fans, as it was the first time

The Z-Peugeot squad for 1987, with many familiar faces but a completely new look for the team uniform.

in over 20 years that the famous white and chequer jerseys were not part of the professional peloton. Instead, the brand was represented by the pop-art shirts of the Z-Peugeot team, sponsored by clothing magnate Roger Zannier, who'd agreed to give Roger Legeay a minimum of three years to come up with the goods.

Retaining most of the old squad, Legeay's men won six races in France and Italy, including the GP Ouest France, thanks to Gilbert Duclos-Lassalle. At the same time, it was supremely ironic that thanks to Stephen Roche's past links with Peugeot, that the Carrera team rode with the Peugeot name on their shorts. Roche duly won the Tour de France (itself, also in a transition period) and the Giro d'Italia, but sadly riding a steel-framed Battaglin bike from Italy! The top Z-Peugeot rider in the 1987 edition, meanwhile, came home well down the field in 20th …

Some subtle changes were applied to the graphics for 1988, with the down tube lettering becoming slanted and losing the chequers, while the stripes that had become something of a Peugeot signature in recent years were toned down a touch, at least on most models – some of them had their own unique style of colouring, but then it's already perfectly clear that nothing has ever been straightforward when it comes to documenting the evolution of Peugeot bicycles!

The domestic 'Demi-Course' grades and tourers were chopped back again, with the PXR80 being one of the casualties. The P531W 'Normandie' randonneur was an attractive newcomer, however, manufactured using Reynolds 531 tubing. The mudguards, carrying platforms and lighting were hardly noticeable, and with 18 speeds, it was a nice tool for everyday use. Incidentally, one should take note of that 'W' suffix, for it was applied to all adult models for the 1988 season.

In the 'Course' category, there looks to be an increase in model numbers, but a lot of it was down to the two-tone paint option (identified by a 'BW' suffix rather the strict 'W' one) or the racy 'DW' colouring, with a white base and contrast paint around the stripes and maker's

Stunning artwork on the cover of the German road-racer brochure for 1988.

name. Anyway, the three 'A'-series models were carried over, with only minor changes in their specification and a new product code – the A500 became the A500AW, the A400 the A400AW, and so on. Likewise, the PY10P (finished in Anthracite) had a similar spec to before, but a new PY MAW code to go with the 'Perthus' name; with the PY10FC gone, the latter was also offered in PY CAW guise, fitted with Campagnolo 'Chorus' components, and priced at 8900FF.

The PX SIS became the 6495FF PX SISW for 1988, inheriting the latest Shimano 6400 component set at the same time, and coming in Night Blue only; the PX SBW was similar, but had Shimano 5000 bits and two-tone paint, while the PX CAW had Campagnolo parts and red paintwork. Meanwhile, the PS10BW 'Savoie' was a new model, with Super Vitus 980 tubing, and Huret and Modolo components.

The PG10PB and PGN10P were replaced by the PG10BW and PG10W, respectively, while the PJ10B, PG SIS and PC10 grades were dropped in favour of a new 3895FF PH SISW grade, which came with a Reynolds 501 frame and Shimano 105 components. The PH501 'Ventoux' was basically carried over with just the subtle graphic changes, but now offered in P501W and P501BW guise; there was also a P501TW version for triathlon use, which replaced the PG10T in the line-up. The PH513 was also familiar, but now called the P513W in its latest form.

The PHE20 was much the same as before (the 'Mont Blanc' model only gaining a 'W' suffix), although the PHE13 evolved into the PE13DW, inheriting Huret derailleurs and the latest paint scheme. While the PHE10 was dropped, the PE10LS became the PE10LW (or PE10DW with graduated paint), and the PE10S1 became the PE10SW, albeit retaining the 'Avoriaz' moniker. In the ladies line-up, the PH15T morphed into the PE15TW, and the PE15BW was added as an alternative, with two-tone paint and racing handlebars. The PH153T became the PE153W, and the old P15 grade was split into two, with the P15W being the same as the 1987 model apart from the frame graphics, while the P15CW version sported drop handlebars.

America offered ten road-racers for 1988, but almost as many ATBs. This was as clear a sign as any that the 'Golden Era' was well and truly over, for it was a similar situation in many European markets, too, with Holland being a good example. It all comes down to practical issues at the end of the day, but function and romance (for want of a better word) will always be two very different subjects, with designers having two very different purposes in mind for their products. Yes, an ATB may be able to take a curb head-on and not break, whereas a road-racer will almost certainly fall to pieces given a similar amount of abuse. However, it's rather like comparing a Hummer with a Lamborghini Miura – the brawny Hummer doubtless has its share of fans, but, even when stationary, the hearts of enthusiasts will always be drawn to the beauty and sheer technical elegance of the Italian thoroughbred until the end of time.

The Peugeot brand was represented by Roger Legeay's Z-Peugeot team and the Belgian SEFB-Peugeot outfit of Ferdinand Bracke during 1988, although the latter equipe (led by a man who'd done so much for

Bernard Chesneau proudly showing off the 1988 SEFB-Peugeot colours and his mount for the season. This would ultimately be his last year as a pro.

Ronan Pensec's team card for the 1988 season.

Peugeot in the past) would only use the French bikes in this one season, probably because the desired results weren't forthcoming. Ronan Pensec took two of the five wins clocked up by the Z-Peugeot team, but sadly there was no silverware from the big three events that catch world attention; Pensec was Peugeot's top finisher in the 1988 Tour de France, coming home in seventh overall, while Denis Roux was tenth.

Looking through the 1989 domestic catalogue, perhaps the biggest surprise wasn't what was in it, but what was missing, for the much-publicised and only recently introduced 'A'-series had already been dropped – a further sign of a struggling road-racer market, which was doubtless the reason behind Peugeot failing to launch the new PFC10 carbonfibre bike it had developed in association with Zodiac Aerospace on time.

However, the loss of the aluminium-framed bikes accounted for just three of the ten 'Competition' grades dropped and, as such, it's pretty hard to figure out what replaced what – a task made all the more difficult by the use of familiar names on bikes that completely fail to tie-up with those from the previous year. For instance, the 1988 'Dolomites' had a Reynolds frame, but the new version had a Columbus one. Likewise, the 1988 'Savoie' had Vitus tubing, whereas the latest model had a Reynolds 531 frame. There is more correlation in the components when comparing nameplates, but even so, it's easier to say the whole range was streamlined in order to give buyers a more clear-cut choice going forward …

With all-new colouring across the board for 1989, perhaps the most interesting bike was the 14-speed C 653 MABZ 'Racing Team' model, which featured Reynolds 653 tubing, and Mavic components. Next in the pecking

Continued on page 159

CARBON PRO
PFC 10 Z
LA VOIE ROYALE.
PREMIÈRE MONDIALE
PEUGEOT.
TOUS TUBES CARBONE
TUBE DE DIRECTION
TOUT CARBONE.
POIDS DU CADRE 1,280 KG.
ÉQUIPEMENT FRANÇAIS.
14 VITESSES.
PEUGEOT

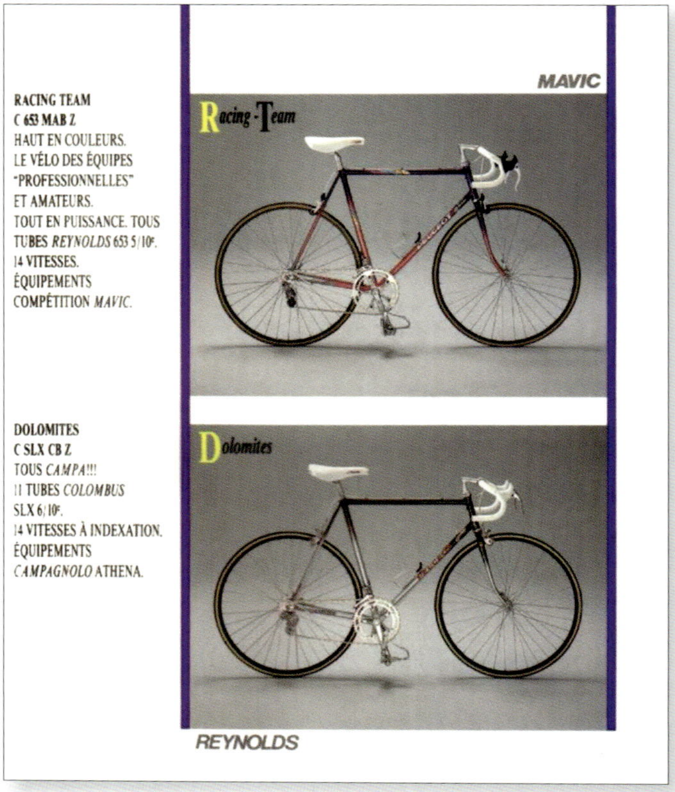
RACING TEAM
C 653 MAB Z
HAUT EN COULEURS.
LE VÉLO DES ÉQUIPES
"PROFESSIONNELLES"
ET AMATEURS.
TOUT EN PUISSANCE. TOUS
TUBES REYNOLDS 653 5/10e.
14 VITESSES.
ÉQUIPEMENTS
COMPÉTITION MAVIC.
MAVIC
Racing-Team
DOLOMITES
C SLX CB Z
TOUS CAMPA!!!
11 TUBES COLOMBUS
SLX 6/10e.
14 VITESSES À INDEXATION.
ÉQUIPEMENTS
CAMPAGNOLO ATHENA.
Dolomites
REYNOLDS

GALIBIER
C 531 SB Z
L'EFFICACITÉ.
14 VITESSES A INDEXATION
SHIMANO ULTEGRA
CADRE REYNOLDS 531 5/10e.
ÉQUIPEMENTS SHIMANO.
GÉOMÉTRIE
DE COMPÉTITION.
PEUGEOT

SAVOIE
C 531 HB Z
L'ASSOCIATION
DES ÉNERGIES EUROPE 1992.
14 VITESSES
À INDEXATION AR.
SERIE SACHS-HURET
ARIS NEW SUCCESS.
CADRE REYNOLDS 531 5/10e.
ÉQUIPEMENTS EUROPÉENS.
PEUGEOT

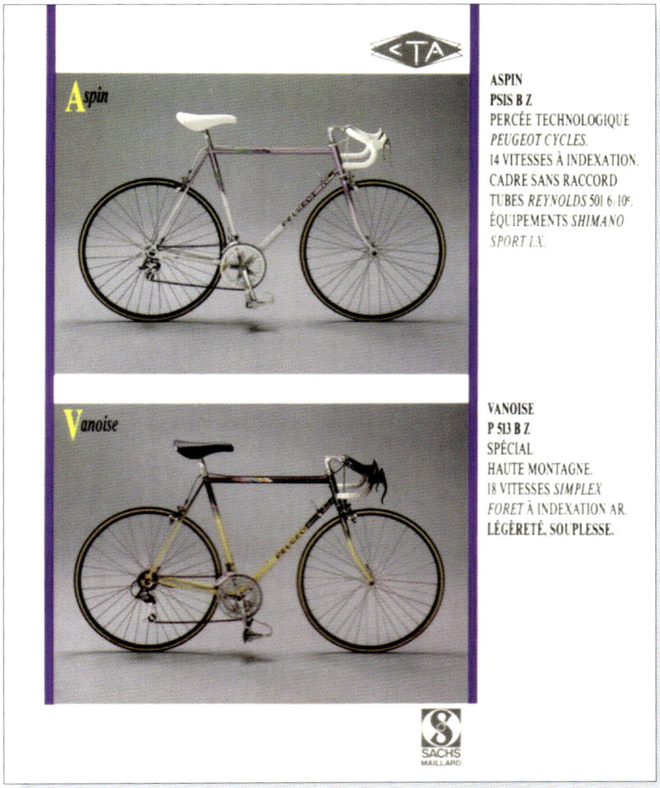

Selected pages from the French brochure for 1989. Please remember that not all bike names were universal, and were often applied to completely different machines from market to market.

Reynolds

order was the C SLX CBZ, with Columbus tubing and Campagnolo 'Athena' components (the 'Z' suffix being common to all bikes for 1989, incidentally). There then followed two Reynolds 531-framed machines, three with Reynolds 501 tubing, three with 'HLE' frame material, and two with Peugeot's lower grade tubing; the four bikes listed for the ladies all came with inhouse tubes to keep production costs and selling prices in check. These frame variations were then offered with different component sets, with the 531s having a choice of Shimano or Huret parts, for instance.

The 'Demi-Course' and randonneur line-up looked familiar, at least, with only minimal changes to fit in with the latest colouring, and a similar grading system to before. The 21-speed 'Cyclo' was new, though, aimed at long-distance touring. It added one model to make up for the three dropped in the 'Ville' and 'Tourisme' ranges lower down the pricing ladder.

The C SLX CBZ was called the 'Athena' in export markets, which made sense, given the groupset employed. Most importers offered ranges that tied-in with those of France, although certain places, like Holland, continued to list the 'Cosmic' aluminium-framed model, doubtless in a bid to clear stocks, as this was to be its final curtain call. Meanwhile, America was listing more ATBs than road-racers. Enough said …

Jean-Marie Leblanc took over as director of the Tour de France in 1989, which would prove to be a good move – Leblanc's vision would create an event that went beyond cycling, in effect becoming what the World Cup is to football. One could argue that this has always been the case, but with the power of television being able to make or break organizations overnight, one has to deliver on a reputation for exciting sport, and keep things that way year after year – something which is easier said than done.

Anyway, Robert Millar (back on a Peugeot after signing for the Z equipe) was the top Z-Peugeot finisher in the 1989 TdF, winning a stage and coming tenth overall; Millar also won the Tour of Britain. However, the four more race victories for the team (including one on the GP du Midi-Libre thanks to Jérôme Simon) was not enough to convince Roger Zannier to stick with Peugeot bikes – with politics playing a part in the decision, the Z team ultimately swapped its allegiance to TVT-made LeMond machinery for 1990.

Opposite: Robert Millar on the 1989 Tour de France. He finished the event in tenth, but did win the Tour of Britain in front of a home crowd. (Courtesy *L'Equipe*)

6. PEUGEOT IN RECENT YEARS

The Peugeot Cycles brand was in for a tumultuous time as the eighties gave way to the nineties, with yet more drama in store in the new millennium. The name would be passed from pillar to post, and fade out only to come back, not only in the shops, but in racing, too. Sadly, the return to competition was to be a brief one, but at least there were some high points that are worth remembering ...

At first glance, the 1990 catalogues were, in the main, similar to those from the previous season. Careful inspection, however, shows a royal mixture of new and old, with totally different line-ups used across the globe adding to the confusion. Some of the old names tied-up, along with a few of the old model codes, but not all of them, and not by a long way in many cases.

Holland, for instance, had a 'Perthus' model with Reynolds 531 tubing and SunTour parts, and Japan had a couple of real oddities in the CY80 (a Reynolds 501 frame with TA and Simplex parts, combined with Weinmann brakes) and P501B/BW (Reynolds 501 tubing with Stronglight, Huret and Weinmann parts).

Designed for winners

The racing pedigree of Cycles Peugeot is unrivalled. It is a success story that stretches back over many years and countless competition triumphs in the world's leading races.

Joey McLoughlin, Sean Yates and the winner of last year's Kellogg's Tour of Britain, Robert Millar, are just some of the cycle super stars who have raced away to victory on Peugeot.

The wealth of experience and knowledge gained from this superlative racing record has enabled us to design and develop what we firmly believe is the finest range of ready-to-race professional speed machines ever produced. A tried and tested range that will prove unbeatable at every competitive level.

At the heart of this magnificent range are the incomparable Peugeot frames, built from the latest Reynolds tubing for super-lightness.

The new geometry and aerodynamics of these innovative frames, designed by advanced technology, take these sleek, streamlined machines into exciting new dimensions of race winning speed and response.

The list of original equipment is the finest you will find, the top quality components that you would choose if you were creating your own dream racer. Campagnolo, Shimano, Look and Wolber are just a few of the world renowned names.

This is a supreme range of craftsman built, ready-to-race cycles, each available in seven different sizes, that any top professional would be both pleased and proud to ride.

The Peugeot Professional Racing Range – designed for winners by winners.

Cover and opening page of a special brochure produced for the UK market.

Meanwhile, Germany was one of the few to continue fielding bikes with Columbus SLX tubing – the CX640 'Dolomites' with a Shimano groupset (the name was usually applied to an SLX/Campy combination), and the CX700 'Vanoise,' which actually was the latter.

With Columbus tubing dropped in most countries, the most important newcomer was the flagship CR1100 (or '753 Chorus'), which featured a Reynolds 753 frame and Campagnolo 'Chorus' components. The old C653 continued in some markets, while others offered a similar bike called the CR700 (or '653 Athena'), fitted with the Campagnolo 'Athena' groupset; the CR800 was another alternative, being the same as the CR700, but equipped with Shimano 'Ultegra' parts. The other 'CR' model was the CR500BY (or '531 Altus'), with a Reynolds 531 frame and Shimano '105' components, although 'Ultegra' bits were used in Germany, thus allowing the 'Galibier' moniker to continue.

Moving down in price, the P SIS BZ was a direct replacement for the PR500 'Aspin,' the PR400 'Izoard' came with HLE tubing and Shimano RX100 components, and the PE300 'Ventoux' had the same frame combined with Shimano 400EX parts. Further down the ladder again was a real mix of codes and names, with the PE10 designation carried over in Japan, for example, but the P100L moniker adopted in many countries. Naturally, there were lots of subgrades – too many to go into seeing as we are now clear of the 'golden era' that is the main subject of this book. Notwithstanding, the general rule of thumb in this new system is a pecking order of CR (or CX on occasion), PR, PE and P, with a smaller number attached to it meaning a lower grade, and vice versa. The 'B' suffix was a paint code, while the 'Y' suffix was a year index.

In general, the interesting thing was the way the lustre seems to have faded on the 'Course' models. All of them had painted forks, which was one sign that the classic era had well and truly ended (along with the leading-edge accessories on offer at the time), but by far the greatest indicator was the American catalogue. While the 'Athena' was dropped, five models were carried over, augmented by a new entry-level grade, but the road-racers were now pushed to the back of the brochure, as ATBs and bikes of that ilk were the strongest sellers. As it happens, the 1990 catalogue would prove to be the last one for the US market, as sales ended there soon after;

The German catalogue for 1990.

Peugeot car exports duly followed suit at the end of 1991.

Thankfully, it wasn't all doom and gloom outside the traditional European outlets, with Canada proving to be a strong sales arena thanks to Procycle's continued efforts. Japan, too, had its fair share of Peugeot fans. By this time, Cycles Peugeot Sales Japan KK were handling everything again, their 1990 catalogue listing 12 adult 'Course' models (including the painfully shy PFC10), and one for junior riders. The brand would have a rocky road in Japan, but the bikes were sold in car showrooms at one point, and have managed to keep a presence in the Land of the Rising Sun to this day.

Meanwhile, on the racing front, the Z team was so determined to secure the services of Greg LeMond (already twice winner of the Tour de France) for 1990, that a special contract was written allowing him to use his own LeMond/TVT bikes. More than that, all riders would be tied into the same deal, thus bringing the Z-Peugeot era to an end. Granted, it paid off, as, with good support from the likes of Robert Millar, Gilbert Duclos-Lassalle and Ronan Pensec, the American won the TdF in fine style. But for Peugeot fans, it was the first time in living memory that there was no-one representing the marque in the professional peloton.

Nothing changed for 1991 and 1992, with the Z equipe's continued use of LeMond bikes, as the man himself was still the team leader. Indeed, even after the team evolved into the GAN outfit, with Roger Legeay still in charge, things stayed the same, with Peugeot kept out in the cold.

The birth of Cycleurope

New seat tube graphics had been adopted by the time the 1991 season kicked off, with the CR1100BY giving way to the CR1000BN, with Reynolds 653 tubing, as a new top-end model. This was destined to be a short-lived variant, for in 1992 it became the 16-speed CR1000PC, which employed a Reynolds 708 frame to take Mavic and Sachs components.

Weighing in at just 9.5kg (21lb), the CR1000PC featured the simplified badging that would filter through the rest of the 1992 line-up, which included three CR-series bikes in France, along with one PR model, three PEs and two P-series grades, as well as four frames and four options for the ladies. While the domestic flagship featured traditional down tube derailleur levers, it was also apparent that this was the era when shifters were starting to become integrated with the brake levers. It would take a while for the revolution to take hold, but it's enough to say that the latter is by far the most common form of shifting mechanism we see nowadays.

Cover of the domestic 'Course' catalogue, along with the CR1000PC page from the same publication.

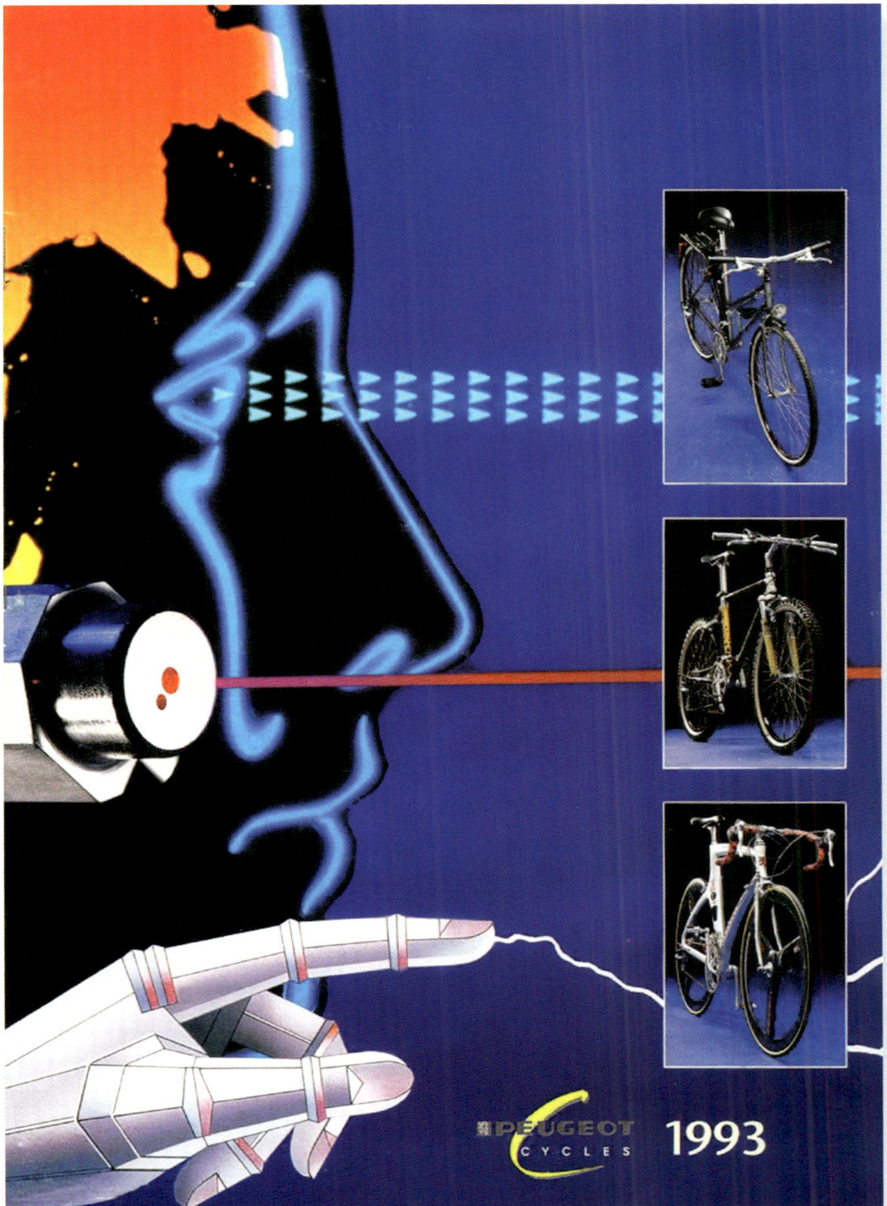

Striking artwork on the Dutch brochure for 1993.

Interestingly, the offer was made by another bike manufacturer – BH (Beistegui Hermanos) of Spain. BH, which had been building bikes since 1923, had secured the rights to the Gitane brand via its purchase of Micmo. BH then secured a licence to build Peugeots, and duly formed Cycleurope as an umbrella company in 1992. A few years down the line, Cycleurope managed to become the owner of the tooling, and was thus entrusted with the manufacture, sales and marketing of Peugeout bikes. With others joining the group, including Bianchi later on, Cycleurope would become to cycling what the Swatch Group is to horology, helping to keep long-established brands alive.

One glance at the 1993 catalogues, with the Vitus monocoque carbon bikes, and we know the face of cycling had changed forever. Yes, one could still buy a traditional road-racer, with Reynolds or occasionally Columbus tubing (albeit with shifters integrated into the brake levers on the latest 'PF'-series models), but the PC1000/TC1000 was the way to go for serious enthusiasts, with Donnay carbonfibre tubes arranged in alloy lugs, and Shimano 105 components.

Chequer patterns were reintroduced for the 1994 season, with iconic blue and yellow paintwork also making a comeback, mated with a filled-in head badge that had first been seen about 12 months earlier on the full carbon bikes. There were still plenty of 'Course'

On the face of it, with such a large range of racers still on offer in France, the bike business was doing just fine. However, sales had been dropping off year after year as the 1980s progressed. With increased overheads adding to the problem, not to mention the competition from cheap imports from Asia, Peugeot's management was right to consider all the options available. When an offer was mooted to hive off the cycle section to a third party, the solution it presented seemed almost custom-made.

British advertising from the 1993 season.

models offered in France, with the PF1002, PF1000, PF800, PF700, PF610 and PF600 grades listed for the domestic market, along with the CP550, CP400, PE300, PE203, CS103, CS100 and CE100 further down the price range. Although no longer the huge employer it once was, the Romilly-sur-Seine factory could still boast that it had 900 workers assigned to the design and building of Peugeot bikes.

A return to racing

The Amaury Sport Organisation (or ASO) took over from *L'Equipe* as organiser of the Tour de France from the 1993 edition. In reality, it was a paper change, for after Émilien Amaury died, his son Philippe formed the EPA publishing house (keeping *L'Equipe* and *Le Parisien* going alongside several other titles), and ultimately ASO, which became part of the EPA group in September 1992. Sadly, there were still no Peugeots present in this iconic race, but that situation was about to change.

It truly was a welcome sight to see the newly-formed Aubervilliers 93 team adopt Peugeot bikes for its first year in racing, the 1994 season (the '93' represents the postal code of the commune rather than a date). Lylian Lebreton won the Tour de l'Ain, with Denis Marie claiming a win in the following year. Yes, these were small steps, but 1996 saw the team take a stage on the Tour de France, while Frédéric Pontier won the Tour de Normandie.

In the meantime, the big news was that the high-flying Festina team would adopt Peugeot bikes with Shimano components for 1995. Festina riders had come fourth and fifth in the 1994 Tour de France using Look machinery, and were ranked 15th in the world (the GAN team, which was doing well thanks to Chris Boardman, was ranked 21st); the team leader was Richard Virenque, who was always devastating in the mountains. In short, with bike development moving fast (the contemporary

Frédéric Pontier in his Aubervilliers 93 team colours, standing behind his Peugeot racing bike.

streamlined time trial machines being a perfect example), thus levelling the playing field to a certain extent, there was every reason to think Peugeot would be put back on the map, despite a large number of changes to the team line-up.

Things started slow, however. Richard Virenque took the La Polynormande, Laurent Dufaux won the Route de Sud and another race in his native Switzerland, and Lars Michaelsen won one in Belgium. By far, the highlight of the season was Virenque holding on his polka dot jersey in the Tour de France (Fernando Escartin was the top finisher in the Tour, coming home in seventh).

Richard Virenque tucked in behind Jan Ullrich on the 1996 Tour de France. (Courtesy *L'Equipe*)

With the team now more settled, 1996 was a much better year, with Virenque winning the Giro del Piemonte in Italy, Dufaux winning in Switzerland, Bruno Boscardin winning twice in France, and Laurent Brochard taking both the Tour du Limousin and the La Polynormande. The Festina guys even did well in America, but it was the results in the Grand Tours that provided hope: Dufaux was second in the Vuelta a España and fourth in the Tour de France, while Virenque was third in the TdF and crowned king of the mountains once again.

The next generation

The range for 1995 was basically similar to that of the previous year, albeit with subtly revised graphics and paint schemes to freshen things up. The 'Professional 1200' was an interesting newcomer, though, with carbonfibre lugs as well as tubing, plus aluminium alloy front forks. There was also a short-lived Team Line service established, rather like the Prestige shop of yore, allowing racing teams to order bikes to meet their specific needs, from unique component mixes all the way up to specialist time trial machines.

The 'Professional 1200' was one of nine 'Course' bikes that made it into the comprehensive domestic catalogue of the following year, including a new 'Professional 1000' grade (often known as the 'Alu Chrono 4000' or 'AC4000' outside France) with a 5086 aluminium alloy frame. These alloy frames, less exotic than their predecessors, were becoming more common within the industry by this time, as the fight for cost-effective weight reduction raged on.

In the background, BH sold off the Cycleurope business to Monark Stiga AB of Sweden in the summer of 1996. Salvatore Grimaldi, an Italian entrepreneur based in Sweden, started buying up shares in Monark Stiga soon after, and, with Bianchi in its portfolio since May 1997, plus a handful of other brands, thanks to the

Laurent Dufaux featured in a Festina watch advert.

Pascal Hervé's team card for the 1998 season.

Cover of the hefty domestic catalogue for 1998.

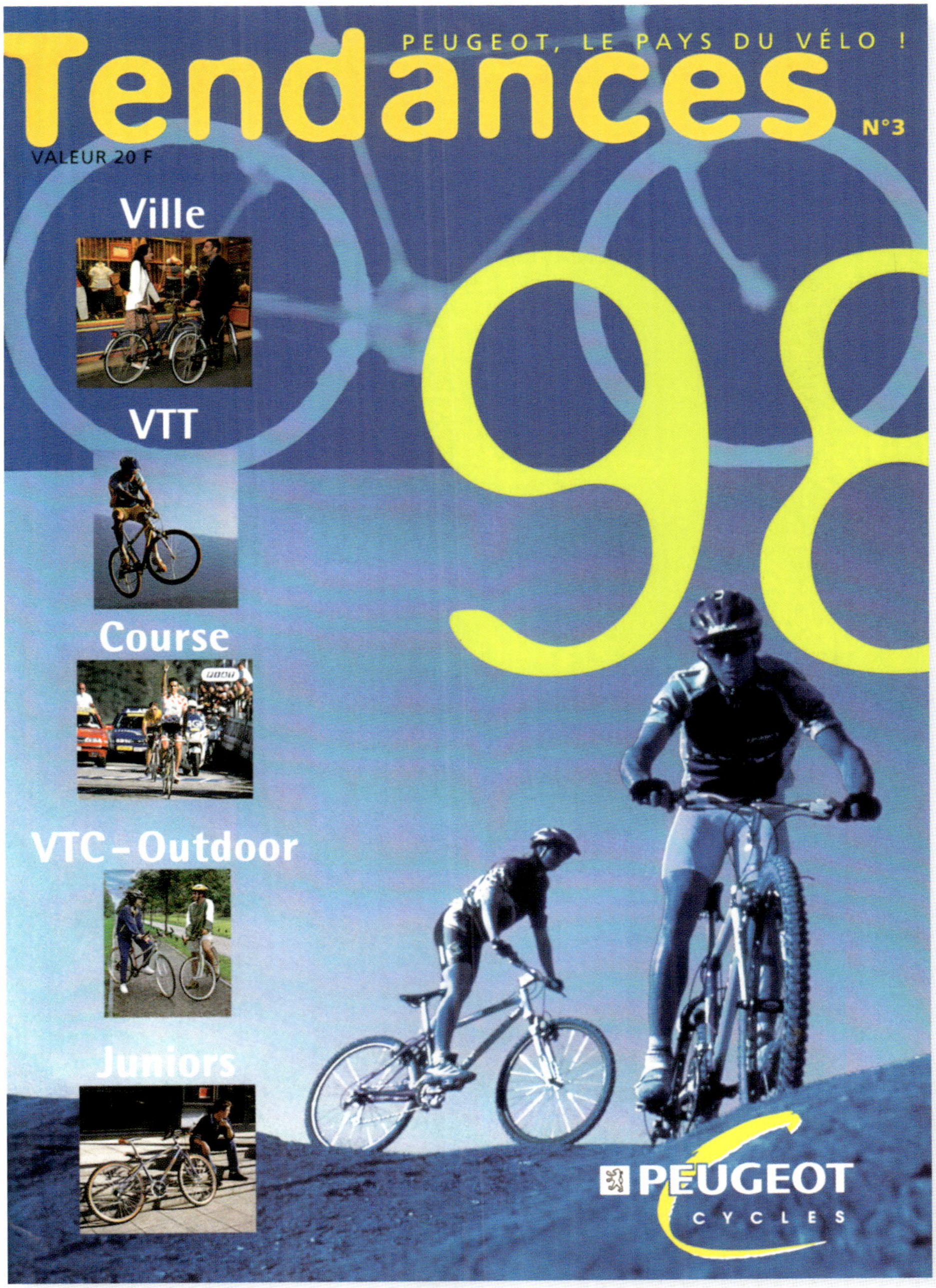

vision of Grimaldi Industri AB, the Cycleurope concern became even stronger.

Festina and BigMat team bikes were offered for 1997, with Reynolds tubing and coming in 14- (PE5000) or 21-speed (PE5003) guise. The Festina model was finished in yellow and blue, while the BigMat one came in yellow and red. No less than 19 'Course' grades were listed, although it has to be said that many were a long way from true road-racers by this time.

The show goes on …

As one will have gathered from the last paragraph in the previous section, Peugeot bikes were still being used

The remarkable Onyx concept displayed at the 2012 Paris Salon.

by two professional teams in 1997 – Festina-Lotus, and BigMat (the successor to the Aubervilliers 93 outfit). The latter won a few stages, but nothing more; 1998 was much better, with three race wins, although the equipe moved over to Look machinery for the following season. On the other hand, Bruno Roussel's job as DS at Festina looked pretty secure. His team won eight races during 1997, with Laurent Dufaux third on the Vuelta, and Richard 'Ricco' Virenque was top climber and second overall on the Tour de France. In addition, Laurent Brochard was crowned UCI World Champion in Spain in October 1997.

In the background, though, the racing circus had been struggling with EPO and other drugs for some time, with widespread usage, but suitable tests for abuse simply not available. As the money moving through the sport increased, there was added pressure on team managers and riders alike, with many taking the 'if you can't beat them, join them' train of thought. En route to the 1998 Tour de France, a Festina team car was stopped at a routine border check, and large amounts of doping products were duly found.

It has to be said that this was not the level of cheating witnessed in the Lance Armstrong camp, literally on a scale big enough to provide Hollywood with storylines, and to think Festina was the only team up to these dirty tricks is extremely naive – the truth has come out in the wash with many riders in recent years, proving the assumption that it was probably harder to find one that wasn't doping to be true. But an example was needed at the time, and catching the Festina team red-handed with so many pills and needles just happened to fit the bill ahead of such a high-profile event.

All Festina team members were arrested at one point, with seven riders ultimately ejected from the Tour. In fact, the Tour de France was a disaster from a PR point of view per se, with several teams pulling out in protest – the only good thing to come out of it was a win for the loveable Marco Pantani, helping to put Bianchi back in the spotlight at the same time.

However, despite the scandal and subsequent upheaval, Pascal Hervé won the GP Ouest France plus two more French events in 1998, and Laurent Dufaux took the GP du Midi-Libre and Tour de Romandie. In addition, Richard Virenque won a race in France, Gianluca Bortolami claimed the GP di Chiasso in Switzerland, Fabian Jeker took the honours in the Escalada a Montjuïc, and Marcel Wüst won a second race in Spain.

By this time, a new Danish equipe – Team Home-Jack & Jones – had joined the fray, choosing Peugeot bikes for its first two seasons. They managed to win a few stages in 1998, but clocked up several wins in 1999, some as far afield as Australia. Notwithstanding, the outfit switched to Vitus bikes for 2000, and would become known as the now-famous CSC ProTeam in later years.

Meanwhile, with Juan Ferdandez Martin and Yvon Sanquer being named as the new bosses at Festina, many of the team members started the 1999 season late due to suspensions following the fall-out from the 'Festina Affair'. Virenque had moved to Polti as well, adding to the team's woes. The Frenchman was hardly made to feel welcome on the Tour de France, which is doubly ironic given the results (later nullified after bringing the sport into disrepute). In the end, Christophe Moreau and Patrice Halgand won one apiece in France, and Jonathan Hall was crowned the champion of Australia – it was little to show for a budget running into millions.

Even though the poor results of 1999 had little to do with Peugeot, Festina moved over to Specialized bikes for the 2000 season, signalling a second end to the French maker's professional competition exploits. Sadly, this would prove to be the last one, too. At least history shows Peugeot to be the most successful cycle racing team of all-time, by quite some margin, as it happens, and this book should stand as a celebration of that fact rather than simply mourning a loss.

A final word

The 1998 catalogues followed the format established in the previous few years, with a range of steel frames (some with oversize tubing) backed up by the odd aluminium one, although carbonfibre frames were no longer listed for public consumption. 1999 witnessed the introduction of carbon front forks and new, ATB-inspired

The Romilly site with the Cycleurope logo upfront.

frame geometry on certain bikes, and things were much the same as we entered the new millennium. Sadly, other than a flurry of colouring revisions, there was not much else to report on the technical side.

However, things were definitely moving on the corporate front. Procycle stopped making Peugeots in 2001, although the brand should be returning to Canada via the Quantum concern as this book goes to print. That may be the catalyst to get Peugeot back into the USA one day, too?

Then, an even bigger bombshell, for the Peugeot family said that it had decided to concentrate on cars in 2002, leaving Cycleurope no choice but to phase out the brand's bicycles; the licence was not renewed in 2004 as a result. Ironically, though, there were bikes made after this date, featured in catalogues sporting the Peugeot logo rather than that of Cycleurope. Sold in Peugeot's car showrooms across the globe (a trend in the industry for a time, using automotive marque names and badges to punt a variety of two-wheelers), although unfortunately, there were no road-racers listed.

Despite this turn of events, Cycleurope still listed its base in France as the Romilly factory, and indeed started building Peugeot bikes under licence again after a new agreement was signed between Cycleurope (via Grimaldi) and the PSA Group in 2010. Many exotic designs would follow, some displayed at motor shows as a form of promotion, others available to enthusiasts of the brand.

In recent years, Peugeot's designers have been teaming up with Cycleurope to focus the brand's direction. Electric bicycles (e-bikes) are increasingly important, as new modes of mobility are examined by forward-thinking car makers in these challenging times, and the promised Peugeot MTB team may help promote them further. The other area of development is the re-issue of 'vintage' machines, especially as cycling is becoming trendy once more – not just amongst Eroica types, but with dedicated followers of fashion across the globe as well. Much of this is thanks to movie exposure, showing a new generation what they have been missing.

At the time of writing, 250 workers were building around 1000 bikes a day at the Romilly site. Interestingly, some of the latest models have adopted badging that readily reminds us of earlier days, back when Romilly was bought to allow Peugeot to keep up with demand – a truly golden era ...

It's good to see Peugeot is making the most of its heritage, with a number of retro-style bikes having been released in recent years. This pair of bikes, and a number of other models, were still available as this book went to print.

A complete buyer's guide to electric bicycles, including the types of bike available, what to look for and why you should buy one. Packed with useful contacts, including importers, websites and magazines, advice on where you can ride, and the law. Also includes battery charging and maintenance info, as well as basic cycle maintenance.

ISBN: 978-1-845849-39-9
Paperback • 19.5x13.9cm • 64 pages
• 101 colour pictures

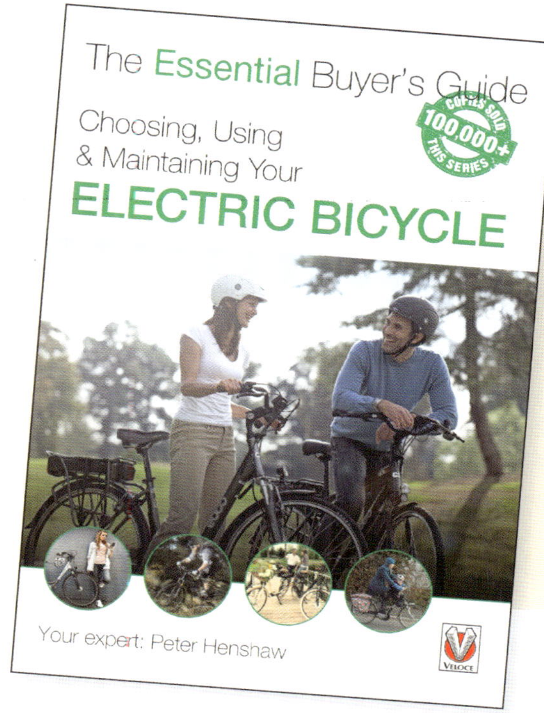

A unique guide to France for lovers of classic and modern cars. From museums and concours d'élégance to motorsport events and track days, it covers 200 attractions throughout the country. From highlights such as the Monaco Grand Prix or Rétromobile to fascinating but less well-known events, there is something here for every enthusiast.

ISBN: 978-1-787110-57-1
Paperback • 21x14.8cm • 248 pages
• 609 colour and b&w pictures

For more information or to purchase, visit www.veloce.co.uk
email: info@veloce.co.uk • Tel: +44(0)1305 260068

INDEX

The Peugeot company, its subsidiaries and products are mentioned throughout this book.